Increasing Hits and Selling More on Your Web Site

Greg Helmstetter

WILEY COMPUTER PUBLISHING

JOHN WILEY & SONS, INC.

New York • Chichester • Brisbane • Toronto • Singapore • Weinheim

Publisher: Katherine Schowalter
Editor: Tim Ryan
Assistant Editor: Pam Sobotka
Managing Editor: Brian Snapp
Text Design & Composition: Pronto Design & Production, Inc.

Designations used by companies to distinguish their products are often claimed as trademarks. In all instances where John Wiley & Sons, Inc. is aware of a claim, the product names appear in initial capital or ALL CAPITAL LETTERS. Readers, however, should contact the appropriate companies for more complete information regarding trademarks and registration.

This publication is designed to provide accurate and authoritative information in regard to the subject matter covered. It is sold with the understanding that the publisher is not engaged in rendering legal, accounting, or other professional service. If legal advice or other expert assistance is required, the services of a competent professional person should be sought.

Library of Congress Cataloging-in-Publication Data:

Helmstetter, Greg, 1967-
    Increasing hits and selling more on your Web site/Greg Helmstetter
      p. cm.
    Includes bibliographical references (p.).
    ISBN 0-471-16944-7 (pbk.: alk. paper)
    1. Internet Marketing. 2. World Wide Web servers—Management.
    3. Business enterprises—Computer networks—Management.
  4. Internet advertising. I. Title.
    HF5415.1265.H45   1997   96-43741
    658.8'00285'467—dc20   CIP

ISBN: 0-471-16944-7

Printed in the United States of America

10 9 8 7 6 5 4 3 2 1

To my father for my spirit,
to my mother for balance, and
to my brother for leading the way

Acknowledgments

I once believed that books were written by experts. I now realize that books—at least, those relating to anything changing as quickly as World Wide Web marketing—are compilations of the knowledge of many experts from many subfields. I have learned at least as much about the Web during the research and writing of this undertaking as I knew when I began. I owe this newfound knowledge to many people who have generously provided time, information, or both.

In particular, I owe thanks (in no specific order) to Ryan Scott and Rosalind Resnick of NetCreations, Ken Wruk of WebPromote, Dr. Brian Wansink of the Wharton School, James Lippard of Primenet, John Audette of WebStep, Thom Reece, Erik Kraft, Ed Hott of Intersé, Rick Brown of Web Traffic Builder, Craig Brenner of QUALCOMM, Stephen Dundas of the Dundas Loom Company, Dr. Cliff Kurtzman of the Tenagra Corporation, and many of the contributors to the Online Advertising Discussion List.

I would also like to give extra special thanks to Tim Ryan, Pam Sobotka, and Brian Snapp at John Wiley & Sons for their hard work at making this book become a reality; Marcia Yudkin for her Small Business Publicity FAQ; Martin Dunsby at Deloitte & Touche, whose technical expertise is matched only by his business acumen; Kate Gerwe at Netscape for showing me their world from the inside; and, most of all, to Pamela "The Research Wench" Metivier for her tireless help, and Dr. Gerald Faulhaber and Farhad Mohit at the Wharton School for introducing me to the potential of the Web before most people had even heard of it.

Contents

Introduction

This book was written for one purpose only: to help make your commercial Web site successful. There is no shortage of books on the market that explain the general business applications of the Internet or how to create Web pages. And most of these books offer some advice on how to draw people to your site and how to display information in a user-friendly fashion.

But these books—in attempting to explain everything you need to know about creating Web sites from a general point of view—fall short of providing in-depth details and how-to examples for refining your site with the singular focus of maximizing revenue. As such, these books only briefly mention many things that need to be addressed in much more detail for readers who are building their Web businesses.

This book gets down to the nitty-gritty dirt. You'll not only read about the things you ought to do, but I'll give you plenty of examples of how to implement the suggestions. You'll see examples and case studies of how others have already tried things, both successfully and unsuccessfully. You'll gain from the experience of those who have experimented and learned about what works and what doesn't. You'll even learn sneaky tricks that few marketers think to use.

The Organization of This Book

I've broken down the mechanics of generating Web revenue into two distinct categories. First, you have to get people to your site. Second, people have to buy once they get there. (Exceptions are also covered, such as business models that depend on advertiser sponsorship). Part I covers important things that you must think about before going online. Parts II and III deal with drawing hits and making sales, respectively.

Drawing hits to your site is primarily a function of promotion, whereas making sales is primarily a function of the design of your site. Most sites will be designed and created before promotion begins, so why have I chosen to talk about promotion before design? The reason is this: Planning your promotion is a fundamental step in the creation of your overall marketing plan, business model, and strategy. Because all of this must be done before you begin to *build* your site, I have discussed promotional strategy before site design. By planning your promotion, you learn much about how to build your site and for whom you will build it.

With that said, I will add that it is not necessary to read this entire book, cover to cover, to derive its intended value. This book has been written to be valuable to newbies and experts alike. All that is required is that the reader has some level of interest in making money on the Web. Since different readers of this book will begin with varying levels of knowledge and experience pertaining to Web marketing, I have to distilled the contents down to their purest, hardest-punching form, labeled as "tips" in most cases.

You might consider skimming through these tips first. If they don't immediately make much sense, then you should probably read through the entire book in a linear fashion, so as to absorb the necessary background information, which will then place the tactics into an appropriate context.

However, if you already have some experience with creating and promoting Web sites, I predict that certain tips will jump off the page and sing to you. That is, you will read a couple and then be struck by one that is *exactly* what your site is missing. I hereby grant you permission, in your feverish excitement, to skip right to that section and read all the juicy details, out of sequence from the rest of the book. After you have implemented these radical and brilliant changes to your commercial site (most likely at two o'clock in the morning), you can go back and read the sections you skipped. I urge you to do so, as there are countless snippets of wisdom embedded throughout the body of this book that will be useful to newcomers and verterans alike.

There's More Than Just These Pages!

That's right, this book has an online companion on the Web. It contains nifty things like links to examples, software, and other resources mentioned in the book; of course, it includes *additional tips and tactics* pertaining to late-breaking technology and market changes.

Visit me at the *Increasing Hits* Web site, located at:

http://www.monsoon.org/book

Let's make this interaction two-way. I am always looking for new and clever techniques for making Web sites more successful. I would appreciate hearing about your experiments, lessons, and successes you've had using these tips or your own clever techniques. Who knows ... if you don't mind sharing your great idea, you might get a lot of free publicity in a future book or magazine article!

I wish you all the best and much prosperity from these very exciting times.

—Greg Helmstetter

P.S. I find it a gross shortcoming of the English language that we are forced to use such unwieldy monstrocities as "s/he," "he or she," "him or her," and "his or her" in order to convey the relatively simple concept of "person." My fondness for efficiency favors the traditional convention of using masculine pronouns alone to convey non-specified gender; however, my fondness for egalitarianism finds this solution less than satisfactory. I propose a novel solution: We invent the missing words, three non-gendered, third-person pronouns:

- zhe, meaning "he or she"

- hem, meaning "him or her"

- hes, meaning "his or her"

Any takers? Contact me at the Increasing Hits site, mentioned above. We'll start a movement. Until then, I've stuck with "he or she," in most cases, for this book. This is not the forum for social upheaval.

DEVELOPING YOUR WEB STRATEGY

THE STATE OF ONLINE
C O M M E R C E :
TODAY AND TOMORROW

So much has been written already about the vast potential of the World Wide Web. Strong words are tossed around, often to sell newspapers and magazines. Unfortunately, in these early days of the commercial Web, data are scarce and opinions drive much of the commentary. There are probably as many writers who dismiss the Web as an over-hyped, under-useful waste of marketing money as there are those who rave about the Web's vast and untapped potential as the perfect marketplace.

How Much Money Do Web Sites Make?

Is the Web a barren field, or is it a street paved with gold? The true answer, of course, is neither. According to the research firm International Data Corp., more than 100,000 retailers had established some sort of Web presence by May 1996. Annual sales over the Web are estimated to have reached $324 million dollars in 1995, and the top one-third sites report being profitable in 1996. If we momentarily ignore the fact that such figures are difficult to measure accurately, these rough estimates suggest that each Web business, on average, has generated about $3,000. That's not exactly a street paved with gold. But it says something important:

People *do* buy over the Net.

Many more potential customers will gain Internet access for years to come. Furthermore, it is reasonable to assume that each person will gradually purchase more over the Net as certain things change:

- Fears of transaction security fade.

- Digital forms of cash becomes commonly used.

- Customers' habits shift toward considering the Web as a place to look for products.

- Browser and agent technology enables more efficient searching and shopping by users (such as automating price comparison).

- More retailers offer more products.

- Retailers learn the subtleties of making their sites more useful and persuasive.

If this prospect for a rosier future—someday—is not enough to convince you to sink your savings into a commercial Web site, only to make $3,000 next year, then keep in mind that these are averages. The problem with averages is that they are only averages—they often throw away too much information to be useful.

Suppose ten people live on an island, and one of them makes $450,000 a year while the other nine each make $10,000 a year. The average income on the island is $54,000, which is a lousy way to characterize the population's affluence. Thousands of current Web sites—sometimes admitting to being "under construction," sometimes not—were thrown together merely as placeholders but have not yet begun to be operated and promoted as serious businesses. These dormant sites may catch occasional, accidental visitors who—low and behold—end up actually buying something. Or they may do nothing more than provide a convenient way to look up an employee's phone number. Not every site expects or even attempts to sell anything. If you browse enough, you will find sites that currently offer no way for you to purchase anything, even if you want to.

These thousands of sites draw the average sales-per-site statistic way down. On the other hand, sites like the Internet Shopping Network and Netscape's home page sell millions of dollars of products over the Web. Most firms hesitate to specify exactly how much their sites cost to create or how much they have generated in revenues, for fear of giving sensitive information to competitors.

For all these reasons, there is no definitive answer to the question, "How much money do Web sites make?" If you do a search on any product category, you will often find that, for each well-executed site, there appear to be about 4 to 10 times as many amateurish-looking sites to whom you would never dare give your credit card number. Even if you believed they were honest, you might have no confidence in their ability to handle your order competently.

Thus, it is true that many companies have not made money through their Web sites. Whenever you read or hear this, take some comfort in knowing that many of these attempts are simply bad attempts—incompetently executed with errors so gross as badly scanned home photography, misspellings in the first paragraph, or links that lead the user to nowhere.

Other sites fail to generate revenue despite having been produced well because they have not been adequately promoted, usually due to an innocent ignorance on the part of the site's owners. It is one thing to expect any project manager—regardless of his or her experience with computers—to meticulously proofread his or her sales copy; it is another thing to expect somebody with little Internet experience to be an expert at promoting the company's site online. (This book attempts to cover both bases—stating the obvious just because some people are so busy that they miss obvious things like proofreading, and covering the not-so-obvious nuances of site design or marketing in a tricky and sensitive culture like the Internet community.)

The simple truth is that making money on the Web is a lot like making money with any other business: It *can* be done, it *is being* done, but it isn't easy, and not everyone succeeds. Although hard rules in this arena are few, virtually all successful sites exhibit the following traits:

- They draw sufficient traffic volume.
- They provide visitors with a reason to stay once they arrive.
- They appear to be trustworthy.
- Their products are things that people want.
- Their products are priced appropriately.

Each of these traits may be obvious, but none is particularly easy to execute.

What About the Big Picture?

If you are interested in Web marketing enough to be reading this book, then I assume that you are astute, industrious, ambitious, and—most of all—progressive in your thinking (it's easy to forget sometimes, but most companies are not yet on the Web). Trying to sell you on the great reasons for going online would probably be like preaching to the choir. The short truth is that there are great reasons for heading to the Web, such as its ability to target narrow markets inexpensively and reduce administrative costs related to making sales or conducting follow-up customer service.

But let's not go crazy. Too many commentaries about the advantages of Web commerce are made by people who are excited about the prospects without necessarily being accountable for cashing in on those prospects. It's good if you are excited—that enthusiasm will help you get through the long hours of work ahead. But, the more excited you are, then the more likely it is that you could use a dose of conservatism.

Perhaps you've heard some of these remarks made about the potential of Web commerce:

- The Mother of All Paradigm Shifts
- The Future of Commerce
- The Second Goldrush
- The Leveler of Playing Fields

Instead of panting with excitement and nodding blindly, let's look at each of these claims with a discriminating mind and an eye toward realism and, most of all, hard-core business pragmatism: What is going on? How can we reach the best possible outcome given the changing environment?

The Mother of All Paradigm Shifts?

The term "paradigm shift" has only recently been used enough to qualify it as an official buzzword. The truth, however, is that paradigms have been shifting since back when a few plant cells in the primordial ooze got tired of competing for scarce sunlight and said "heck with this" and started eating fellow plant cells instead. Animals were born. A paradigm shifted.

In the grand scheme of things, that was probably more significant than Netscape walking off with the de facto Web interface standard, in broad daylight, right under Bill Gates's nose.

We are indeed at the cusp of a significant change in the way people conduct their daily lives—but, for a sense of perspective, think about the degree to which other, relatively recent innovations have affected people and business. Agriculture, written language, antibiotics, and railroads have all had a far more significant impact on humanity than Web commerce is likely to, even with virtual reality thrown in.

But I promised to keep this discussion pragmatic. These examples serve as a point of reference for our thinking, and for an important reason. If you focus only on what is happening today, you will probably fail at Web marketing or at least *fail to excel* at Web marketing. As the saying goes, "Assume that whatever people can think of today will be possible tomorrow and assume that whatever is *possible* today will be *affordable* tomorrow." In the midst of running your day-to-day business, devote some time every now and then to studying, at the very least, what is possible (but still expensive) today.

> **TIP:** Avoid being taken by surprise: Periodically ask yourself the question, "If such-and-such suddenly became cheap tomorrow, how would that affect my business?"

The Web is most significant in its ability to synergystically combine the existing power of current technologies and practices. If you think about it, the Web does little on its own except substantially beef up the usefulness of our computers, our phones, video, and even FedEx. How earth-shattering would it be that people can now receive a catalog and order something in minutes online, if they still had to wait six to eight weeks to receive their order?

To imagine the near-term boundaries of the Web's potential commercial impact, imagine that *every* business in the world, no matter how small,

- Could be easily located online

- Offered immense, searchable, hyperlinked volumes of all non-sensitive company information

- Were connected by bandwidth that supports two-way, full-screen video

If all companies were connected in such a way, it would mean amazing things for everyone. And the Web would even qualify for paradigm-shift status. But would it be the Mother of Them All? No. Is it the most significant change in our lifetimes? It might be the most significant change *for commerce* in most of our lifetimes (depending on how long one lives), but it is not difficult to imagine the *social* impacts of the Web changing our lives and world more significantly, such as with telecommuting, education, and even dating.

The Future of Commerce?

Is the Web the Future of Commerce? Yes, yes, yes. Partly. By that, I mean that nearly all businesses will require Web connection as a standard element of doing business. If for no other reason, firms will be forced to go online because Web communications are likely to merge with or supplant traditional telephone communications.

Second, the *intra*net (a company's internal, private information network) is rapidly emerging as a primary driver of Web growth as firms begin to realize the tremendous efficiencies made possible by connecting all their workers and making documents easily accessible.

But, saying that *all businesses* will be connected to the Web does not mean that all *commerce* will take place over the Web. I doubt than anyone has ever said that *all* commerce will drift toward the Web, but there is certainly disagreement among experts as to the degree and rate of migration. You've probably heard it before, but people don't usually like buying clothes that they haven't yet tried on. What about clothier catalogs? That's a good point—*some* people will buy clothes without first trying them on in a dressing room. But recognize that the $60 billion spent in all catalog sales in this country accounts for only 3 percent of all retail sales. This number will probably increase somewhat due to the sheer number of "catalogs" that can be accessed online for virtually no incremental cost. Rather than looking for online commerce to replace traditional retail commerce, expect to see Web-enhanced ways in which companies sell products with hybrid distribution models, such as being able to try clothing on in a store to assure fit and then see color options, for example, on the store's computer. The store could then offer greater variety while lowering inventory holding costs, and manufacturers could respond to demand for particular stock items in real-time—eliminating much unnecessary waste and lowering costs, particularly in industries where fashions and preferences change quickly, such as apparel.

Nearly all firms will be hooked up to the Web eventually, so a more useful question is, "*When* will they be hooked up?"

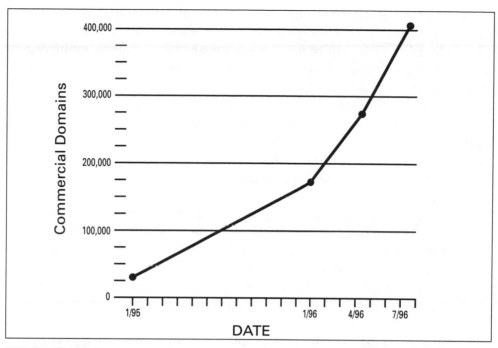

FIGURE 1.1 The registration of commercial domains continues on a steady climb as more companies come online. Source: InterNet Info (http://www.web com.com/~walsh).

One of the simplest, if crude, ways to measure the number of business Internet connections in existence is to see how many entities have registered ".com" domains (meaning "company," such as in a Web address: http://www.cocacola.com). According to InterNet Info, as of July 19, 1996, more than 419,000 commercial domains were registered with InterNIC, the organization that grants new domains to organizations who request them.

For several reasons, the total number of commercial domains is an impure measure of commercial Web proliferation. First, many companies doing business on the Web do not possess their own domain, such as "tenants" using one or two pages of another company's online mall. Second, many companies have Internet connections (for e-mail, etc.) but no publicly accessible Web site, and possibly no plans to create a site. Third, many companies have preemptively registered domains for future use, even though they have no current Web presence. For example, leading consumer products manufacturers have registered the names of each of their brands to keep somebody else from using the name. At some point in the future, Nabisco might have 50 different Web sites with distinct names, such as http://www.fignewton.com. (As unique names become more scarce, InterNIC, the entity that grants domains, is beginning to discourage single organizations from owning multiple domains—see Chapter 6, "How to Register Your Domain.")

Because the number of domains is not necessarily an indicator of how many businesses are online, it is helpful to look to other information sources that estimate the number of commercial Web sites in particular, as well as the rates of change in these numbers. As of early 1996, the research firm MIDS estimated that there were 80,000 commercial Web sites in existence.

Different studies give different estimates of how many commercial Web sites exist, sometimes varying by more than 50 percent, making exact numbers impossible to pin down. However, looking at the *rate* of domain registration and Web site growth tells a more complete story. As you can see in Figure 1.1, the number of commercial domain registrations jumped from roughly 171,000 to over 419,000 during the first six months of 1996.

If we were to extrapolate these numbers on their current exponential path, we would soon predict there to be more commercial Web sites than people on the planet. That makes no intuitive sense, even if there were a separate site for every product of every company. Therefore, this growth will inevitably begin to level off. Marketing analysts and statisticians are attempting to predict when the growth curve will begin to flatten. They will use, as reference, historical data of the adoption rate of previous technologies such as fax machines, computers, voicemail, and so on.

Your primary reasons for studying how many other businesses are online are to do the following:

- Gauge competition

- Know how far ahead of the pack you are (and duly pat yourself on the back)

- See how far behind you are (and duly get your rear into gear)

As a means of studying competition, these macro-scale statistics don't really help you much. It is more important for you to see what specific firms are doing and to assess how their actions will impact your narrow segment of the Web marketplace. Studying your Web business's competition is discussed in Chapter 2.

Estimating the number of potential online customers can be even trickier than counting businesses. For instance, a survey by the research firm Find/SVP estimates the number of Internet users in the United States to be 9.5 million, while findings by Nielsen Media Research initially put the number at 24 million (for United States and Canada), only to later adjust that number down to 19 million after industry analysts criticized Nielsen's analysis of the data.

The Numbers Keep Changing

The unprecedented growth rates of the Internet as a marketplace have prompted industry insiders to speak of the Internet in "Web weeks" or "dog years," meaning seven years' worth of change happens in one calendar year.

As such, almost any marketing statistics you see in print will likely be outdated by the time you read them, including those in this book. Be careful—if you have read that 30 percent of Web surfers are female, for example, then the real number may have reached 50 percent by the time you read it. If up-to-date numbers are important for your marketing plans, then attempt to locate such data online for the most timely information.

For links to some of the leading sources of current Internet business statistics, see this book's companion Web site at:

http://www.monsoon.org/book

The Second Goldrush?

Is this period of marketing history really a goldrush? It depends on what you mean by using that analogy. The goldrush mental picture summons images of tens of thousands of people from all walks of life quitting their jobs, spending family savings on picks and shovels, and heading for the hills in highly speculative ventures that promise huge returns to a very few lucky individuals and bankruptcy to everyone else.

That last part is, I believe, responsible for the overuse of this metaphor—large returns to a few and failure for the rest. While that analogy might describe the CD-ROM development market reasonably well, it has very little to do with the Web. Certainly, some firms have made substantial and newsworthy returns (Virtual Vineyards, for one). And many firms have not made money. But, unlike our goldrush scenario, the instance of commercial Web success is not all-or-none. And failure usually doesn't necessarily spell bankruptcy. The simple truth is that experimenting with Web-based business does not have to be extraordinarily risky because the costs of playing the game are low for many entrants. There are plenty of Web sites that don't generate much money, but they do consistently cover their low, monthly operational costs and create supplemental revenue for their owners. Gold mines usually don't work that way. Certainly, plenty of big-budget sites are taking a much more aggressive gamble. But, for each of these, there also exist low-budget, wait-and-see-what-happens sites created by more cautious businesses.

The notion of quitting your job to head for the hills of the Web deserves scrutiny as well. Most commercial Web sites are ancillary marketing functions of existing companies. That's not selling the farm; it's more like selling apple pies from the farmhouse while the crops out back sustain business as usual. Even many of the brand-new companies formed to seek Web profits are the brainchildren of moonlighting entrepreneurs, gainfully employed elsewhere during the day.

There are, of course, exceptions to this. There are people who invest large amounts of money (from $100,000 to over $1 million). There are venture capital-backed enterprises recruiting executives from Fortune 500 firms to manage big, expensive Web upstarts even as you read this. Some of these large investments will fail; others will succeed. But for now, it is still possible for college students, Mom and Pop, moonlighters, and tiny businesses to enter the realm of Web marketing without betting the farm. I emphasize the words "for now" because all of this is going to change, at least for a portion of the market (read on).

Leveling the Playing Field?

The Web has been heralded as the best thing to come along for small businesses since the ... well, the best thing *ever* to come along for small businesses. Here are some of the reasons that others have given to back up this claim:

1. Customers can now find small companies as easily as they can locate large companies.

2. Small firms with specialized, niche-oriented products can target individuals in narrow market sectors based on their unique interests.

3. Small firms can look big.

For the most part, all of these reasons are true. But let's look closer at each one of these reasons with an eye toward the future, say, the next two years.

Customers Can Now Find Small Companies as Easily as They Can Locate Large Companies

In one sense, this claim is true. Traditionally, it has been difficult or impossible for small businesses to access many markets (such as distant cities or foreign markets) due to the high costs associated with promotion, attracting distributors and rep organizations, securing shelf-space, and so on. The Web certainly opens the doors, at a very low cost, to many potential customers throughout the world. According to a story in *The Wall Street Journal*, the owners of a site that sells nothing but hot sauces (http://www.hothothot.com, described later in this book) spend about $100 per month for Internet access and draw as many new customers as if they had spent $50,000 a month on mailing catalogs.

But beware, this "leveling" of accessibility does not apply evenly to all businesses. Hot sauce is a great niche product—some people love it, they can't find 450 varieties anyplace else, and they understand what the site is all about with just two words: "hot" and "sauce." But, instead of starting a business that merely coexists next to huge corporations, suppose you were actually to compete with them, head-to-head. If you began manufacturing ordinary tires for cars, would the Web allow you to begin siphoning market share from Bridgestone and Goodyear? Probably not, unless your tires are unique and appeal only to a small segment, such as antique automobile collectors. The important distinction here is that you would no longer be competing *directly* with the giants.

> Direct competition against a big opponent is just as risky on the Web as it is in traditional markets because they can still outspend your site development and promotional budgets.

In the earliest days of commercial Web sites, a company stood a reasonable chance of receiving visitors merely by being present. Surfers would get excited simply because someone had come up with an incredible innovation ... selling flowers on the Internet! Or baseball cards—how ground-breaking! Gosh, if somebody included a snazzy graphic, then surfers would tell all of their friends to go check out the cool graphics at http://whatever.com.

But eventually, each surfer had seen cool graphics enough times that he or she was more interested in looking for something in particular, like the current skiing conditions in Snowmass. Surfers who were around in the early days can remember searching for something reasonably ordinary and coming up with *zero* hits on search engines such as Yahoo!. That used to be normal. I can imagine, years from now, my grandchildren asking me how we used to check the ski conditions back before the Internet. Imagine the confused looks on their faces when I tell them, "We used to call the radio station." (Come to think of it, that seems dumb even now. Oh well, maybe I'll just tell them we just rode up to the mountains on our horses and hoped for the best. They won't know.)

Things have come a long way in just a couple of years. I'm pretty easy-going, but I would consider firing the marketing director of any ski area that did not have, at least, a modestly functional Web site in operation by the autumn of 1996. Many consumers now *expect* this sort of information to be available, at least for certain categories of companies, such as ski resorts. AJ's Transmission, just down the street, might be another story, but we will eventually expect to find small local companies online just as surely as we now expect to find them in the phone book.

What does this mean? Well, back at the beginning, it was often *easier* to find a small company than a large company on the Internet because there were one or two small companies (in each industry) that employed someone who enjoyed playing around with computers during his or her spare time. We all know the type—they had their own Web sites chock full of baby pictures before the words "World Wide Web" had ever been uttered on CNN, and well before CNN had its own Web site.

During those days, many bigger companies (excluding technology firms) had no idea what the Web was, and getting permission, let alone money, to create a corporate Web site would have been virtually impossible. As recently as the fall of 1994, I asked a couple of brand managers at a leading consumer products company what their plans were for experimenting with advertising on the World Wide Web. Their reply: "Whaddya mean?" I was shocked. None of them had even heard of it! So I said, "You know, the *Internet*?" And then one of them suddenly looked less confused and said, "Oh, I've heard of that."

I would have understood if these people had been cattle ranchers or airline pilots, but, folks, this was one of the largest consumer product, brand management companies in the world. They are big, and like most big companies, they are conservative and feel more comfortable doing what has worked for them in the past. It was during this time that, yes, it was just as easy to find small companies as large on the Web. If you did a search on "facial soap" you were more likely to find a Web site for *Pure Oregon Honeycomb and Pumice* facial soap than you were to find *Ivory*.

But let's think about this for a moment. Isn't it also just as easy to find small companies by using the free 800 directory service (1-800-555-1212)? Any company with an 800 number is listed. The problem is, you have to know the name of the company first. What if your customers don't know your name? No problem; the Web allows us to search by category. But what happens, in the near future, if you do a search on some topic such as

```
"hiking boots"
```

and come up with a *thousand* hits? (At the time of this writing, this search yielded 163 hits on Infoseek). If you're bored, you can read all thousand of them until something strikes your fancy or until you find a specific company that you had in mind when you began. But since most people have no desire to check a thousand sites, they are prone to do one of two things:

1. Narrow the search by using more specific words.

2. Be drawn by advertising related to their search.

You will most likely narrow your search, which is addressed in the section below. If you don't narrow your search, there is a reasonable chance that you will cast your attention toward the nice-looking graphic at the top of the page (see Figure 1.2). Suppose the graphic is an ad for a maker of hiking boots. If the ad were appealing, would you click on it? Maybe, maybe not. But you are certainly more likely to notice this ad than you are to notice an obscure link, perhaps number 283 down on your list of a thousand links. If you see the ad but not the buried link, then you are more likely to actually click on the ad and visit that manufacturer's Web site.

Relating this back to a discussion of leveling the playing field for small businesses, I ask you, who is going to be placing these prominent ads with the search engines? Small businesses? Not usually. If the potential reach of an ad is large, then it will be expensive. That means large advertising budgets. That means big companies.

In this way, the Web will not be as level as some people have promised. But what about all of those people who tried a new search, with more specific parameters? This question leads to the second reason why the Web is claimed to be the leveler of big and small businesses.

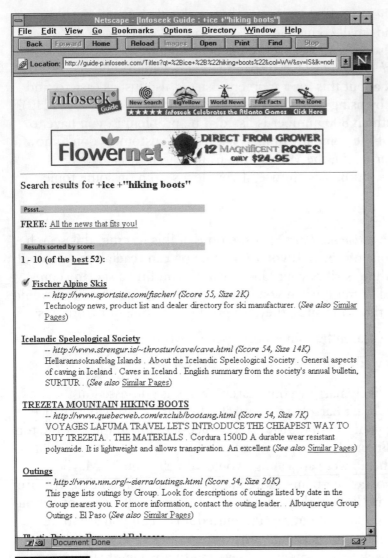

FIGURE 1.2 Today, a random flower ad accompanies a search for hiking boots. Soon, more of these ads will be directly related to your search subject.

Small Firms with Specialized Products Can Target Individuals in Narrow Market Sectors

No user wants to investigate a thousand sites related to hiking boots, so he or she will probably choose to narrow the search. Suppose our searcher is an experienced outdoorsman who seeks hiking boots that will provide superior insulation in extreme cold-weather conditions. If he were searching on Infoseek, he might narrow his search by entering the following:

```
+ice +"hiking boots"
```

This search would bring up only Web sites containing both "ice" and "hiking boots"; at the time of this writing, this narrower search reduced the number of results from 163 down to 38.

Thirty-eight listings is a reasonable number for someone to scroll through, reading down the list of brief descriptions or excerpts from the site, in order to decide which sites to investigate further. While some of the 38 search results may contain private pages with stories of somebody's recent backpacking trip, some commercial sites will remain. More importantly, some commercial sites will have been excluded, particularly the more general, mass-market-oriented sites. That's bad if you're in charge of marketing Nike outdoor products. That's good if you're marketing Asolo expedition footwear.

Even if a niche-player manufacturer of high-end outdoor footwear didn't happen to mention "ice" in its Web site, our searcher will still find stores such as The Village Cobbler (http://www.aalive.com/cobbler/) that sell "hiking boots" and "ice" climbing gear. The user can skip past the link to Popular Surplus (which sells "hiking boots" and "ice" chests) and visit The Village Cobbler, expecting to find information that is closer to his target. It is reasonable to assume (and usually accurate) that a small, specialty shop will carry more specialized merchandise such as cold-weather hiking boots of the highest quality available. The shop may provide information about the products it carries, as well as links directly to its manufacturers' Web sites.

In this way, the Web perhaps even goes beyond *leveling* the playing field for small businesses; you might even say it gives them a tremendous advantage over big businesses who depend on large, homogeneous groups of people who all want essentially the same thing.

Business analysts and futurists have had a field day mentally exploring where this will lead in the future. Some say there will be a renaissance of cottage industries in which couples working out of their homes will be able to earn a living making custom-fit sandals out of recycled tire treads by selling them to a geographically dispersed group of customers brought together by their common interests and the Web.

Others predict that Big Business will adapt to meet the challenge and find other ways to provide more specialized products and services. My favorite "way out there" example is that of being able to walk into The Gap, have your measurements taken, and sip cappuccino while a computer-controlled laser plotter cuts denim cloth and somehow assembles a perfect-fitting pair of jeans, while you wait. We'll see.

Regardless of which of these two pictures most accurately describes the future (and both may happen simultaneously), one thing is certain: The trend is moving toward ever-greater specialization. It is now passé to discuss "niche marketing" (marketing to specific, small groups) in the new, technology-enabled enterprises who think in terms of *"sliver* marketing" (resolving product attributes down to the preferences of individual consumers).

A survey of firms that have been successful with Web ventures reveals discouragingly few golden rules. Instead, success is usually determined by attention to a thousand small details—the most important of which are detailed throughout this book. But one rule appears over and over which applies to most small businesses.

> **Golden Rule of Web Marketing for Small Business:**
> Go after narrow, well-defined niches.

This is about the strongest foothold and most defensible position for a Web enterprise with minimal financial resources. Niche marketing on the Web is discussed more fully in the next chapter. Large businesses (that is, those with big budgets) should, in the short term, pay more attention to the law which appears to be most useful to large business.

> **Golden Rule of Web Marketing for Large Businesses:**
> Use the Web to cut costs and boost efficiency.

This also is discussed at greater length in Chapter 2. To be sure, both large and small businesses can follow both of these rules to some extent, so it is more a matter of emphasis and degree as opposed to deciding which rule to follow at the exclusion of the other. But lower costs, and therefore lower prices, are the greatest defense that non-niche-marketers have against niche players—There will always be a portion of the buyers who don't care so much about the particulars of a product if they can get it at a lower price, just as there will always be customers who are willing to pay more for exactly the right thing.

As a tool to aid those who market their wares to subcategories within subcategories, there has never been a more useful medium than the World Wide Web. The Internet's origins as a way of coordinating specialized research groups has, in effect, led to a design optimized for targeting people with specific interests. In enabling such high degrees of niche marketing, the Web truly has been a leveler of playing fields between large and small businesses. I must regretfully offer words of caution, however, when speaking of this state of the world. Owners of small Web businesses may not need to worry about this for a couple of years, but perk up your ears anyway.

> **Warning to Niche Marketers:**
> Technology will enable big companies to enter niche markets.

Mark my words on this. There is only one reason why Walmart doesn't currently stock recycled-tire-tread-soled sandals: limited shelf space. A Walmart store has physical, measurable, finite square footage. They will stock any and all items that promise the highest revenues for that square foot of shelf space. If they find an item that will outperform an existing item, they will bump the existing product in favor of the new product (except in special cases such as loss-leaders, which draw people to the store).

If only five people in a town with a population of 150,000 want this kind of sandal, then Walmart won't carry the sandal if the same amount of shelfspace could sell ten weed whackers.

But, aha!, this is where Web niche marketers come in, right? Right, people who need those sandals order them online from small businesses. For now anyway. But what happens, a few years down the road, if 20 percent of Walmart's sales come from online orders? If that were the case, then instead of fine-tuning the mix of items stocked in each individual store, Walmart wouldn't worry about it. They will just fulfill orders from some huge warehouse built next to the runway in a hub city of one of the overnight delivery carriers. Suddenly, Walmart can economically carry many more items, in more sizes, in more colors for the very same economic reason that there has always been more variety in a JCPenney's catalog than there ever was in the JCPenney's department store at the mall.

As you read this, larger firms are investing in technology such as huge, relational databases and software that can remember customer histories such as your name, age, foot size, and favorite NBA team. Once these systems go online and begin data-mining all known sources of marketing data (particularly the habits you exhibit while Web surfing), there isn't much to keep Walmart from attempting to meet the world's demand for tire-soled sandals. If Walmart is able to use technology to consolidate enough demand for this or any other specialized product, the company's aggressive buyers will shop around to find the lowest-cost manufacturers. They might even require quantities of sandals so large that our couple working out of their cottage could not even begin to produce enough. Suddenly, the eco-sensitive footwear is being produced in Malaysia for pennies.

To defend against this possible future, the niche marketer (or manufacturer) should ask himself or herself a critical question.

Niche-Businessperson's Heads-Up Question:
Would I be able to compete effectively if my product suddenly became so popular that fierce competitors entered my market?

Occasionally, pioneers who develop entirely new product categories from virtually nothing end up getting squashed once the category grows strong enough to attract serious competition. (Anybody out there want to buy a used Osborne computer?) It is one thing to develop a great new product. It is quite another thing to hang on to the majority of the market share of a great product category.

And finally, let's discuss the third reason people have given to describe the Web as a leveler of playing fields.

The Web Can Make Small Companies Look Big

This statement is basically true. In fact, I find this to be one of the most encouraging of the "democratizing" claims made about the Web.

As savvy consumers, we all know that there are good companies and bad companies out there. Often, the very good small companies end up growing into bigger companies. It therefore makes sense to feel more comfortable and secure when dealing with a big company because they must have done something right to become big.

We associate big companies with the notion that we will deal with professional people because big companies are supposed to have processes for screening applicants and training employees. We assume that things will get done right because big companies have systems and processes in place that are designed specifically to do things right. We assume that the customer's satisfaction will be important to the company. We also know that big companies have more to lose from bad publicity. One motivated, upset customer can do much more damage to the image of a Fortune 500 company than he or she could ever hope to do against Bob's Radiator Repair.

There is much less certainty, however, when dealing with small companies. When is the last time you saw a sign that read "All Sales Final" in a national grocery chain? I never have. But I have seen them in Mom-and-Pop fruit stands and non-franchise, dinky, owner-operator convenience stores in every part of the country. Dealing with small businesses is a crap shoot; you just don't know how it's going to turn out until it's too late. If the owner couldn't give a damn about customer service, then there's a decent chance the person behind the counter isn't too worried about it either.

As cautious consumers with limited time, we cannot afford to call the Better Business Bureau every time we try out a new dry cleaner or bagel shop. But it's hard to get ripped off at a bagel shop. The worst thing that can happen is the bagel comes out of the toaster a little burnt and the manager won't give you another one for free. Total cost? About a buck. But what about when you go to buy a new TV? Would you feel comfortable buying a $700 item from a tiny storefront in a strip mall? Will the store even still be there in three months? Even on big-ticket items, we don't bother to call the BBB because it's easier and still more assuring to make the purchase at Circuit City or Best Buy. Without bothering to read their return policies or talking to a manager, we just assume we'll be taken care of properly should something go wrong.

This prejudice of judging a company by its size is rational, but it is a prejudice just the same. That means that two types of errors can occur. First, we can still have a bad encounter with a big firm, even though we thought we were safe. Second, we pass up many opportunities for dealing happily with highly reputable and professional businesses who just happen to be small. The Web largely eliminates both of these types of errors for one reason: We don't see the size of Web companies, but we *do* see whether they're professional.

To me, this wonderful feature of Web commerce is similar to the cessation of the practice of attaching a job applicant's photograph to his or her resume (though the practice continues in many countries).

Right now, you or I could browse the Web and find a company whose site looked so amateurish and cheesy that it would be good money to assume that other elements of the enterprise were not particularly professional either. We could also find a great-looking, well-written, well-designed, and highly professional Web site and assume that the company had its act together.

In both cases, we are exhibiting prejudice again—we assume, from appearances, that the company is well run before we deal with it personally. As before, this means that we could be wrong in our assumptions. The great-looking Web site could actually be a money-laundering front for gun runners. The bad-looking site could belong to a top-notch company but was constructed as the pet project of a manager who had not yet read this book.

But these exceptions are rare. In general, the correlation between the professionalism of the site and the professionalism of the company will be reliable. That's simply because professional companies do things professionally, by definition. So we're observing a much better indicator of the thing we would really like to know than we do when we gauge the size of a company to infer its degree of professionalism.

Because the Web allows such a high degree of one-on-one interactivity with surfers and customers, the most successful Web companies, large and small alike, will be those that exhibit the best of both worlds: the high professionalism that is expected from large firms and the personalized attention exhibited by small firms.

Conveyance of a professional image has always been good for any business, and that fact will not change, even if the Web does change. Sadly, however, I am afraid that it will soon become difficult for small companies to present exactly the same *type* of professionalism as their big-budget competitors.

Technology is racing forward, and Web browsing software accepts more advanced "plug-ins" (JAVA, Shockwave, VRML, etc.); now an unlimited number of extensions can be made to the capabilities of the browser. As mentioned before, Web sites are being used as customer-friendly storefronts to massive back-end databases that can deliver customized information on the fly. Together, these technologies mean that it is becoming possible for a Web site to do some pretty amazing stuff. Imagine, for instance, a Web site that knows you've been to the site before, remembers what you looked at, and creates new pages with new information or product configurations that no other customer has ever seen before or will ever see again.

> JAVA is a programming language that allows Web sites to offer as much interactivity as ordinary computer applications. JAVA-equipped sites can do much more than ordinary sites and, accordingly, they cost more money and take more time to develop.

As more advanced Web features such as JAVA applets start to populate commercial Web sites en masse, we will begin to see the first, large-scale separation between the kids and grown-ups of Web commerce. The first sites to feature frames or streamed audio were worth checking out—even if the frames or audio weren't used particularly *well*—merely because they demonstrated a new technology. Similarly, the added functionality provided by the first few sites sporting JAVA was noteworthy simply because it was novel.

> Interactivity is the degree to which user actions change the content of a Web site. Clicking the "back" button of your browser changes the page, which is a very low form of interactivity. Filling in forms that lead to a custom-generated page is medium interactivity. Chatting in real-time with other users and playing multiplayer games are examples of high interactivity.

But the real power of JAVA is that it makes the Web much more *interactive* for the user. This will enable marketers to interact with customers in ways yet undreamed of, at the complexity level of a fast-paced video game, if need be.

Currently, small business owners can create their own Web pages by learning to use simple HTML. The added possibilities offered by JAVA and powerful databases means that high-end Web site production is going to become the exclusive domain of highly skilled programmers. If businesses wish to stay on the leading edge of Web site functionality, then today's do-it-yourselfers will eventually need to hire these specialized skills, either by bringing on trained employees or contracting with outside vendors. While these added costs will not make site production cost-prohibitive for all, it will increase the financial risks for those firms that wish to continue looking like a big company online.

If this didn't increase the stakes for Web marketers enough, don't worry, it gets worse. In time, your local cable company will be able to provide users with Internet connection, with one added feature: *huge* bandwidth. Your computer's modem will be replaced by a cable-modem, able to receive full-screen video and stereo sound, just like regular television, only digital and interactive.

That means that shoppers visiting your site, instead of reading text and seeing a few small pictures, will be able to click a button and instantly start watching a 30-minute infomercial featuring your product, or a five-minute glitzy commercial, customized for their interests, featuring Hollywood-caliber visual effects.

But wait a minute. That sounds like an expensive Web site to produce. Doesn't it?

> The Inevitable Future:
> Most of the best Web sites will cost a great deal of money to produce.

There will always be exceptions to this. First of all, the next generation of development tools (such as user-friendly JAVA programming tools and video editing software) will go a long way toward bringing production costs down, just as desktop publishing tools made high-end print production more affordable.

Second, there will always be some great new idea that is so strong on its own merits that flamboyant presentation is not necessary to attract attention. Of course, ideas this good (and the success that they bring) generally attract investors—catapulting college students to multimillionaire status in some cases. Then the simple site based on a good idea quickly becomes a state-of-the-art, extravagant site based on a good idea. Even without outside investment, Web marketers who discover a gold mine are wise to re-invest some of their booty back into the site if they wish to continue adding to their success story.

All Is Not Lost

This picture of the future need not scare you off. I expect it will excite some of you who see the changes for what they really are—opportunities. More advanced technology equates to more ways to reach people, more ways to provide value, and more ways to make money. The stakes for entering the world of Web marketing are about to get higher, meaning fewer people will possess the resources or guts to give it a try at the high end of the spectrum.

If you're serious about doing business on the Web, then this could actually be good news. The trick is to learn enough and gain some experience while market entry is still reasonably cheap. This book is intended to help speed up that learning process. Success from any venture you begin now will help fuel further advancements in terms of money, experience, and confidence.

And for the less aggressive, I should emphasize one important fact: There will always be important value provided by a simple, low-tech commercial Web site.

As stated earlier, eventually, every business will be expected to have some rudimentary form of Web presence. The majority of business sites may never operate as more than a passive, online business card, merely waiting for people to seek it out to find something as mundane as a store's hours or location. At the very least, you will be able to outsell these small firms by focusing more attention on the design, quality, and update of your site. Your aggressive promotion will also draw more traffic to your site than their passive inactivity will draw to theirs.

Even in the future Internet world of highly interactive, broad-bandwidth Web sites, consumers will be interested in dealing with firms that offer only a simple, lower-budget site, so long as they feel that they are dealing with a professional outfit. The Web will continue to provide consumers with access to millions of small firms that continue to outniche and outspecialize the Walmarts of the world by sheer creativity and entrepreneurial talent.

The fact that you are reading this book now means that, at the very least, you are far, far ahead of the laggards, if not the pack. You will learn ways to bring more people to your site and make your site work better for you. The experience that you gain now will allow you to ease into bigger and bolder Web ventures later if you choose to take an incremental approach. By experimenting with the ideas from this book, from other sources, and from your own creativity, you will become more comfortable with the technology and medium now, perhaps more comfortable than most people ever will become.

COMPETITIVE
ADVANTAGE

W eb-based businesses are one of the easiest types of commercial enterprise to create. In the language of business, one would say that "barriers to entry" are virtually nonexistent. That means that anybody, with almost no money, no prior knowledge, no contacts, and no friends can get an Internet account, snip and edit pieces from other people's Web sites, and go into business for himself.

Competitive Advantage in a Market with No Barriers to Entry

The ease of entry is good news if you are looking to get into business on the Internet. It is bad news if you are already there because it means that anybody who wants to can become your direct competitor in a matter of days.

If you are the first to get a particular, truly great idea—one that starts earning huge sums of money within days of going online—then, just as soon as your venture is written up in a magazine, you can bet there will be other entrepreneurs close behind you, watching everything you do, trying to figure out ways to do it better.

But rather than bemoaning the difficulty of maintaining a competitive edge on the Web, it is far more constructive to focus on why the state of reality is good for you, and how to best defend against competition on the Web in the short and long term.

Why No Entry Barriers Is Good for You

First and foremost, the lack of significant barriers to entering a Web-based business is good for you because it also applies to *your* market entry. Whether you are creating a business from scratch or simply adding another channel of distribution to an existing company, you can enter the market with much lower financial exposure than most traditional venues allow. In the simplest case, you can pay a hundred dollars or less to an existing Web business, say, an online mall, and have them provide you with a Web page that describes your product/service and gives visitors information they need to contact you, such as your phone number or e-mail address.

Second, even though you don't want direct competitors coming online if you can help it, you do want good Web sites to populate the Internet as quickly as possible. If your site were the only site on the Web, nobody would be browsing because there would not yet exist a critical mass of rich content to draw users online. It is true that users have limited time and attention and that all sites conceivably compete with your site for that limited attention, but, at least until every consumer regularly browses the Web, be happy that other firms are out there, collectively making the Web a more interesting and useful place to be. They are all helping to draw in a larger potential audience for you.

Mechanisms for Defending Against Competition

There is nothing to stop everyone who chooses to do so from creating a business on the Web. But that doesn't mean that there is nothing you can do to keep them from encroaching on your cozy, little, profitable corner of the Web.

If you currently have an online business, consider the following defensive strategies for making it difficult for newcomers to compete with you on your turf. It's not good enough to simply be better than the competition. You must be better in some way that is difficult for them to copy.

If you are looking to expand your Web activities, or if you are in the early planning stages of a new Web enterprise, consider these strategies as not only a way to defend yourself once you're established, but also as a way to potentially outperform or seize market share from existing Web enterprises that have failed to patch any gaping holes in their armor.

Real Estate

Have you ever seen the movie *Far and Away*? It is about Irish immigrants participating in the great Oklahoma land race in the 1800s. At the end of the movie, actors Tom Cruise and Nicole Kidman pound a stake into the ground and win the deed to a prime piece of land, their little slice of the American dream. Why did they win the land? They got there first.

It wasn't because they paid more money, because they were smarter, or because they passed a settler's aptitude test. The land went to whoever got to it first, and Tom Cruise beat everyone else. Today, descendants of those who participated in the real race may still possess large tracts of land in their family holdings because, unlike cars, real estate increases in value. But immigrants today don't even have the opportunity to race, much less win, a contest for free land. So what makes those Irish immigrants in the 1800s more deserving than immigrants today? Absolutely nothing. However, They got there first. Fair or not, that's the way things are.

Success on the Web is a numbers game. If a consistent percentage of visitors to your site purchase your products, then you want to get as many people to your site as you can. Even if you sell no products, if enough people visit your site, then you can make money showing advertisements to them. Either way, you want traffic.

The best way to create a steady stream of traffic is to provide something that lots of people want to visit. Ideally, they will want to visit frequently, even daily.

In the 1960s, a visionary real estate developer named Robert McCulloch bought thousands of acres of cheap land along the banks of the Colorado River, which separates Arizona and California. He then literally bought the London Bridge, had it shipped from London—stone by stone—and reconstructed it on his property. This attracted thousands of people to his master-planned community, known today as Lake Havasu City.

Having discovered a golden formula, he purchased 12,000 acres of cheap grazing land in the Arizona desert near Phoenix, perhaps 30 miles from the nearest gas station. He then built a man-made, 28-acre lake, in the center of which he constructed the world's tallest fountain (500 ft.) and started selling homes in his new community, called "Fountain Hills." Today, even the homes far from the lake go for millions of dollars.

> Stake a claim. Then give people a reason to visit.

The best virtual real estate you can own on the Web is that which thousands of people will visit daily without even thinking. All of those selections at along the top of your Netscape browser (What's Cool?, What's New?, Search, Destinations, etc.) are hotlinks to Web sites of the company, Netscape (see Figure 2.1)

If you look very carefully, you will also see a big, giant ad by sponsor Toshiba, which paid in the neighborhood of $20,000 per month to have this eye-grabbing rectangle cycled onto several of Netscape's pages, along with ads placed by other advertisers. The ad received approximately 750,000 exposures during the month that it was displayed. That's good real estate.

Method for Claiming Real Estate #1:
Build a new browser.

Netscape doesn't own the only prime real estate on the Web or even the only browser. Consider PointCast Inc. (http://www.pointcast.com). If you haven't heard about it yet, you probably will. Through its Web site, you can download its specialized browser (which can run completely independently of Netscape Navigator). With the PointCast Network, you customize the special browser to act as an agent that seeks out news information of interest to you, including historical stock charts, company information, industry news, sports, and weather, all for no charge.

Better still, the software acts as a screen saver that begins displaying news items, specific to your interests, whenever your computer isn't in use. It can save a great deal of time for people who would otherwise need to sift for this specific information. The entire service is sponsored by advertisers whose logos appear next to your news clips while the screen saver is active.

PointCast has, with its independent browser, essentially created a new piece of real estate. Once people go through the effort of customizing the browser to search for specific topics (which takes about ten minutes), they never have to do anything else—PointCast comes to them.

Method for Claiming Real Estate #2:
Build something that millions of people will need to visit frequently.

All of the major search engines have staked a claim for online real estate. Yahoo!, Infoseek, Alta Vista, Lycos, Excite, and Magellan are all services that many people use daily. Even though it is possible to access these pages directly (thereby avoiding an unnecessary step and circumventing Netscape's site) they derive much of their business from being on Netscape's Search page.

Naturally, building a new browser or a better search engine is beyond the scope of most Web entrepeneurs. I offer these as extreme examples to illustrate the concept of building real estate where none previously existed. I find it helpful to remind myself that the most massive and heavily trafficked Web sites were created out of thin air, by people with nothing but an idea—and sometimes by teams much smaller than you might imagine.

There are still plenty of ideas which have not been thought of. You might consider building a useful new utility that nobody else offers. For example, VersionCheck (http://www.versioncheck.com), seen in Figure 2.2, was created to provide a free and simple way for anybody to find out what is the most recent version available for any software. This may sound like an extremely narrow focus, but remember, niche-oriented strategies tend to work well on the Web. The narrow focus of VersionCheck makes the concept simple to explain with few words, and the site is frequently mentioned in the press and has generated a great deal of word-of-mouth advertising, all of which lead to higher traffic.

FIGURE 2.1 By distributing its Navigator browser to millions of users, Netscape has made its home page one of the most heavily trafficked plots of real estate on the Web.

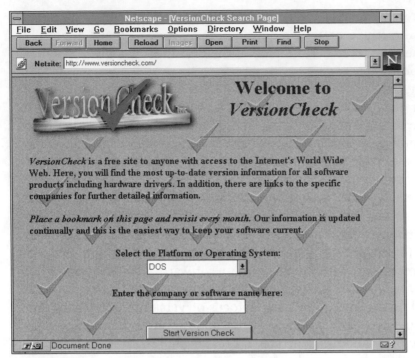

FIGURE 2.2 By offering a free and useful software look-up service to Web users, VersionCheck (http.//www.versioncheck.com) has developed a popular piece of Web real estate.

Once people look up the version of a particular piece of software, they can link directly to the software publisher's site for more information—provided, of course, that the publisher has paid for a link, which is how VersionCheck makes its money.

> **Method for Claiming Real Estate #3:** Ask users to select your page as their home page.

Users can assign your page to appear, by default, each time they log on to the Web. It can't hurt to ask. Naturally, it will help if you provide a reason that would make them want to visit your site automatically, such as a joke of the day, clues for a contest, and so on. (see "Building a Repeat-Customer Base," Chapter 14).

> **Method for Claiming Real Estate #4:**
> Ask users to bookmark your page.

Again, it can't hurt to ask. If users bookmark your page, they may not visit your site frequently, but they are much more likely to visit *again* than if they didn't bookmark your page. And if all visitors to your site visit one or two more times than they would have otherwise, the increase in traffic will be substantial.

> **The Most Important Method for Claiming Real Estate:**
> Make it your mission! Say you'll do it. Act with fervor.

Whether your business involves something in a highly competitive arena like sunscreen lotion, or something more obscure like aboriginal art, whether you're providing tangible products or pure information, give yourself a mission statement and make it guide every other action you take! If you are selling aboriginal art, then describe your site to everybody as:

> "This is *the* site on aboriginal art. On the Web, *we* are *it*. The ultimate."

Repeat this like a mantra and let it build *an attitude* which guides every step of your development and promotion stages. Design the site as though it is *the number one site* of its kind and promote it with this attainment as a foregone conclusion.

If this sounds corny or motivational or hypish, that's okay. If your closest competitor has this degree of fervor and zeal about his site and you don't, in head-to-head competition, his site will probably outperform yours. Don't think of it as hype, think of it as staking your claim.

First-Mover Advantage

In many traditional businesses, there are advantages to being the first to enter a market. The most obvious advantage relates to the section above about staking a claim to a market you're calling yours. If you moved onto a tiny island that had fifteen obstetricians and no dentists, would you rather practice obstetrics or dentistry? A wise businessperson would choose the latter. Many claims have been staked on obstetrics, so it makes sense to stake out a new claim, one with unmet demand and guaranteed work.

If you make a loud enough splash in one niche on the Web, you will scare off many would-be competitors. If they think they can do it better than you, they'll try to. But if they think there's *no way* they can do it better than you, they'll look for something different; something which isn't already being done so well.

When companies hire me to look at their Web business strategies and help them through the early ideation stages, one of the first questions I always ask is something like: "What are the three or four existing sites out there that are closest to your proposed site?" I like to ask them this in person so that they have to answer immediately, with no time to go do some extra homework. Invariably, I get one of two types of responses:

Type 1: "Well there are only two that come remotely close. The most serious-looking is an outfit in Connecticut who carries a lot of the same manufacturers but gears everything to the high-end customer, with pricing that reflects . . ."

Type 2: "Uh . . . I'm not sure." (At this point, the guy usually looks over at someone else and says, "Have we looked to see who else is out there?")

My purpose for asking this question is not to make anybody look bad, although it does sometimes have that effect. It can also scare them enough that I feel like I've earned my entire fee in five minutes. And if they wish to retain me further, I know where to begin my work. I do what the "Type 1" people have already done, and what you should do:

- Conduct an exhaustive search of every Web (and, where appropriate, non-Web) business who directly competes in your intended field.

- List the companies in order of how closely they compete with you.

- For those who compete most directly, assess the strengths and weaknesses of their sites and anything that can be inferred about their business models and promotional strategies.

> **TIP:** If your competitor sells advertising space, check to see if a rate card is available at the site. This will tell you not only what they charge for advertising, but also information about their site traffic and, possibly, visitor demographics.

If one of the greatest advantages of being the first to enter a market is unchallenged claim-staking, then one of the biggest disadvantages for the first-mover is that there is no one to provide an example, or a benchmark against which you will compare yourself. Trailblazing means not having a path—getting cut by occasional thorns and frequently not knowing which direction to turn. When you are the second firm to enter a market, you are able to infer a lot about what works and what doesn't by watching what the first-mover does, and more importantly, what it no longer does. You may avoid some of the mistakes your competitor has made.

Before the Web came along, a great way to gauge whether your competitor was having success with his or her business and advertising methods was to observe, over time (six months, for example), whether he or she continued to run the same ads in the same publications. Logic suggests that if the ads weren't working, he or she would stop wasting the money every month. Astute observers have used this method to figure out which magazines work best, what size ads work best, and what type of ad works best—all without spending a dime on advertising.

While this method can be mimicked on the Net to see if other companies are deriving benefit from paid ads they place online, the method doesn't work with regard to being able to guess whether another company's actual *Web site* is successful as a marketing expenditure. Keep in mind that it can be fairly cheap to *maintain* a site once the initial work is done. A site that cost $5,000 to launch may cost only $30 per month to keep online, if no changes are made to the site. An unsuccessful site may therefore stay on the Web for a long time.

However, it is a good bet that a Web site is doing well if the site is frequently updated (such as every two weeks) over a long period of time (such as six months). I don't recommend delaying your business plans by waiting months just to see if competitors keep changing their sites. However, you might think back to some sites that you visited several months ago—perhaps some of the first sites you encountered when you had just begun browsing the Web. Make a note of which ones are still in existence and which ones have vanished.

Of the sites that have remained open, next identify which ones have changed significantly. Have large, new sections been added? Has the site undergone a design facelift? In particular, has any new interactivity been added, such as a search feature? Does the page say it was "last updated" within the past two weeks? (Check "View" then "Document Info" with Netscape Navigator to see if a "Last Modified" date is available.) Any of these suggests that a site might be drawing enough revenue for the owner to justify continued expenditures on site development.

But you don't necessarily have to study your competition to learn what works on the Web. You can keep reading books like this one and spend time each week browsing to see what different people are trying. If some clever idea seems to be working (that is, if they keep doing it) for a player in a different industry, then maybe it will work in your industry or niche.

Many Web marketers get so bogged down with the details of running their sites that they give up a formerly time-hogging passion—aimless browsing. This is dangerous. Browsing is probably what educated you about the Web in the first place. It is also one of the best ways to learn new ideas and stay informed about trends.

There was a time when it was smart to wait and see what fate befell other online marketers before jumping into the game. For example, before the Web exploded in popularity, it was far less clear whether a company should risk dabbling with online transactions over the major online services (AOL, CompuServe, etc.). Things have stabilized enough to suggest a likely future for electronic commerce. The time for "wait and see" is gone.

Because the costs of experimenting with most Web marketing ideas are, for now, reasonably low, I usually recommend that just about any company that is considering going on the Web do so right away. Every now and then, a unique idea comes along. But, chances are, somebody is already doing something similar to what you've got in mind. Don't expect to be the first or one-of-a-kind in a big category. Rather, focus on a subcategory that nobody else has yet thought to exploit. This strategy gives you the best of both worlds; role models to follow from your larger category and your own claim to a unique subcategory. Even though some firms will enter the market with the approach of being "the same, only better," I would advise people to do the following:

- Differentiate yourself as much as possible from the very beginning.

- Look for an idea that is as original and creative as possible.

- Look for ways to add real value to people who visit your site.

If you have an idea, begin today. You can learn a lot and do a lot before you actually start spending money. Your idea will change and grow during every step of this process. As you talk to other people, your idea will continue to change, sometimes becoming more refined sometimes leading down a slightly better path that you hadn't originally considered. Here is a brief list of reasons why you should start right away (actually, a summary— many of these reasons you'll find elsewhere in this book):

1. Staking your claim first may deter competitors from entering.

2. Novelty gets press, and press is key to gaining dominant market share. If your site comes out just after a similar site, you may be seen as "me too" and get much less press.

3. If you keep costs low, then you can safely learn while you refine your site and business model.*

4. Even if you are not profitable at first, the market is growing as more users gain Web access. As long as you experiment and continue to learn, your extra year of experience with Web marketing will pay dividends later.*

Even though I've argued that you should strive to create a Web business that is totally original and unique, I realize that many people will still find compelling reasons to enter niche categories in which competitors have already staked a claim. If you are one of these so-called "second-movers" or latecomers, I offer these words of advice:

1. If you must adopt a "the same, only better" attitude, make sure to focus your efforts on the "better" portion of that statement and strive to find *visible points of differentiation*, such as lower prices, more customized service, better selection, and so on. Realize that the aspects of your business that are identical to somebody else's will be aided by your competitor's actions as he or she broadens the market of your general category. For example, Wrangler benefited when Levi's revived the popularity of jeans in the early '80s.

---

*Warning: See the sidebar in this chapter, "An Argument Against Incremental Growth."

An Argument Against Incremental Growth

Throughout this book, I talk about the good reasons for starting out small (in terms of the size and complexity of your Web site) and growing gradually. But there is a potential risk in doing this. Slowly adding functionality and improving your Web site gives competitors time to mimic and improve their sites based on your ideas.

However, if you, all at once, spring a massive and fully mature service onto the market, then the sheer weight of your accomplishment can psychologically and practically impair would-be competitors. If they witness that your huge investment in time and effort (and probably money, in this case) makes your site the "best of its class" by a wide margin, then they will think long and hard before attempting to come out with something better. They know they will have to invest even more than you did.

But despite this, in most cases, I believe that the arguments for building your site gradually prevail. The reason I've downplayed the above argument against incrementalism is that "fully mature" is a state that never actually occurs. There will always be upgrades and improvements, even with complex and giant sites like Yahoo!. Also, even if a site doesn't change for six months, it may change on the seventh month. Thus, all sites are perpetually "under construction." If you wait to reach perfection or critical mass, you could find yourself waiting indefinitely, always looking for that last bit of improvement. If you wait too long before releasing a new site or feature, then you run the risk of watching somebody else do it first. Even if their implementation is not as refined as yours, they may derive some of the first-mover advantages mentioned earlier in this chapter. If you must wait, don't wait too long.

2. The incumbent firm or firms may not notice your entry into the market. Of course, the more you promote your site, the more likely they are to discover you. But, for example, you may register your site with search engines, begin drawing modest traffic, and refine your site for weeks before actually launching a big promotional splash. In talking with commercial site owners, I've discovered an interesting point. While most of them do diligent reconnaissance work *before* going online (checking out the competition), they seem to neglect this activity *once they go online*. They get too bogged down by the details of running a business to look over their shoulder at who's coming at them.

Keeping abreast of the competition sounds important but, in practice, often becomes a low priority. This may be an opportunity for you. If you undercut your competition on the price of a popular item, for example, users who are adept at comparison shopping may find out about you long before your overworked competitor finds out.

And it goes without saying, that once you get bogged down with the details of running *your* business, you won't let anybody sneak up behind you ... right?

Intellectual Property

All of the strategies mentioned above for securing a competitive foothold are nice, except for one thing. They aren't indefinitely sustainable. Perhaps nothing stays constant forever, but on the Web, very little stays the same for even a month.

There are very few things that you can do to outsell your competition that he or she cannot copy in a short span of time. If you implement some new feature meant to draw traffic to your site—perhaps a job board—there is nothing to stop your competitor from implementing a similar job board. How nice of you to give them the idea. They may even do it better than you. And then, not only are your sites competing, but your job boards are competing.

But there is hope—intellectual property lasts a long time. The term refers to patents, copyrights, trademarks, and trade secrets. For our discussion, we'll concentrate on copyrights, trademarks, and an additional topic (my personal favorite), exclusive agreements.

But first, some things need to be said. Although I once talked my way out of a parking violation before a judge, I definitely am *not* an attorney. Nothing in this book should be regarded as legal advice. If any part of the next section jumps out at you as being relevant to your Web business, then I highly recommended that you talk to a lawyer to make sure you're protected, both from unscrupulous others and from your own mistakes.

If you'd like to contact an attorney who specializes in intellectual property and Web commerce, check the links at this book's online companion: http://www.monsoon.org/book.

Copyrights

At the risk of stating the obvious, one of the most defensible Web business strategies is to create a site that people like and tell their friends about. Others may copy your ideas, but they can't legally copy your words or images. If you have a gift for telling stories, being persuasive, or making people laugh, then, by all means, use it! Such gifts are rare.

Good material can be stories, jokes, recipes, advice, Tip of the Day, Word of the Day, or You-Name-It of the Day.

First, consider the value of pure information—bland, dry text. There are people who make a good living conducting e-mail surveys, compiling the results, and selling the findings to companies who advertise on the Web. These analysts and researchers do a lot of hard work at the beginning, compiling information that doesn't exists anyplace else. They release some of the most newsworthy highlights as press releases. Anybody who wants the full report can then pay $500 (and often much more) for a printed, 50-page copy. Buyers of these expensive research reports typically do not turn around and redistribute the information because they have paid a lot for the report and they want to keep the contents to themselves, they don't want their competitors to learn the same information, and the report is difficult to reproduce because it is in a printed format rather than electronic.

That's just one way to make money—selling nothing but statistical data. Imagine the infinite variety of useful tips, beautiful graphics, or entertaining words that you could use to draw people to a Web site. The possibilities are limited only by your imagination. Sure, there are already hundreds of funny, bizarre, brilliant, or otherwise memorable sites out there, but there are *hundreds of thousands* of sites that almost nobody would be interested in visiting. You want to be one of the relatively small group of sites that people actually tell their friends about.

Regardless of your chosen business model, creativity will be one of the biggest determinants of how well your site performs.

If your site makes money based on advertiser sponsorship, then you will need to draw large numbers of visitors. Aim for a gimmick or some compelling aspect of your site that hooks people instantly. Something that people immediately understand—something called "high concept".

An example of a high-concept site is "Find the Spam" (http://sp1 .berkeley.edu/findthespam.html). Visitors to the site attempt to find the Spam in a picture, but the Spam is so ridiculously large that you could never miss it (see Figure 2.3). It's very gimmicky, and it works.

Netscape - [http://sp1.berkeley.edu/findthespam.html]

File Edit View Go Bookmarks Options Directory Window Help

Back Forward Home Reload Images Open Print Find Stop

Location: http://sp1.berkeley.edu/findthespam.html

-- Sanitized for your convenience.

Welcome to Find-the-Spam

• SPAM • SPAM • SPAM • SPAM • SPAM • SPAM • SPAM • SPAM • SPAM • SPAM • SPAM • SPAM • SPAM •

Somewhere in the picture below is spam.

If you think you've found the spam, click on it to find out whether you're right. A word of caution: It's not as easy as it looks. Most people find it best to stare directly into the image for two to three hours before they have the confidence to find the spam on their own.

For those of you using a text-only browser, here is the non-graphical version of Find-the-Spam. Select the one which is Spam: Spam ... **a moose**

If you've tried and tried and still can't get it, there's a Spam Help page.

http://sp1.berkeley.edu/maps/spam.map?197,264

FIGURE 2.3 High-concept and clever gimmicks are a good way to draw traffic, as with sites such as "Find the Spam" (http://sp1.berkeley.edu/findthespam.html).

While "Find the Spam" is not a commercial site, there is no reason why the trick could not have been masterminded by a Web operator at Hormel or a neighborhood deli. (Again, check with an attorney about things like using another company's trademark in such a fashion—you might even be able to get them to *pay* you to promote them in such a way.) High-concept sites are some of the most successful sites at receiving "What's Cool" links (see Chapter 8) and generating tremendous word-of-mouth promotion.

Trademarks

While most entrepreneurs and commercial Web site owners understand that having a trademark provides them with some protection against knock-off companies, they stop short of realizing the true value of the trademark and its business extensions. Don't think of your business in terms of its name and logo; think in terms of the *brand equity* you build each day.

Brand equity is a phrase that embodies everything your customers have come to associate with your business. If your name and logo conjure up feelings of professionalism and exemplary customer service, then that is part of your brand equity—an intangible but very real asset.

If you are creating a new company, then you have little or no brand equity built up yet. Nobody has heard of you. The words you choose for your name might trigger some automatic response among some people, but that is a far cry from what the words "Harley Davidson" mean to nearly everybody. Harley has huge brand equity, which, unlike Coke, Pepsi, and AT&T, was built not by immense advertising expenditures, but by the loyalty and devotion of its customers.

Your Web site should have an identity.

A large portion of your brand is called "corporate identity," or simply "identity." If you walk into a design firm and ask for a basic corporate identity package, they will assume you want a logo, letterhead, and business cards. If they are good, they will ask you what sort of image you want to convey. They should ask you who your customers are—for example, industrial buyers or end consumers? They should ask if you want to appeal more to sophisticated audiences or plain, everyday folks. They will get a feel for your company and its strengths and then craft an identity that conveys that essence in a glance.

Similarly, you want people to assume a lot of things subconsciously about your business just from seeing your site's home page. They should also feel as though they have stepped into a recognizable place. See Chapter 14 for tips on how to do this.

If your site is the online marketing mechanism for Annabelle's Antiques, you might just name your site "Annabelle's Antiques Page." That might work, especially if thousands of people are already familiar with your business. In this case, chances are, only people who drive by your store each day are familiar with the name. In other words, your accumulated brand equity is small and very localized. Wouldn't you rather visit a site called "The Treasure Chest"? Perhaps that's taken already. How about, "Grandma's Attic"?

When people visit "Grandma's Attic," imagine they are met with beautiful, subtle graphics and icons that convey the feeling of arriving in an old, long-forgotten attic. Perhaps icons of antique items are used as the links to other pages within your site. Perhaps there is a "locked desk" page; in order to open this page, visitors must find the key (a password) somewhere on your site.

If you start with a strong metaphor or "virtual place," then the creative ideas will begin to flow naturally, as your mind envisions such a place. If you brainstorm with two or three people, you will have more great ideas than you have time to implement.

The list below is made up of Web sites that have a strong identities. They possess their own names, distinct from the company that created them. Some are the creations of small companies; some are from large firms. In the cases of sites created by large companies that have significant, established brand equity (such as Silicon Graphics), the sites make their relationship to their parent company obvious by incorporating the parent's logo or mentioning the parent in small print, as in Figure 2.4. In this way, the site has a life of its own while piggy-backing on the established familiarity of its parent company.

Sites with Names of Their Own

"Silicon Surf"	Corporate site of Silicon Graphics
"Planet Reebok"	Corporate site of Reebok
"Sound Advice"	A site about using sound on the Internet
"CDnow"	A site that sells music

A site that is merely given the name of its parent company doesn't immediately convey the "feel" of being its own entity. "Joe Boxer" may

FIGURE 2.4 Silicon Graphics has created a separate identity for its site by giving the site a name of its own, "Silicon Surf" (http://www.sgi.com).

interest people who are into the bizarre line of undergarments, but something a little more creative like "Joe Boxer's Hangout" (featuring cool underwear hanging on a clothesline) would give the site visitor a greater sense of entering a special place than the current name/identity does (see Figure 2.5).

Sites Named after Their Company

"Joe Boxer"	Corporate site of Joe Boxer underwear
"TreEco Products"	A firm that sells eco-friendly products
"Metropolitan Museum of Art Gift Shop"	Pretty self-explanatory

Notice the last example. In this case, it makes great sense for the Metropolitan Museum of Art Gift Shop to keep its real name as its Web site name because it is already the name of a real place, with established brand equity. Now shoppers can visit the virtual version of the same place.

FIGURE 2.5 Joe Boxer has simply named its site "Joe Boxer," perhaps missing an opportunity to build the site into a "place" with its own identity.

Exclusive Agreements

Like copyrights and trademarks, you can defend your marketing position with the use of special rights that you have and that nobody else has. The best example is that of an aggressive, Web-marketing-savvy firm partnering with an established company that has strong brand equity but no knowledge of the Web. The online company can negotiate the exclusive rights to be the electronic distributor of the company's products. I know several people who have wanted to create online businesses, but they had no product to sell. They managed to find partners in the form of existing companies that wanted to go online but were afraid to invest in unfamiliar technology or to hire employees who knew about running commercial Web sites.

If done properly, these deals can be a true win/win. The Web marketers must meet agreed-upon minimum performance criteria, or they lose their exclusive license to act as the manufacturer's Web marketing presence. The manufacturer agrees not to let anybody else use the company logo on other Web sites.

Being Smarter

Finally, one of the best ways to maintain a competitive advantage is simply to do things smarter than the other company. If this sounds so obvious that it doesn't need to be mentioned, then I will remind you that many firms do dumb things. Perhaps more frequently, they don't do anything dumb, but they fail to continue looking for ways to act smarter every day. This entire book is about trying to be smart. To summarize some of the categories of ways to be smart, consider the following.

1. **Be proactive**—Don't wait for something to go wrong before you change things. You already know that the Web market changes at lightning pace, in every way from technology to accepted practices to customer habits.

> If you find a formula for success, assume it will not last longer than a few months.

In 1995, Netscape shocked Yahoo! by removing it from the most prominent position on Netscape's Search page. This was an unexpected and damaging blow to Yahoo!, whose hit count dropped sharply. Shortly thereafter, Yahoo! (and the other directory services shown on Netscape's Search page) began to strongly encourage its visitors to bookmark the Yahoo! page so that users could circumvent the unnecessary step of going through Netscape's Search page. If Yahoo! had been doing this all along, it might have avoided losing a great deal of traffic.

As the old saying goes, "expect the best and be prepared for the worst."

2. **Experiment constantly**—Management guru Tom Peters used to emphasize that "excellent" firms practiced regular goal setting. Over the years, Mr. Peters has changed his tune. Acknowledging that the environment now changes so quickly that long-range goals can lead people down the wrong road, his new message for managers is that they do the following:

   1. Try "stuff" all of the time.

   2. See what works.

There has never been a marketing medium more well suited to experimentation than the Web. Your product's pricing, description, packaging, and even its *name* can be altered moment by moment, if necessary, and the resulting changes in inquiries and sales can be seen within hours (and sometimes even in real-time).

3. **Seek out efficiency**—Almost every commercial Web site manager or Web entrepreneur whom I know has told me basically the same thing: "I wish I could clone myself."

   There are so many things that must be done that many of these people have half-jokingly commented that their eating, social lives, and personal hygiene have gone down the tubes since they've begun their Web project. First of all, there are many tiny details that must be addressed for things to work at all. Most people handle these details capably but then become overwhelmed with all of the extra things that they *could be doing* to promote their site. Should you work just a couple more hours and ask a few more sites to provide links to your site? Some of them will do it, and there might as well be an infinite number of other sites out there that you could ask.

   Web marketers who are successful in the long term will be those who embrace new tools and technologies that allow them to do more things in the same amount of time. I discuss a number of these later in this book.

4. **Be Creative**—Yes, I said this at least once already. I really mean it. If you aren't creative, hire or partner with someone who is. In fact, an ideal team for this business might be one brilliant, creative person and another meticulous, number-crunching person. If these two can manage to work well together, they just might make some money.

SCALE AND SCOPE: HOW BIG
DO YOU WANT TO GET?

A s you begin to develop your strategy for creating a successful Web-based business, it is natural to begin by thinking about your business model—that is, what you will sell, how you will make it, and how you will sell it.

Almost all non-Web businesses require a substantial investment before doors can open for business. The Web is exceptional in its ability to let people start up for almost nothing. However, many Web start-ups do require substantial investments for one reason or another. Before we delve too deeply into what you'll sell and how you'll sell it, you must answer one big question first: How big do you want to start out?

Before you start designing a business around your site (or a site around your business), you will need to decide what your site will be able to do, who will run it, how often its content will change, how much all of this will cost, and how much customer traffic will be required to support your venture. While these are concerns for all businesses, if you are a self-funded entrepreneur or a very small company, they become immensely important.

Business Risk vs. Personal Risk
Bigger investments mean bigger risk, but it's probably not all your personal risk. Smaller investments mean smaller risk, but a lot of it is probably your own personal risk.

To some extent, Web sites are scalable—meaning a small project can gradually grow into a large, complex operation. Practical realities, however, separate most sites into two camps, which I'll call "big" and "small," referring to the size of investment and scope of the project.

You must choose the degree of commitment at which it makes the most sense to begin. This is not just a financial, technical, and strategic question; it is a personal one as well. What exactly do you want out of this? Are you willing to risk a lot of money on a possibly slim chance of making a fortune? Or would you be content with some additional income with little associated risk? Is this an experiment or a passion? A hobby or your livelihood?

Big Site versus Small Site

If you had to be an animal in the Canadian wilderness, would you rather be a moose or a field mouse? If the objective were longevity, it's not clear which animal you should choose. Each has advantages and disadvantages.

The advantage to being a moose is that you are so big that nobody messes with you. The disadvantage is also that you are big—so big that you have to look everywhere for enough food to sustain your massive weight. Wolves won't kill you, but you may starve to death. The advantage to being a field mouse is that you are very small—so small that you can live plentifully off the seeds produced by a small patch of land. On the other hand, you wouldn't put up much of a fight against even a wolf cub.

This moose/mouse perspective is an appropriate analogy for businesses and, more specifically, commercial Web sites. Small businesses do not require huge revenues to support bureaucratic organizations and massive infrastructure such as those found in large corporations. A public relations consultant working out of his or her home can make a comfortable living serving just one good client, but there is a limit to how much money this person can make without growing the size of the business. Larger companies, however, have the upside potential of earning enormous income. The downside is that, when sales are low, large organizations lose money like a severed artery loses blood—fast. For this reason, behemoth firms like airframe manufacturers either make or lose a billion dollars on any given year, depending on whether they win or lose a couple of key contracts.

Web site economics operate under a similar set of rules. As the Web marketplace unfolds, we're seeing two broad categories of commercial sites:

1. **Small-investment commercial Web sites**—A small-investment site might be created by one or two people, housed on the server of a

local Internet provider, and created by the site's owners for less than $1,000 up front and less than $100 per month. These sites may pay their service provider one-time fees to set up custom interactivity, such as forms allowing secure transactions. The owners may modify the text and graphical content of their sites at any frequency they desire, but due to limited resources (particularly time) these sites usually remain under 40 pages and are generally updated weekly or even much less frequently. Daily or continuous content updates require dedicated personnel or custom computer programming, which is not usually an option for small-investment sites. The simplest of these sites can be easily managed via modem from a home-based business.

2. **Large-investment commercial Web sites**—These big-budget sites can have initial start-up costs ranging from $50,000 to over $1 million. When such sites are created as new companies (as opposed to being an adjunct operation of an existing firm), outside financing (either debt or equity, such as venture capital) is usually required. With so much at stake, these ventures need total control over their own server/s and usually either partner with a competent technology company or hire dedicated technical personnel and house their own machines. These large and complex sites can have hundreds or thousands of Web pages, and they often generate custom pages on the fly. Such sites are often built by a team of full-time employees, such as an in-house graphics department, Web page designers, copywriters, JAVA programmers, and others. These tasks are sometimes outsourced to specialized Web development firms, but it usually becomes more economical to bring the capabilities in-house if content or site design is expected to be updated frequently. Large investment also means money is available for traditional promotion (such as television or radio advertisements), which are an expensive—but potentially effective—way of generating substantial traffic.

(Chapter 5 describes ways to cut costs regardless of your business model and regardless of whether your site is big or small. For now, think about the strategic differences between sites that can be operated by a handful of people versus those that are built and maintained by a large group of people.) In all likelihood, the more expensive of these two types of site will have more features and functionality, which will help it draw more traffic. That's the good news for big site owners.

> Bigger sites offer more content. More content means there is something for everyone. Therefore, big sites are usually able to draw more traffic.

The bad news is that a large investment site *must* draw more traffic if it ever hopes to break even. According to Forrester Research, in 1995, Time Warner Inc. lost $8 million on its massive Pathfinder Web site. Other large publishers are continually revamping their business models, one day offering their services for free (advertiser-sponsored), only to switch the next day to charging for subscriptions, and so on. These policy changes are a desperate attempt to find any formula that will cause their sites to make money, and many large sites are not finding any formula that works.

Whether you are just beginning to come up with ideas for a potential Web business or you have already written a business plan and begun to build your site, consider the following rule of thumb:

> The larger the investment ... (upside) the more money your site can potentially make, and (downside) the harder it will be to become profitable.

Just like playing blackjack in Las Vegas, investment size is a sort of multiplier—betting big means you will probably either win big or lose big. There are exceptions, of course, but the rule generally holds. Unlike Vegas, however, risk does not necessarily scale in a linear fashion on the Web. Good data are rare due to firms' unwillingness to disclose financial information, but many of the "most successful" large Web sites have not earned a profit yet. Presumably, these sites consider themselves successful because they have drawn heavy traffic, won critical acclaim, and have earned revenues at or above projections. Such sites are often "on target" to become profitable at some future date. Many small-investment sites, however, by sheer virtue of their low start-up costs, managed to be profitable in days or weeks. Of course, "profitable" does not mean they are making *a lot* of money, just that they are making *some* money after the site's bills are paid each month.

Therefore, I recommend that most firms take a smaller, more conservative approach with an emphasis on keeping costs as low as possible without sacrificing professionalism. Exceptions do exist, and sometimes moving fast with a big investment is the only way to seize a brief window of opportunity. Or you might be the first person to have a truly great idea that really can't be scaled from small to big—meaning you must make a big investment to launch your idea properly. For most commercial sites, these all-or-none, do-or-die scenarios don't apply.

Be bold in your thinking, cautious in your spending. When considering how large a commitment to make, you must also consider that inexpensive sites can often sustain success simply by drawing new people. Expensive sites not only must draw new people, but also must keep repeat visitors coming back.

This profound difference will impact every facet of your strategy. Think about a small Web business that sells a special type of fishing lure. If a minute fraction of all the world's Web surfers stop by and purchase enough lures for the site to cover its costs and earn a profit one month, then the site may continue to be profitable month after month simply by drawing a small percentage of the ever-growing number of people hooking up to the Internet. Simply put, growth of the overall user base could make this company's profitability sustainable for several years at least. If so, anything that causes customers to revisit and purchase again will add incrementally to the site's profitability.

On the other hand, large and expensive sites that have been in operation for less than a year generally do not report being profitable so soon. With such high initial development costs, some sites do not expect to be profitable even for a couple of years. This might sound as if the site's managers do not expect the site to generate much revenue until some future date, perhaps when more people have learned about the site or when the Internet's customer base has grown larger. This is not necessarily the case. In many instances, sites need to quickly begin generating revenue so that they can, at the very least, cover the monthly expenses associated with maintaining and updating the site and keep paying the bills. Once this positive cash flow is created, the company can begin paying off the site's initial, up-front development costs.

When deciding whether to go big or small, make a distinction between one-time development costs and ongoing maintenance costs. In general, the sites that are more expensive to create will be more expensive to maintain and update. However, the type of business model you choose will determine what your life will be like for the next couple of years, so give it some careful thought. Consider the cost structures in Figure 3.1.

1 Low Start-up Costs/Low Ongoing Costs

Example: A simple yet elegant site attracts visitors who are interested in hiring an executive search firm. The site provides much

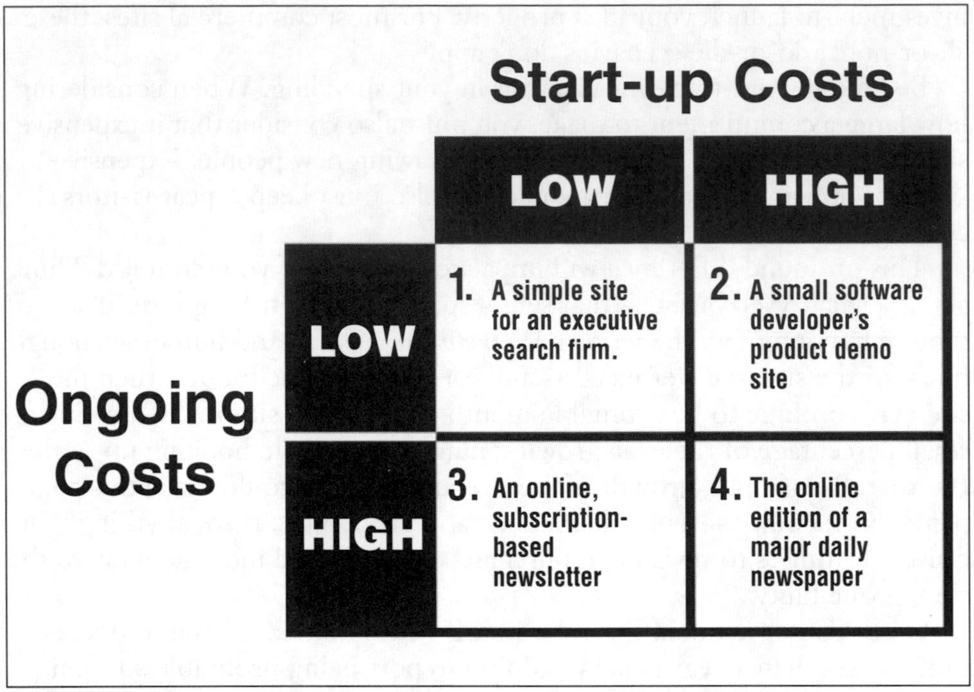

Start-up Costs

	LOW	HIGH
LOW	**1.** A simple site for an executive search firm.	**2.** A small software developer's product demo site
HIGH	**3.** An online, subscription-based newsletter	**4.** The online edition of a major daily newspaper

Ongoing Costs (row label spanning LOW and HIGH rows)

FIGURE 3.1 Different business models lead to dramatically different cost structures.

information about the company and its services, but little interactivity, essentially inducing prequalified clients to call the firm directly.

Pros: The costs are low all around. A site like this could be created on a shoestring budget and might need to be tinkered with only on rare, special occasions.

Cons: The upside potential of such a site is limited. Without adding additional features or online services (such as resume preparation services), the site will not be able to create new revenue sources.

2   High Start-up Costs/Low Ongoing Costs

Example: A small, one-product software developer creates a complex, interactive site that allows visitors to see demonstrations of what the software can do. Demo JAVA applets, downloads of demos, full products, and upgrades are available online, as are credit card transactions. A searchable FAQ (list of Frequently Asked Questions) allows visitors to seek specific information.

Pros: The nature of the business and product is such that the site does not need to change often, except when product updates become available, for example. The site has enough functionality that most potential customers will be able to find the answers they need to their questions without tying up sales representatives on the telephone.

Cons: The initial development costs of a site with this degree of interactivity is higher than many small businesses would need to spend. Even with positive monthly cash flow from the site, it will take longer for this site to recoup its investment and begin to earn a profit.

3 Low Start-up Costs/High Ongoing Costs

Example A, Small Company: An online, subscription-based newsletter provides a clean and simple format for visitors to read timely and industry-specific information.

Pros: The initial site design may be simple enough that the small business owner was able to create the site without hiring experts. Basing the business on a paid-subscription model helps maintain an active customer base, once those customers are obtained.

Cons: The owner/writer of this newsletter is a slave to his or her active customer base, and the words "running on auto-pilot" will have no meaning to this site's owner as they do to some Web marketers. The ongoing costs associated with keeping the site alive (writing each week's new articles) are probably impossible to automate without adding staff, meaning the ongoing costs are expensive in terms of either time or money.

Example B, Larger Company: A 2,500-employee company creates a nonautomated registry that allows both insiders and outsiders to look up the telephone number of employees, departments, or sales representatives.

Pros: By creating this registry in a nonautomated fashion, the start-up costs might be inexpensive (relative to other site start-up costs), even if the data were entered by hand. This might be a good option if the information were not expected to change frequently.

Cons: If the information were to change frequently, then manual edits in this nonautomated system would begin to add up. Such ongoing costs would be virtually nonexistent if a larger investment had been made in the beginning and the site had originally been built as an interface to an existing company database.

4 High Start-up Costs/High Ongoing Costs

Example: The online version of a major metropolitan newspaper.

Pros: The strong brand awareness that already exists will make it easier to draw big traffic initially, as well as the ability to capitalize on print/online cross-promotions. Such large traffic volume will create a good piece of online real estate that the company may use in any number of imaginative ways, meaning the upside potential income may be extremely high.

Cons: The breadth, scope, and complexity of the site will make this one of the most expensive sites to be found anywhere. The extraordinarily high start-up costs mean the venture will succeed only if the online newspaper consistently draws high traffic. This means that building a base of regular, *repeat* customers is crucial and that the venture will fold if site visitors never return after their first visit. Keeping so many people interested in returning means that fresh, new content must always be replacing the old. This is a dangerous situation because the site owners must continue to pour massive resources into the site's upkeep. If traffic begins to wane, management will be in the difficult position of deciding whether to (a) spend more, in order to re-energize the business, while risking throwing good money after bad, or (b) spend less in order to slow down negative cash flow while hoping that other efforts (such as promotion) will help to boost site traffic—risking that the lower quality of content will bore existing and new visitors.

> **Something to Consider:**
> Naturally, everybody wants repeat customers. However, the bigger your investment, the more likely it is that you will *require* repeat customers just to break even.

(For specific strategies related to building repeat visitor traffic, see Chapter 14.)

Degrees of Site Complexity

When referring to Web sites, "complexity" generally refers to categories such as size of the site, number of elements, frequency of updates, and degree of interactivity.

- **Size**—The size of a site is usually measured in number of pages. Larger sites naturally take more work to create and maintain than smaller sites. "Large" is a relative word, depending on the resources available. For a small company in which only one or two people maintain the site, a site over 20 pages could be considered large.

- **Number of elements**—"Elements" refers to anything that users see or do on the page, such as small graphic icons, larger photos, headlines, articles, clickable links, downloadable files, audio clips, forms, and so on. Somebody has to create and keep track of all of these elements, as well as link them all together in an HTML document.

- **Update Frequency**—Revising a simple site every day doesn't make the site more complex, but it contributes significantly to the complexity of *managing* the site once it is up and running. Some sites remain commercially viable with very infrequent updates (such as once every couple of months), depending on the nature of the site, the business model, and the customers. Other sites offer continuously revised information, such as stock quotes or weather forecasts. Information that is updated daily or more frequently usually involves some type of automation. Such automation can be complex and expensive to install, but it cuts costs in the long run and simplifies the day-to-day management.

- **Degree of Interactivity**—The degree to which user input affects what happens at the site is what people most frequently refer to when describing a site's complexity. All sites offer some degree of interactivity, even if merely providing links between pages or a link to send e-mail to the company. Allowing the user to download files and fill in forms is about as interactive as a site can be without employing customized programming called CGI scripting.

CGI (Computer Gateway Interface) scripts are instructions between the Web site and the server. For example, a form might allow a user to enter information about herself such as her three favorite music artists. Custom CGI scripts would then deliver that information to a database on the server that examines her musical preferences and makes recommendations for other performers that she might like. That information could be sent to her as e-mail or even in the form of custom Web page, generated on the fly, with names, images, and prices of CDs that she could then order.

Because this type of programming is beyond the technical capabilities of most Web site designers/administrators, and for server security reasons, CGI scripting is usually performed by whoever maintains the server. This means that, if you want customized interactivity, you will either need to own and operate your own server or pay other people to add custom scripts to their server. Even if you write your own CGI scripts and provide them to the company that maintains your server, they may insist on conducting a security audit of your scripts, which they may bill at their standard consulting rate.

As an example, many Web businesses are physically maintained on the server of another company such as a local Internet provider. If these providers offer encryption capabilities (for credit card transactions, for example), they will typically charge their client, the Web business, a one-time set-up fee of perhaps $100 to create the necessary CGI scripts for enabling secure online transactions. Keep in mind that this is a very common request and that the programmers are sometimes just making slight modifications to existing scripts and doing the "custom" work in less than an hour. If you want something that's never been done before, expect to pay a hundred dollars (or whatever your provider charges) for *each hour* of custom programming.

> **T I P :** Seriously consider bringing customization capabilities in-house if your business model calls for a site with high interactivity or frequently changing *functionality* (as opposed to content, which can be changed frequently and easily).

While significantly more difficult than learning HTML, creating CGI scripts with PERL or C++ is learnable by the more technologically adventurous and hands-on marketing mortals. And there are sources for public domain, prewritten scripts on the Internet. Keep this in mind if you are considering maintaining your own server either now or in the future. If so, you will either want to learn these skills yourself or hire someone who possesses them. Even though this book is geared more toward marketing than technology—or *because* it is about marketing—I emphasize the need to acquire these skills internally for a specific reason. That is, being able to experiment inexpensively with new features and functionality on your Web site will make you consistently better able to outflank your competition.

Imagine you get a great idea for adding a new interactive feature to your site. If you, your partner, or a company employee is available to implement the idea—even in a scaled-down, experimental mode—you will be able to learn quickly whether the feature is helping your site and whether you should implement the full-blown version. And maybe you're the kind of person who gets these great ideas almost every morning in the shower. If you have to contract with an outside firm every time you get a new idea, you might as well accept right now that most of those ideas will never get tested. Even if you have development funds at your disposal, contracting with another company means it takes longer, requires tight specifications at the offset, means spending more time coordinating and communicating, and your pet project risks being placed in the bottom of your contractor's In basket, meaning it takes a few days rather than a couple of hours.

Experimenting with your site must be cheap and convenient. There are simply too many potential competitors out there, ranging from big firms with dedicated technical personnel to the lone, enterprising student operating out of his college dorm room, who possess the technical capabilities to make their sites interactive in ways not yet conceived. Chapter 5 goes into greater detail about whether to outsource different components of your Web operation.

Big Company or Small Company?

Bigger companies will tend to have larger Web sites. Large firms have more resources to which they can devote Web development dollars. Large companies also have more employees who can regularly contribute to the company's own intranet. Corporate intranets are fast becoming efficient and economical ways for businesses to organize their information flow. To the extent that portions of intranets are accessible to the general public, big companies will have bigger sites.

However, company size and Web site size must not necessarily correspond with one another. For example, a large manufacturer of automobile subassemblies may have a site that is accessible by its one and only customer ... Ford. This type of site may dispense with the gimmickry intended to lure surfers. As such, the site may be relatively small for the size of the company. Alternately, many start-up firms whose only business existence is on the Net may be comprised of two-dozen Web designers and technicians who create massive sites based on public-domain data sources, for example.

Because you are involved with either a big company or a small company, company size is probably a constant rather than a variable in your business plan. But it is an important point to consider when developing the plan because the size of your organization can have a strong impact on what may work well, or not so well, on your commercial site.

(If you are involved with a small company, the next section is for you. If your firm is large, read it to see what you are up against.)

Exploiting the Primary Advantage of Being Small

Big companies are like elephants. Elephants fear nobody—not lions, hyenas, or crocodiles. Nobody—except mice and ants. There is a species of ant that runs up the nostril of an elephant's trunk and kills it by eating its brain. Nasty, to be sure. But these ants are just using a technique that military strategists and marketers refer to as guerrilla tactics—a small group ambushes or penetrates an adversary's defenses by moving quickly and with stealth to make a targeted and devastating strike against the opponent.

> If you are small, use your smallness as your strategic advantage.

While your large competitors are busy throwing massive budgets at risky investments, you have the opportunity to try small things on a daily basis that require few people's (or nobody's) approval. Use this advantage. Making a mistake is usually acceptable because the Web is fluid and flexible. If you try something bold and discover that it makes no improvement to your business, you can change it back to normal the next day. Most of your site visitors will never even know.

You *can* be nimble, so ... *be* nimble. This means constantly trying new things, no matter how different or unconventional—remember, Internet users expect new things to constantly wow them. Test different ways of drawing traffic to your site. Constantly play around with things. It might mean putting up multiple Web sites catering to different audiences. It might mean cooperating with tangentially related businesses and leveraging each others' resources. That's the sort of thing that can be extremely difficult to implement in large companies without a royal decree from top management.

Think back to the days before every record company was promoting its musicians on the Web. Imagine two cases: Big Record Company and Little

Garage Band, each of whom had its own Web site. If someone in Little Garage Band had the idea of putting a snippet of a new song they were recording on the site as downloadable audio, the idea would have been tossed around and everyone in the garage would have said, "Oh, that'll be cool. How fast can you do it?"

But if the Webmaster at Big Record Company got the idea of making public a yet-unreleased piece of music of a major artist, imagine all the people who would have immediately become concerned. They might all end up approving the idea eventually, but it probably took at least eight weeks to get sign-off from all of the relevant people. Will the artists like the idea of having material leaked before the final cut is perfected? Will radio stations be upset that they didn't receive something first? Will the company show its cards to competitors, who will then have more time to respond? Is this covered in everyone's legal agreements? Will piracy keep people from buying CDs? Will people with 8-bit soundcards think the CDs are poor quality? The questions are endless when you're more concerned about covering your rear than trying something different.

While daily content changes may be a regular part of the job for Web managers at a big company, frequent substantive changes are not so easy. By "substantive," I mean to entirely new features and sections. Changing the joke in a joke-of-the-day section is not substantive. However, adding a joke-of-the-day section to a site that does not have one *is* substantive. As a small business, you could add an entirely new section or promotional feature to your site, such as a contest, in a matter of days after coming up with the idea. At large companies, historically, it has been difficult to get even a basic Web site up and running—and extra features only make matters worse.

Lumbering Giants?

In early 1996, it was possible to do an Infoseek search on "Nike" that yielded 818 search results. There existed Web sites ranging from home pages of American college students who like shoes to Japanese athletes discussing their sporting events. But there was no actual Nike home page to be found. To be fair, Nike was, at that time, busy putting together a very nice site related to its involvement with the summer Olympics in Atlanta. The site turned out to be very well produced and substantial in scope.

But for months, customers could not e-mail Nike, while they could send e-mail to Ryka. Ryka (http://www.ryka.com) is a small, yet successful manufacturer of exclusively women's athletic shoes. It has a modest, sim-

FIGURE 3.2 Ryka managed to put a simple site together on a shoestring budget months before giant competitor Nike was anywhere to be found online (http://www.ryka.com).

ple site that does little more than provide a forum for discussion of women's issues and links to women's sites; see Figure 3.2. But with resources that are essentially nothing compared to mighty Nike's massive marketing budget, Ryka had an online presence long before Nike. It begs the question, "why?"

In Internet time (see "dog years" in Chapter 1), Nike was way behind Ryka, despite Nike's possessing almost 37 percent of the U.S. market for athletic footwear and being the world's largest shoe company. Most surprising of all, Nike has a reputation for using new and different marketing approaches. But no Web site. Tsk tsk.

Why So Slow?

Outsiders can only speculate about what took Nike so long to get its online presence established. And delays coming from creating a complex and extraordinary site (see Figure 3.3) are not a good excuse because a very nice "placeholder" site could have been erected in a matter of days. Executives may have argued against putting anything online before the whole thing was ready to unveil, but I surmise that others felt that there should be *something* online—*anything*—if for no other reason, to facilitate e-mail from customers and avoid embarrassment whenever somebody asked "What's your Web address?"

Moreover, people who did try to reach the company were likely to find themselves instead at the home page of college students who were all too eager to talk about the company. Do you suppose Nike's director of public relations or marketing communications intended this—disseminating information to investors and the market through college students with bizarre hobbies? I rather doubt it.

Regardless of Nike's reasons for waiting, the truth is that most companies who are lagging behind in establishing an online presence are late simply because they started late and/or it is taking a long time to implement. Late starts are often due to lack of foresight, a situation endemic in perhaps most large companies. Long development cycles are also frequently due more to bureaucratic friction than technological or marketing

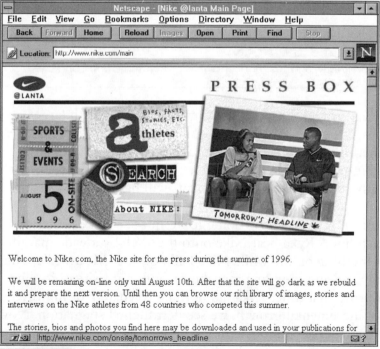

FIGURE 3.3 Nike was late to arrive on the Web, but its Olympics-oriented site was top-notch (http://www.nike.com).

problems. Just imagine the headaches for all sorts of different divisions and departments (accounting, production, marketing, distribution, and so on) that could be created if Nike were suddenly to allow direct online ordering, for example.

The Small Company Advantage

The primary advantage for small firms is their ability to sustain profits earned from pursuing narrow niches with small markets. As discussed earlier, however, this is not the same as direct competition with large companies. If you own or work for a small company and you must compete directly with a Goliath, then ditch your slingshot because your best weapons are speed and agility.

- **Speed**—Anything you do takes less time because you don't have to coordinate activities between as many groups of people or receive approval from as many layers of management.

- **Agility**—You can be flexible in your approach and try things that are more daring than what you would expect to see coming from your larger and more conservative competition.

> **Application of Speed and Agility:**
> Try new things constantly, and test concepts even when they're still unrefined.

Speed and agility are not just "a good way" to compete with larger opposition; they may be the only way. If you try to beat bigger businesses at their own game, they will be able to outgun you with more dollars, more manpower, more power in distribution channels, and so on. If, however, you apply speed and agility, the giants will have difficulty copying you.

Don't just do it once. Never stop doing it. To quote a Nike poster, "There is no finish line." Ryka beat Nike onto the Web by a wide margin because it had something online while Nike had nothing. Meanwhile, Nike was taking a long time and spending megabucks building a site of its own. Unfortunately, during that time, Ryka did nothing to change or improve its site. Instead of incremental growth, we see detrimental stagnation. Now, Ryka's site looks amateurish and bland next to Nike's. (For more on small versus big company advantages, see the discussion of "Leveling the Playing Field?" in Chapter 1.)

Exploiting the Advantages of Being Big

As in traditional business, Web business tends to confer certain advantages and disadvantages to larger firms. Some of the more notable advantages are these:

- Access to more resources (money, labor, knowledge)
- Greater clout with other players on the value chain (vendors, distributors)
- Established reputation with customers (brand equity)

Almost all of the disadvantages stem from organizational inefficiencies:

- Resistance to change
- In-fighting
- Poor internal information flow
- Simple processes take longer

In short, these problems are best addressed by fixing the organization in general, as opposed to just looking at the problems from a Web perspective. There is no shortage of books dealing with topics such as Business Process Reengineering, as there is no shortage of consultants willing to tell you what to do—witness the spate of "just-right-sizings," to put it euphemistically, that have occurred in the past couple of years. With that said, the following recommendations refer specifically to commercial Web concerns.

Implement an Intranet at full-speed!

Private corporate intranets are one of the best ways to fight the problems associated with large company inefficiencies. Because large companies have so much to gain by streamlining any aspect of their operations, the emphasis need not be restricted solely to improving customer-related functions such as marketing and customer service. However, these should also certainly be included in any company's analysis of how to improve its business with the use of an intranet.

One of the best defenses against niche specialization is to offer more general products at a lower cost. Large companies, with their larger volumes, are better at exploiting economies of scale and learning-curve effects to create products at a lower cost than their smaller rivals can. There is probably no end to the ways that intranets can be used to cut large company costs, but here are a few of examples given by Mike Elgan, Editor of *Windows Magazine*: "You can use an intranet to give employees access to company documents, distribute software, enable group scheduling, provide an easy front end to company databases, and let individuals and departments publish information they need to communicate to the rest of the company."

Additionally, intranet Web pages can be made accessible to non-employees (either publicly available or with passwords) for purposes such as:

- Coordinating just-in-time delivery with vendors and distributors
- Automating information access so that customers can look up their own information rather than using live operators
- Conducting marketing research (see below)

Niche Marketing

Large companies may never be able to outperform small companies in highly specialized market segments, but this shouldn't keep them from trying, at least in cases where individual customers can be engaged through automated processes. For example, a bank could provide statements via the Web and customize individual statements to reflect unique customer preferences. Special promotions could be automatically targeted to customers who have shared marketing information about themselves through online questionnaires.

Leveraging Brand Equity to Promote Security

One of the primary factors keeping many people from buying over the Web is their concern that they are not dealing with a reputable company on the other end. This fear vanishes if people are already familiar with the business.

> **TIP:** If your company is a household name, then it never hurts to remind people that they're dealing with a known quantity by using phrases (particularly on order forms) such as: "...with all of the quality and customer service you've come to expect from XYZ Corp..."

Using the Web for a Familiar Friend—Marketing Research

Larger companies are famous—or even notorious—for conducting marketing research. It often seems that, the larger the company, the more research it conducts before moving forward on a given decision. I have mixed feelings about this because, on one hand, research is great for helping managers make decisions, and many companies would benefit remarkably if they did more of it. On the other hand, big companies (and government agencies) often seem to suffer from "paralysis by analysis," studying so much that they never actually do anything, or proceeding at an agonizingly slow pace. (Unfortunately, this tendency has much to do with managers being more concerned with covering their butts should things go awry than it is an attempt to make decisions based on perfect information.) Perfect information will never be available, and the longer you search for the answers in the controlled environment of a lab, the more the questions will have time to mutate out in the real world of the marketplace. This trade-off between timeliness and accuracy of information is nothing new to marketers. But since the Internet marketplace is screaming along in accelerated dog-years, timeliness of market research is probably more important than ever, relative to its accuracy. Using research to reduce the risk of going online is discussed in Chapter 5.

The Web is one of the best media to ever come along for doing fast market research. For a number of reasons, small companies historically have not conducted much first-hand research. The reasons given usually have to do with firms' shortage of manpower and money. More often, I suspect, the failure to conduct research has more to do with underestimation of the massive benefits of research and lack of expertise in conducting research and analyzing the results. This small business bias against *primary* research (meaning research that is conducted firsthand, as opposed to buying published reports) creates a huge opportunity for small firms who bother to learn how to use these big guns.

Many large companies, however, are already accustomed to doing research—indeed, they occasionally have a bias for doing too much, in my opinion. Nevertheless, along comes the Web and suddenly research becomes easier, much faster, and much cheaper. Because big companies value the results of research, because they are already in the practice of conducting it, and because they have employees who know how to conduct it, they will likely become adept at using the Web for this purpose. The insights that they gain about customer preference, will give them a real advantage over firms that don't do research. I accept it as a foregone conclusion that large firms will use the Web to conduct marketing research. For this reason, I speak of research as an advantage that large firms have over small firms. I must emphasize, however, that small firms can and should conduct marketing research on the Web.

If small companies merely *attempt* to do this, they will go a long way toward reaching parity in the marketing arms race against larger competitors. But most of them won't do it. I say this with confidence because certain types of affordable and useful research have always been available to small businesses, yet they are typically ignored. When is the last time you received a questionnaire from your barber shop or hair salon asking you such things as what hours you wish the store were open? This just doesn't happen very often. I actually received such a questionnaire recently, but it struck me at the time as extraordinarily rare for such a small company. Good for them; too bad for their competition across the street.

Additional Tips for Implementing a Web Site in a Large Company

I've said it before, and I'll say it again—the Web is fluid and flexible. I repeat this over and over because so many firms put up a site (sometimes good, sometimes bad) and then forget about it. True, this is certainly better than having no Web presence, and there are times when a site does not need to change. But I believe that most firms with stale Web sites do not continually develop their site for one reason: It never occurred to them.

It's as though the president of the company read *Forbes* one day and declared, "We need a Web site." And that was that. Perhaps the site didn't get much response and the company concluded "Web sites don't work" without even analyzing *why* theirs didn't work. Or maybe the site had a favorable response, but nobody was assigned the task of creating new and better opportunities out of the medium.

The problem with capitalizing on the Web's flexibility in large companies is that large companies are not known for being flexible themselves. I'm speaking of firms so large that their first Web-related move is to assemble an "ad hoc Determinization Team for long-term strategic Web Imperatives." Translation: a dozen people spend about three months trying to figure out if the company should have a Web site, and maybe even what that site should do. A "go" decision after this lengthy process is better than no site at all. The problem is that, three months later, the questions have already changed and therefore the recommendations have become partly obsolete.

Assuming your big company has determined that it does need a site, then all efforts should be made to keep this sort of bureaucracy-laden decision-making process from interfering with the site's continued development and management.

> **Tip for Big Companies:** To capitalize on the Web's fluidity, circumvent bureaucracy by having the company's Web site manager report *directly* to top management, regardless of the size of the firm.

A firm large enough to have a Public Relations department may have pre-approved content continuously spewing out, frequently enough to make the Web site updater's job simple. However, in firms this large, it is often a procedural nightmare to attempt to experiment with anything remotely innovative because new things require someone's approval, often many people's approval. By the time the simple, two-day "experiment" has been approved, it will often have grown into a two-month initiative requiring feasibility studies, benchmarked objectives, approval from lawyers, token input from irrelevant entities for political reasons, and so on. Yuck.

Big or Small, One Thing Is Certain...

In the final analysis (pardon this gross generalization), small companies seem to come up with fresher ideas, but they can't always afford to make anything come of it. Big companies have money and resources but have difficulty implementing changes quickly due to their own glacier-like inertia. But no matter how big your firm, how much money you've got, or how rapidly you can respond to the changing market, one thing is certain. You must offer something that somebody wants. Deciding what you'll offer—selecting and refining your business model—is the subject of the next chapter.

THE MOST IMPORTANT
DECISION YOU WILL MAKE:
CHOOSING YOUR
BUSINESS MODEL

his book is designed to help you to get people to your site and to help them decide to make a purchase once they're there. But it is up to you to determine what type of product or service you will attempt to sell. You probably already know what it is if you're reading this book. But even if you know exactly what it is you will be selling (or currently are sell-ing—in which case, I hope you know what it is), I encourage you to look over the discussions of various business models for one simple reason:

> Multiple business models can coexist on one site.

You may have your hands full selling widgets from your site today, but eventually you will probably want to look for additional ways to make money from all those people visiting your site. Maybe you will start offer-ing advertising space to widget integration specialists; maybe you will start offering custom widget design; or maybe you will start selling financing for widgets. You get the idea. If you have not yet developed your business model, then you must read on. If your Web operation is already up and running, or if you already know exactly how it will be working, then relax your brain and read on for ideas about how you may expand your opera-tions in the future.

> **TIP:** No matter how busy you are, frequently ask yourself, "What other ways can our site bring in money?"

If you can't think of any new ways for your site to bring in money, then your head is too full of today's plans and concerns. Relax even more. I have not met with a single Web business owner for whom I could not come up with a list of brand-new ideas for generating additional revenue with his or her site. I wish I could say there was some magic to it, but the only trick I brought to them was an outsider's objectivity. Some of the ideas on those lists seemed painfully obvious after they were stated, but nobody had thought to try them—usually only because they had been too busy to ask themselves the question. The Web moves fast and you must constantly put yourself into the "what else can we try?" mental mode, no matter how busy you become implementing the great ideas you came up with yesterday.

Great Promotion to a Great Site Won't Sell Something Nobody Wants

Jalapeño flavored body paint. Would anybody buy this? Beats the heck out of me. I can imagine not selling a single jar, and I can imagine it becoming the hottest (heh heh) craze on the Internet. (If anybody actually does this, please drop me a line and let me know how it goes.)

Your promotional efforts may draw crowds to your site, and your site may be so appealing that each visitor explores it thoroughly and tells his or her friends about it. But if they don't want your product, you won't make much money. Take some comfort in knowing that *if* you draw large enough mobs and *if* your site is incredible, then it is very likely that you *will* sell something—the law of large numbers and the sheer weirdness and diversity of the Internet market suggest that somebody out there will want your stuff, no matter what you sell.

Getting your first sale will give you a thrill, but if it's the only sale, the thrill won't last long. Your product has to create enough appeal for enough people to create a steady stream of ongoing sales revenue. If you are adding a site to an existing business, then the potential returns may already be limited by the nature of your product or the size of your market, which is not necessarily bad, particularly if these limits are high.

If you are looking for ideas about what to sell, then you can afford the luxury of choosing something that is most perfectly suited for Web-based sales. (Realize, however, that regardless of whether yours is a new or an existing business, the Web's inherent flexibility will allow you try multiple things, which you probably should do even if you already have a top-selling product or service.)

We know that perhaps all businesses have some potential use of the Web. Grandma can sell hand-crafted teddybears. American Airlines can let passengers book their own flights. You can order a pizza from down the street or check the whereabouts of your FedEx package. People use the Web to sell music, poetry, wholesale Maine lobster, army surplus, strip-o-grams, software, bookkeeping services, and just about everything else.

Many people who speak about Web marketing emphasize that a Web site must add value, or in other words, give people a reason to visit other than merely displaying your wares and letting them order online. At the risk of upsetting every expert in the world, I disagree. Sometimes showing your products is enough, particularly if they are products that people want but can't find elsewhere. Additional site features are a great bonus, and the really creative stuff *will* help generate word-of-mouth, but let's face it, all of the site extras ranging from cute gimmicks (find the Spam) to useful little online programs (like mortgage calculators) will probably only help you draw traffic—important, but only half the battle. If you don't offer the right things for sale (at the right price) then you are going to be disappointed, no matter how much traffic your site pulls in.

It's Not Just *What* You Sell, but the *Way* You Sell It

Suppose you sell written information of some sort to customers who find you over the Internet. Think of how many different ways you could deliver such a product.

- Will you mail them a printed report?

- Will you send an automated fax to them?

- Will you e-mail it to them?

- Will you grant them access to your site for a year once they've paid an annual subscription fee?

- Will you just charge them for each time they access your site?

- Will you allow free access to most of your site but charge for peeps at the juiciest parts?

Information products, such as written reports, are perhaps the most flexible type of product because there delivery of the product does not have to include a physical component. Services and tangible products can also be offered in many ways that will affect whether people choose to purchase.

For example, professional services or service contracts can be sold on an á la carte basis, a quoted-job basis, an hourly rate or, a flat fee. Tangible products can be bought outright, bartered, leased, sold directly, sold on consignment, sold through an agent, shipped directly, shipped from a fulfillment center, drop-shipped from an original manufacturer, and so on. These are all things that you should consider, particularly if you are creating a new business. Examples of various business models, both simple and creative, are included at the end of this chapter.

What Is Your Hook?

It is said so frequently that I almost hesitate—your site must have a reason to make people visit. For some sites, the product you offer for sale may be adequate to generate interest. For example, the Hot Hot Hot (hot sauce) site sells 450 kinds of hot sauce, and that alone is enough to make thousands of people interested in visiting the site. The site is clever and educational, but the appeal of these stylistic features is nothing compared to the basic concept.

Other sites may offer something useful and appreciated, but the subject matter is not sexy enough to generate much interest or differentiate the site from similar others. For example, imagine you had a site that listed all the homes for sale in a metropolitan area (many such sites currently exist). Suppose the site is well designed and useful for anyone looking to purchase a home in the area because it allows them to search by several criteria such as square footage, number of rooms, pool/no pool, location, and so on. If other competing sites offer the same functionality, then why should people choose your site? What would make them tell their friends about it? Imagine that you added something no other real estate site offered, such as a demographic/psychographic personality questionnaire with questions about what kind of car you drive, your favorite brand of beer, and your favorite television shows. Then imagine you ran the questionnaire through a marketing demographics database (which you license from another company—perhaps for free in exchange for access to your survey results) and generated a recommendation of neighborhoods where your customers were virtually guaranteed to feel right at home—avoiding the need for these relocaters to spend days driving around an unfamiliar city to find their favorite areas. Suppose then you also overlaid maps of the city showing statistics that realtors don't always volunteer, like geographic incidence of violent crimes, the high water mark of the century's worst flood, or whatever you can think of that relocaters would like to know about.

And then, promote your site as this wonderful thing that will keep people from making the worst mistake of their lives—choosing the wrong house. This high-concept angle could be emphasized to a degree that might generate considerable publicity in traditional media, for example. You would not only cash in on people's inherent anxiety about relocating to an unfamiliar city and purchasing a home, but you would also be offering a solution to that anxiety—in other words, creating value for your customers.

> A bizarre product can be its own hook. A mundane product must be given a hook.

Strong hook concepts will result out of any good brainstorming session about your site. Just keep asking yourself two questions:

1. Why would people want to visit my site rather than a similar site?

2. Why would a magazine want to mention this site?

If you can think of no reason why a magazine would want to mention your site, then you need to stop and rethink things. First, if you get no publicity, then it will be harder to draw traffic. But more importantly, if you can't even think of a single idea that would make you worth mentioning in some publication, then it's very likely that Web surfers wouldn't be too interested in your site either—and they certainly aren't going to tell all of their friends about it. Make it a goal to generate interest among editors of traditional media, and you will probably emerge with a concept that will ultimately draw enough traffic that your site has a chance of becoming profitable.

What if there is just no hook? If you think, and think, and can come up with absolutely no way of making your product or service newsworthy (remember, it can be still be useful without being newsworthy), then consider creating a standard, all-purpose hook such as a contest, a Homer Simpson quote of the day, or something similar. If possible, gear the gimmick to your product category; otherwise, you will draw "bad traffic"— people who will never buy, no matter what. For example, posting pictures of swimsuit models might draw tons of traffic. But if you sell refurbished grandfather clocks, the hordes of prepubescent males visiting your site are not going to buy many clocks.

An exception to the "bad traffic" warning occurs when your site is advertiser-sponsored. In this case, more traffic is usually better because you can boast higher "page visit" counts to advertisers (see Chapter 10). However, you also risk diluting the quality of your site visitors, and advertisers of niche products will be more interested in advertising on your site if you can deliver their niche audience. Admittedly, this variable is more difficult to measure than simple volume of traffic.

One last comment on hooks: A site can have *more than one hook*. Each great hook you create for your site is another reason for you to circulate a press release, another reason for an editor to mention you, another reason for somebody to visit. The site "Sound Advice" (http://www.monsoon.org/ sound_advice) shown in Figure 4.1, provides all sorts of information about

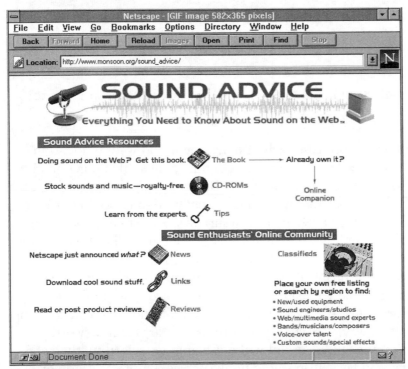

FIGURE 4.1 "Sound Advice: Everything You Need to Know About Sound on the Web" (http://www.monsoon.org/sound_advice) is a one-stop shop for sound enthusiasts. The site offers several "hooks," hoping that at least one resource will appeal to each member of the target audience.

using sound on the Internet. The site generates its revenue by selling a book and stock-sounds on CD-ROM. Because these two items alone would not generate much traffic, the site was designed to become a sort of "community of sound enthusiasts" by offering what amounts to several small hooks:

- Sources for downloading free sounds
- Sources for downloading free software
- Tips from industry experts
- Product reviews from other visitors
- A geographically searchable job board for sound and music-related professionals

Any one of these might provide the hook needed for an editor to give some free publicity, to secure a link from other high-traffic sites, to win a "What's Cool" listing, to make somebody visit, or to make a visitor tell their friends.

New or Existing Business?

Perhaps one of the most fundamentally important variables influencing the development of your Web business will be whether you are creating a brand-new enterprise or creating the Web extension of an existing business. Naturally, new businesses are more flexible because you can do anything you want, whereas Web extensions to existing firms will primarily exist to support the ordinary practices of the company, at least in the short term.

Existing firms may choose to use the Web for a variety of purposes, ranging from merely giving company information to providing online sales and after-sales support. Keep in mind that many existing companies do not try to sell directly online. They may decline to pursue direct sales for any number of reasons. For example, it may be in their best interest to instead use the Web to encourage customers to visit the company's physical retail location, or if the company is a manufacturer, they may direct customers to retailers who stock the company's products.

Possible Web Site Objectives for Existing Firms

The following is a partial list of activities for which the Web might be used to augment the current operations of existing businesses. These suggestions are limited to *external* company communications and do not include all of the ways in which intranets can be used to make companies operate more efficiently (see Chapter 3 for more about intranets). Naturally, new companies can use these suggestions as well, but new Web-oriented companies may have no physical retail location or they may wish to focus their near-term Web developments on generating immediate revenue, thus making some of the following suggestions non-applicable.

- Provide basic information—Phone number, address, hours of operation, company history, etc.

- Encourage customer-initiated communication—Solicit e-mail and provide online questionnaire forms

- Develop company-initiated communication—Daily faxed menus, adding people to direct mail lists (for printed catalogs, etc.), announcing special promotions via e-mail

- Build company image—Describe community/philanthropic activities, post personal employee pages, include information not intended to initiate a sale (describing commitment to research and development, for example)

- Facilitate investor relations—Annual reports, current/historical stock price, articles in the press which spotlight your company

- Facilitate press relations—Make high-resolution images downloadable; allow editors to subscribe to a press release e-mail listserv (see Chapter 11 regarding publicity and Chapter 13 regarding listservs)

- Promote business partners (enhance the image of vendors, distributors, and dealers)

- Solicit resumes and post job openings or application procedures

- Provide online assistance such as after-sale customer service—Product instructions, warranty information, trouble-shooting, and recommendations for company's or third-party accessories

- Sell merchandise directly—Online order forms, 800 phone numbers, fax numbers

- Provide product information (specifications, options, etc.)

- Direct customers to another company that stocks the products—Lists of retailers searchable by region, city-wide maps, phone numbers, retailers' hours of operation, and so on

Creating New Business for Existing Companies

Existing companies should try, whenever appropriate, to use the Web to reach new, targetable niches. A marketer of portable, personal misting systems (canisters used to keep people cool in hot, arid conditions) might traditionally have developed a good business selling misters to athletes and sporting event attendees in the United States. While high costs might have formerly made geographic expansion unfeasible, the Web now makes it possible for this manufacturer to sell personal misting systems to construction workers in the Middle East. Even if English were used on both Web pages, imagine how a page aimed at hot football fans would differ from one geared toward construction workers. The same product might also appeal to fishermen, or a dozen other niche categories, opening up endless opportunities for the company to reach new markets and increase sales.

A Warning to Existing Businesses

The Web, like many other new technologies, sometimes eliminates jobs. This is good for efficiency, but bad for morale and bad for the displaced worker. The irony is that there are probably more opportunities on the Web than you will have time to pursue. Ideally, a customer-service telephone operator who is no longer needed could be put to use in the implementation of a Web project, which quite literally can constitute a thousand details requiring the attention of interested people. In practice, however, skills do not always transfer, and some people do not embrace new technologies. The risk in providing such lateral opportunities to those who resist change is that theirs often becomes a mission to prove that the new way doesn't work. This person can be dangerous to the success of your plans.

My advice, therefore, is to preferentially select people with the change-embracing attitude rather than those with modestly more applicable job experience or technical skills who do not possess such an attitude. The Web is so new that few experts are available. This means that almost anybody will require training of some sort. You are better off training those who are excited about learning something new.

Will You Seek Advertiser Sponsorship?

Chapter 10 is devoted exclusively to the techniques of buying and selling online ad space. For now, just consider the impact on your choice of business model of whether you hope to earn revenue by selling ad space. Many sites which serve as specialized directories, such as listing all of the bed-and-breakfasts in Alaska. In this model, in which the ads and links to other sites are one of the primary reasons for people to visit your site, Web sites can be profitable by charging a relatively low amount (such as $100 per year per advertiser) to a large number of businesses.

Another, less promising advertising-based model goes something like this: "We'll create a site that provides such-an-such for free, and once thousands of people are visiting, we'll sell advertising space." Potential problems to this approach include the following:

- This model suggests no way to make any money prior to attaining "thousands" of visitors, which is no small task in itself.

- Obtaining and retaining advertisers remains tricky in this new medium. Many advertisers have not yet dared to venture into the unknown world of Web media. Standards don't yet exist for verifying or comparing traffic statistics, and even those media buyers who are willing to experiment online are just beginning to learn how to gauge the effectiveness of their dollars spent.

- If you've got thousands of people dropping by regularly, then, even if you do sell ad space, you are probably passing up additional sources of revenue. For example, even free newspapers have revenue sources beyond selling ad space, such as 900 number singles' voicemail services.

- Ad revenue alone might not cover your costs.

A recent advertising rate card from Netscape's site offered banner ad rotations on some of their more popular pages for $30,000, which buys you an estimated one million impressions per month, or a cost per thousand (CPM) of $30.

Assuming you are able to command a $30 CPM (a pretty big assumption), and assuming you have 100,000 visitors per month (which is a lot), then you will make only $3,000 per month from one advertiser. You would make more if each visitor saw several different ads, but these numbers provide a starting point for a somewhat grim analysis. If an average visitor saw three different ads during his or her visit, you'd make a total of $9,000 per month. After expenses, this amount might provide a reasonable income for a one-person, home business. But the odds are that if you are drawing

100,000 visitors per month, every month (remember, that's a whole lot) your site probably offers more than your family recipe for chili. In fact, you'd probably have a complex site with lots of stuff that changes frequently, which means you'd probably have several employees constantly maintaining the site. This could very well be a formula for losing money every month.

Ahh, but what about Netscape and all of the other advertiser-sponsored sites? With some exceptions, most fall into one of two categories: those that also make money some other way, and those that are losing money. Netscape sells lots and lots of software and just so happens to sell some ad spaces on the side. Pocket money. Large publishers of online newspapers are starting to charge for online subscriptions because they're often not profitable from advertiser sponsorship alone. Both of these spell out one piece of wisdom: Ad revenue is supplemental; it's a nice bonus if you can get it.

> Don't base your business model on ad revenue alone.

Again, there are always exceptions. If your costs are low enough and your traffic is consistently high enough, then you could make money on just selling ads (see "Directories" later in this chapter). But you would still be overlooking opportunities for creating additional sources of revenue.

Forrester Research estimates that 1996 Web advertising revenues will total $74 million, which comes to an average of less than $1,000 per commercial site. While this is not enough to support most sites, there is clearly some money to be made selling ad space. You might as well try to sell some if your site draws heavy traffic.

How Will Your Business Operate? An Overview of Some Popular Models

There are probably as many methods for making money on the Web as there are in the real world. If you have not already decided how your site will earn a living, then read the following business model descriptions for ideas. Even if you already know what your site will do, read on—one site can have more than one way of generating revenue.

Tips on Niching

TIP: Pursue niches that are both *strong* and *targetable*.

Niche Strength

The strength of a niche is determined by how easily a person could answer a definite "yes or no?" question. For example, "Do you own a cat?" is easy to answer with a definite yes or no, whereas "Do you have long hair?" is more ambiguous. Does "long" mean shoulder-length or midback length? And short hair on a woman might be relatively long on a man. The answer might also depend on where that person was from or the age of the person. Your site will have more immediate appeal for any visitor who hears about it or arrives at your home page and instantly realizes, "this is for me."

Niche Targetability

"Left-handed, blue-eyed mothers of two children three years apart" is a strong niche, but it's not very targetable because this subset of the population doesn't congregate in one place or make themselves otherwise easy to identify. The best you could do would probably be to target two groups, left-handed people and mothers. One of the best ways to identify the most targetable groups is to scan all of the newsgroup names in Usenet (see Chapter 12). You will find narrowly defined forums for groups such as horse-lovers, spelunkers, underwater welders, HIV-positive individuals, adopted people seeking their birth parents, and so on.

Niche Size

"Users of Microsoft Windows" is a strong niche and a fairly targetable one, but it is such a large group that "niche" is really the wrong word. It's almost synonymous with saying "Internet users." The advantage of targeting smaller niches is that members of that unique group will feel a stronger connection with your message. You may also discover less competition. The disadvantage of targeting small niches is that your potential market is smaller, which can place an upper limit on potential sales. Larger companies are often forced to focus only on larger niches because smaller markets simply aren't large enough to support big companies' revenue requirements.

TIP: Pursuing two narrow markets can be better than pursuing one big market.

However, to optimize under all of these conditions, I recommend that many smaller companies go after *multiple* narrow markets rather than one larger market. In a larger market, they will encounter fiercer competition, and they will not appeal as personally to individuals in that large group of customers.

It may not always be easy to find multiple niches for an established product, but many companies have re-purposed existing products (such as renaming, repackaging, and changing minor attributes) and successfully introduced them into entirely new markets. If all else fails, put your existing product in a watertight yellow plastic box and sell it to watersports enthusiasts. Chapter 14 describes some specific techniques for designing a site around multiple narrow niches.

Virtual Business Agreement

I list this model first because it is one of my favorites for entrepreneurs on a small budget. It goes something like this: You want to run a commercial site, but you don't have an existing business or any product or service to sell. Find an existing business with a narrow, targetable segment, or a unique, high-concept type of product—but select a company that has little knowledge of the Web. Negotiate to obtain the exclusive rights to market this company's wares online, including some split of gross online revenues between you and the actual company. You essentially become the Web marketing arm of an existing organization, and the degree of ongoing interaction between you and the firm will be determined by your unique situation.

I have seen this arrangement work very well in diverse situations, including a graduating college student who started his own business as the exclusive online marketing venue for a brand of fine cigars. There is no shortage of companies that could benefit greatly by somebody just "handling it" for them, particularly with small, older businesses run by technophobic or overworked sole proprietors (see Chapter 5 regarding working with other firms in order to save money).

The particulars will vary from case to case. You may occupy an empty office in the existing business, or you may choose to work from your home and do little more than finesse your site and promote it, meanwhile only forwarding orders to the existing company, which handles order processing, mail-order fulfillment, returns, and all of the other things that they are already accustomed to handling. So long as you have an appropriate way of separating which orders your site generated, you may have little involvement with the daily operation, but you will periodically deposit a commission check made out to you.

You essentially become an independent rep who earns a sales commission. The advantage of this arrangement to you is that you worry about one thing only—making sales. The advantage to the existing company is that you are more highly motivated to make sales than someone hired to become the company's Webmaster might be. Best of all, because you are not involved with the day-to-day running of the existing business, you may have enough free time to allow you to repeat this model with additional companies.

Variations on Virtual Businesses

Recognize that nearly any business activity you can think of can be outsourced to a competent specialist in that field. It has been said that Heinz no longer grows tomatoes, makes bottles, prints labels, ships anything on trucks, or even makes ketchup. Yet that doesn't stop Heinz from selling ketchup. It outsources nearly every aspect of its operation.

The relevance to small, start-up businesses is that you could sell a product over the Internet, while having another business receive 800-number phone calls, handle the credit card transactions, assemble your product, package your product, stock inventory, and ship directly to the customer. Of course, they charge a fee for doing all this, but they are often so efficient that they can actually save you more money than if you had done the operations internally. For links to these sorts of order fulfillment companies, see this book's online companion at http://www.monsoon.org/book.

Also consider partnering (that is, splitting revenue) with companies that possess the capabilities you lack (this is discussed further in Chapter 5).

Information Publishing Models

Online publishing is big business and very attractive for one reason: Information has virtually zero unit cost. Once something is written (this applies to software also), it can be distributed electronically an infinite number of times without costing more money. Unfortunately, information must be delivered before people can know its value (and, hence, whether they're willing to buy it). But if they've already heard or read the information, then they don't need to buy it. One solution to this problem historically has been to make information free or very cheap (newspapers) and to sell advertiser sponsorship (discussed—uh, discouraged—above). So the trick is to get people to pay for something they haven't read yet. Here are some of the ways people have been using.

The One-Time Fee

Users pay a one-time fee for a one-time delivery, such as a book on how to make money on the Web. Because online customers don't have the luxury of flipping through the product's pages, representative samples of information and endorsements are useful for selling these products. It is also effective to tell them what they'll learn, without teaching it to them directly, such as "Learn the experts' five secrets for guaranteeing a tender steak" or whatever.

The Subscription Model

Users pay a one-time fee, such as $10 for a year's worth of monthly newsletters, delivered by e-mail, for example. Because the user is taking a risk by paying up front, this works best with well-known information products. Since most Web products are new (hence, not well-known), a free sample issue is almost always required.

The Pay-Per-Access Model

Users pay each time they visit, such as paying a fee for downloading naughty images or historical stock data. Customers feel safer with this model because their risk is limited to one access at a time. Unfortunately, the model is not as effective at securing long-time customers, such as those who pay more for an annual subscription.

The Cable Model

As the name suggests, this hybrid between the models mentioned above allows users to access portions of a site for free, other portions if they've subscribed, and/or other areas on a per-access basis. These payment options correspond to basic cable channels, premium channels, and Pay-Per-View, respectively. I see high hopes for this model on the Web of Tomorrow because it has evolved through years of painful trial-and-error in the world of cable and now seems to be relatively stable.

The Coin Model

The user invokes some form of electronic currency in tiny increments (such as 25¢) and can make small purchases of impulse items. Imagine seeing "read this page of OJ's diary for twenty-five cents" to get the idea. The technology is not available at the time of this writing, but digital coins are promised to become available by the end of 1996. However, it will likely be some time after that before these electronic tokens are commonly used and accepted. Once they are, however, look out—the opportunities for creating revenue on the Web may explode like nothing we've seen yet.

Directories

One of the more familiar Web business models is that of Web directories
such as Yahoo!, Infoseek, Alta Vista, and hundreds of smaller directories
(see Chapter 8 for more about these services). These services build and
maintain their databases either by using automated programs to crawl
across the Web looking for pages or by allowing Web site owners to register their sites with the service's online registration form.

These procedures allow many directories to grow rapidly without the
high costs associated with creating new content for other types of sites,
such as online newspapers. If the directory draws high traffic, then these
factors combine to create a situation where advertiser sponsorship alone
may make the site profitable. Competition is fierce between the major
directory services as companies invest heavily, improving their software and
hardware, in order to become the "directory of choice" among Web users.
However, many smaller, niche-oriented directories appear every day, and
there are probably many opportunities remaining to be seized.

Value-Added Sites

Technically, any site could be called a "value-added" site because providing
information of any sort creates value to some site visitors. However, this
term is most often applied to sites that use more interactivity and programming to do something customized for people. Examples include:

- Stock lookup services

- E-mail greeting card services

- Mortgage calculation

Value-added sites let people fill out online forms, and then an automated procedure does something for them, such as e-mailing them specific information or generating a custom Web page on the fly. For instance, a user may enter his weight, body measurements, fitness objectives, and so on; then a computer program would generate a Web page detailing the user's customized exercise and diet regimen.

The service could be conducted for a fee or provided for free as a device for building traffic to the site. Any idea that provides customized value could be beneficial to your site, but the best ideas will either do something new and different, or make something familiar more convenient for people.

Brochure Sites

I arbitrarily define brochure sites as those whose purpose is to generate further communication with the company, such as prompting the visitor to make a telephone call to a sales representative. (For our purposes, this is contrasted with sites that sell directly, which are covered later in this chapter.) Brochure sites may offer some value-added services to help draw traffic or build repeat business (remember, these models can and should be combined when possible), but the primary objective of a brochure site is to provide information. Unlike printed brochures, space is virtually unlimited on a Web site. This means that more information can be made available than you would expect a single customer to read. Take care to avoid overwhelming the customer with this information by carefully organizing your site's logic and navigational features (see Chapter 16).

Remember also to have an actionable objective for your site. Just because the site isn't intended to sell anything doesn't mean it can't be crafted to persuade the visitor to do something else, such as pick up the phone or send you an e-mail.

Brochure sites are very appropriate for marketing products that are too complicated to sell directly online, such as customized projects that require a bidding process. These sites are also useful for marketing services that cannot be conducted directly over the Web, such as many professional services.

Direct Product Sales

At last, the fun stuff. Perhaps the most exciting of all commercial sites are those that actually let shoppers buy things from you and charge their credit cards, even while you sleep. If you spend some time surfing the Web, you will probably find a few different formats which people are using to sell things.

You will want to structure your direct sales site differently depending on factors such as these:

- The type of information the customer requires to make a purchase

- The amount of information the customer requires

- Whether the product category is familiar or unfamiliar

- How many product categories you offer

- How many products you offer in each category

- Whether the purchase is likely to be one-time or ongoing

Depending on your particular mix of the above variables, you can choose from several site design models. The following designs are diagrammed and explained more thoroughly in Chapter 14, "Building a Site Around Your Business Model":

- Billboard sites

- Infomercial sites

- Catalog and shopping cart sales

- Online malls

Mix-n-Match the Models

You may find that the most flexible approach is to combine elements of any of the above (or other) business models to suit your needs. Some of the most interesting Web sites follow a hybrid of many models, which I'll call the "Community Central" model because it is a grab bag of everything, centered around some online community (or market niche) such as enthusiasts of a hobby, members of a profession, or residents of a geographic area. By focusing on one theme, various aspects of a community site maintain unity even if different sections offer different points of interest—some for free; others for sale using a multitude of business models.

Vanity Sites

Many companies seem to have created sites for no particular reason other than to have one. I've stumbled across sites for businesses that neither sold anything nor gave me a way to contact them. Baffling—I have no idea why these sites exist.

> The most insidious business model—*no* model.

Many managers sense that "this Web thing" is important, or that it will be important. Having a site seems to be the trendy thing to do, and nothing else. Some people call these sites "vanity sites" because they are there for looks only and aren't expected to do anything.

That is not to say that such sites can provide no benefit—indeed, they frequently do. But vanity sites, by my definition, are not *required* to meet any performance objectives. They are established, the investment is assumed to be written off (or lumped in with advertising, perhaps), and people wait to see if anything happens. Revenues or other quantifiable benefits are treated as a bonus. An informal survey reveals some interesting reasons for the creation of corporate vanity sites:

- "The boss thought we should have a Web site."

  (In one case, the boss had never even browsed the Web or sent e-mail, and he had made his decision based solely on hearing a story about the Web on the evening news.)

- "Our competition has a Web site."

- "We thought that 'http thing' would look cool on our business cards."

- "We want to look technologically progressive."

- "We don't expect much to come of it now, but we wanted to learn about it. If Internet commerce takes off, we don't want to be left behind."

This last reason is probably the best reason to move forward with a Web project that has no specific revenue objectives. Unfortunately, this means that most vanity sites have no stated objectives *of any sort*. That is a mistake—just because a site is not expected to draw revenue does not mean that it cannot have any quantifiable measure of success. Firms that miss this point frequently relegate the Web site's development to the status of "so-and-so's pet project," funded (maybe) with allocations of money and manpower that have no correlation to any projections or objectives. These projects are typically created one piece at a time, thrown together during someone's spare time, perhaps at night, after everyone else has gone home. Such sites come together in a haphazard, shoddy fashion—and it shows. Fortunately, a little bit of planning and management can avoid this. The solution is simple: Vanity sites should still be given performance objectives.

The idea is not only to focus on *a reason* for implementing the site, but to make sure that the site is executed *professionally*. Otherwise, the site might actually tarnish the company's image. Here is a sample of such objectives and requirements. As with financial and other types of targets, it is always helpful to attach numbers and dates to the objectives, wherever possible.

Requirements for Vanity Sites

The following specs are Examples only; your numbers will vary.

1. One person must be held accountable for the following requirements unless otherwise noted.

2. The site must conform to company standards of quality and corporate identity. (See "Identity," Chapter 14.)

3. The first stage of the site will contain, at a minimum, the following pages:

   - Company home page
   - History
   - Products overview
   - State map of service outlets
   - Jobs
   - Contact us

4. The first stage of the site will go active by February 15.

5. Each department manager is responsible for approving copy within 10 days of receiving proofs. Managers who fail to approve copy within 10 days are responsible for the copy "as is" and any errors contained therein.

6. The site will be registered with 10 leading search engines by February 28.

7. Twenty-five solicitations for strategic, non-paid links to the site will be e-mailed by March 12.

8. E-mail comments and questions from visitors will be read by (employee's name) and responded to within 10 working days. Messages that require forwarding will be answered with a "your message has been forwarded" response within 3 working days.

9. The site traffic targets are as follows:

   May 30: 600 cumulative hits* from outside companies

   Aug 30: 1500 cumulative hits from outside companies

   * (The term "hits" should be defined in the document.)

Budgets must also be specified so that decision makers have realistic expectations about what their site will look like and what it can do. Vanity sites that are thrown together haphazardly usually have not been subjected to the discipline of a budget, in addition to not being planned properly.

Finding ways to minimize the costs associated with going online—regardless of company size, site size, or the business model used—is the subject of the next chapter.

MINIMIZING YOUR
INVESTMENT

T here are two sides to the profitability equation. Most of this book is about one side—increasing sales. However, the other side— decreasing costs—is just as important. It is never too soon to begin think- ing about how to keep your Web project's costs down.

The "1 in 10" Rule

A venture capitalist once told me that he expects only 1 out of 10 ventures to be successful. This number seemed surprisingly low. On further discus- sion, I learned an important lesson:

> One winner more than makes up for nine losers if the other nine attempts were *inexpensive.*

This man's recipe for success was counter-intuitive at first glance. I had always thought of entrepreneurship (or new product introductions, in the case of existing companies) as primarily an effort to identify the single most promising idea, to gather the necessary data to build a strong business plan around that idea, and then to invest whatever budget the plan called for in order to make the idea successful.

This is how most entrepreneurs go about building businesses—and it makes sense for a lot of reasons. First and foremost, entrepreneurs are managers of a process, and their efforts will largely be responsible for either success or failure of the venture. But there is still a problem with this approach: It means putting all of your eggs in one basket.

From the venture capitalist's perspective, it would be foolish to put all the eggs in one basket. That is the antithesis of diversification. And, in particular, the venture capitalist is not always involved with day-to-day operations (unlike the entrepreneur) and therefore has an interest in minimizing risk relative to his or her own lack of control over the management of the project. That is why venture capitalists often install their own senior management teams whenever they invest larger amounts of capital.

What does this mean for the entrepreneur or Web marketing manager? Does this mean we should embark on speculative Web projects with a cavalier, "oh well, we'll see what happens" attitude? Not at all. As direct managers of these projects, we are unlike the nonmanaging venture capitalist in one important way: What we do every day impacts the bottom line.

To a very large degree, the success or failure of a new Web enterprise will rest on the shoulders of the person in charge. If that's you, then how you choose to spend your hours each day will influence the outcome, down to the words you use in the e-mails you write. But that does not mean that there is nothing to learn from the wise venture capitalist's "1 in 10" rule. As the rule applies to Web marketers:

> You can try more things if you keep the cost of each attempt to a minimum.

Recall something important about the inherent nature of the Web—something that I've said before and is a recurring theme throughout this book: The Web is fluid, and the Web is infinitely flexible.

You are not investing in dies and molds for manufacturing fiberglass boat hulls. You are putting up a Web site. There is a big difference between the two. If you start selling boat hulls and discover that your boats, oh... *sink*...(or whatever it is that defective hulls do) then you are in serious trouble from a financial perspective. Retooling your production line could wipe you out.

But if you launch a Web site, what's the worst thing that can happen? Maybe nobody shows up. Maybe users show up, but nobody buys anything. Maybe you accidentally offend somebody in Idaho because you make an off-color potato joke. The point is, there isn't much that can go wrong (and *nobody*, to my knowledge, has ever *drowned* from a defective Web site.). There are unusual risks such as the threat of being infiltrated by malevolent hackers, or simply from doing something irresponsible like wantonly violating copyright laws or transmitting child pornography. Assuming that you don't break the law and have adequate network security, your risk is essentially limited to the amount of money you have invested in your venture.

The average cost of the commercial Web site is climbing as larger corporations embark on more ambitious Web undertakings. But the notion of risk, when applied to your Web enterprises, needs to be looked at carefully.

Must You Risk a Fortune on a Hunch?

The simple answer is "no." Let's look at both parts of this question.

A Fortune?

First, many, many commercial Web sites are produced for very low out-of-pocket costs (under $500, if you do the HTML yourself). These sites may not feature the interactive wizardry found at some other sites, but there are still plenty of successful sites that are profitable simply by selling things to people who have a hard time finding them anyplace else.

> Many individuals and small businesses who have begun pilot Web sites report that, by far, the most significant investment has *not been money*. For many sites, the biggest investment is *time*.

Whether this statement applies (or will apply) to you depends on who does the work. So many entrepreneurs and businesses report time as the main investment because they are doing the work themselves. Anybody could hire a Web consulting firm or freelance HTML/graphics person to create a site and pay them anywhere from $25 to $100 per hour. In that case, very little time is invested, but quite a bit of money can be. The decision to create your Web site in-house versus outsourcing its production is discussed later in this chapter.

I have stated earlier that commercial sites in the future will cost more to launch than they do today. Even though a bare-bones, no-frills site will still be cheap, it probably won't stand out as much in tomorrow's sea of glitzy, interactive sites. It is also possible that lower budget sites will come to be automatically associated with smaller firms that lack professionalism, much in the same way we feel whenever we see a cheap-looking business card.

But, remember the axiomatic "Web sites are infinitely flexible"? That means something else: Web sites are scalable. If you create a Web site with a modest budget right now, nobody will think less of your company because the absence of interactivity, video, and so on, is presently the norm for many commercial sites. Remember, the Web is flexible. That means you can add bits and pieces of functionality over months and years. In fact, you should plan to do so as an ordinary aspect of business. Besides, it may be more appealing to company controllers to earmark a small amount of money each month for "Web upkeep and maintenance" than it is to have you plead for a huge lump sum to do all the work at once.

Web sites are scalable in the most extreme sense. For example, your site may reside today on the server of your Internet service provider. If at some point in the future it makes sense to do so, you can relocate the site to your own server in your building without the rest of the world ever knowing the difference. In this instance and all others related to going online, be conservative at first. If you discover you need to be moving faster, the Web will let you do so.

T I P : Start small and build up your site incrementally. But see the warning, "An Argument Against Incremental Growth" in Chapter 2.

Starting small and building from there is the single best way to limit your financial exposure.

Should This Investment Be Made *on a Hunch?*

Again, the answer is "no." If you have an idea for a Web venture, it may be possible to implement that idea fully with very little money. In fact, if you already pay a monthly fee to operate one site, the monthly expense of adding another site can be virtually free.

Web service providers don't care how many pages your site contains. Once you have paid a service provider the initial set-up costs associated with going online, then you can add pages to your heart's content, with some exceptions, as seen below. Because you are free to add more pages, you can essentially create entire, additional Web *sites*, with their own distinct look and feel (see "Multiple Web Presences," Chapter 14). Of course, creating a new add-on site to your existing site will require the one-time creation of HTML coding, graphics, and CGI scripts (if new interactivity is involved). If the site is not revised often, then once the site is developed, additional ongoing expenses are nonexistent except in the circumstances described below.

Another Domain Name Is Added

New domains require domain registration fees. For example, if your existing Web site, "The Dive Shack," is located at http://www.diverstuff.com, then you could create another site called "The Shark Shop" at http://www.diverstuff.com/sharkshop without having to pay domain registration fees because both sites are using the same domain (diverstuff.com). However, if you wanted a completely separate domain and URL address (http://www.sharkshop.com), then you would have to pay about $50 per year to secure the additional domain.

> **T I P :** Also consider the time or expense of registering new sites with search engines and directories so that people can find the new site (see Chapter 8).

Significantly More Disk Space Is Required

Most package Web site deals obtained through Internet service providers include ample hard disk space for a simple site (i.e., 10 megabytes). As your site grows, additional space can be rented for a small monthly fee, such as $25 for each additional 5 megabytes. If 10 megabytes doesn't sound like much space, realize that this would allow you to make available 200 Web pages at 50 kilobytes each. If, for whatever reason, your site requires disk storage quantities far beyond these amounts, then you should consider making special arrangements with your service provider or housing your own server.

Significantly More Data Transfer Is Required

If your site becomes so popular that millions of people are downloading your pages daily, then your service provider (assuming you aren't housing your own server) will charge you for high volumes of data transfer, such as $10 per gigabyte transferred. This is a good problem to have if your visitors are paying. But if they're downloading thousands of large-file-size video clips for free, then you might end up paying extra for your visitors' entertainment.

This ability to add new pages or sites cheaply means that the Web marketer who comes up with an idea one evening can sit down and throw together a "proof of concept" Web site. It might lack the fine polishing of a final site, but it can be enough to gauge public interest (see "Test Your Product Concept First," later in this chapter).

But suppose you don't know HTML and you outsource all of your site development and maintenance. You still don't have to commit to investing development dollars on a hunch. You can perform some impromptu marketing research to test the waters. You can see if there is interest on the Net for your idea in ways such as:

- Looking for similar sites

- Sending e-mail to select individuals for their opinions; ask them "What would you think about a new site related to such-and-such?"

- Posting inquiries to related newsgroups (see Chapter 12 to learn about newsgroups)

These types of marketing research are free (except for your time), and you may be surprised by the quantity and quality of the feedback you receive from total strangers. These activities will often yield the information you need to decide confidently whether you should take the next experimental step, such as creating a modest, proof-of-concept site.

Piggy-Backing to Save Money

All businesses have some start-up costs. The costs of setting up the books, hooking up phones, printing business cards, and even just paying fees to the government can add up to a daunting sum for some entrepreneurs—all before they ever hire their first employee or actually make anything.

> **T I P :**   If possible, consider building your Web business onto an existing company.

This tip obviously applies to Web sites being created for existing businesses, but it is a smart idea for new Web businesses as well.

One of the safest ways to enter a new business is to avoid paying for any start-up costs. If you already have a company, you can build your Web business as an offshoot to your existing enterprise. Even if your Web business sells something entirely different from that of your existing concern, wherever possible, try to share overhead expenses.

What if you don't already own your own business? Look for somebody who does—perhaps somebody who would allow you to occupy an empty office in exchange for his or her own page on the Web, which you could provide. This is simple and cheap to do if he or she doesn't require his or her own Internet domain since the page could be located under your domain. Such a symbiotic relationship could flourish as you provide them with a risk-free way of migrating onto the Web while they provide you with a low-risk way of going into business. Perhaps you provide free weekly updates to their informational Web site, and they allow you to use space, phones, furniture, and the Xerox machine. Naturally, more complex arrangements are imaginable (joint ventures, for example), and the possibilities are bounded only by your creativity and ability to find somebody with just the right needs and things to offer.

Test Your Product Concept First

For some Web marketers, the site exists as an avenue to sell a product or service, such as flowers and real estate. For others the site *is* the product, as in the case of subscription-based newsletters, Web dating services, and advertiser-sponsored sites. Therefore, it means different things to different Web marketers to speak of testing the "product concept" before a full-scale rollout.

Testing Traditional Products or Services Now Sold on the Web

Again, Web is an ideal medium for testing new ideas. This is true for three reasons. First, the costs of trying something new are fairly low. Second, the time associated with testing an idea can be quite short, including the amount of time it takes for results to come in. Third, if you should happen to test an idea that turns out to be unpopular, you can test your ideas in isolation so that the rest of your customer base is not aware of the tests.

Suppose, for example, that you operate an online gift card store. You are considering purchasing a dedicated hardware and software configuration that will allow you to begin laser imprinting cards with the recipient's name or custom messages. Before you restructure your entire fulfillment process, you might want to run a test to see if people even want such a service.

In an instant, you could add a link labeled "Customize Your Greeting" to your site. That link would shift users to a page that describes the customization service and offers prices. First, you could watch the counters and see if anybody was hitting the new page. If you watched for an hour and observed that 4 percent of your site visitors were checking out the customization page, that would be useful information. If, in that time, two visitors actually ordered a custom greeting card, then you could begin to make financial projections under the assumption that the service was always available.

At the end of an hour (or a day, or a week), you could remove the new link. Any later visitors to your site would never know there had been any reference to a custom card service. Why would you remove the link? It is very possible that you would calculate that demand for the custom card service did not justify the investment in new technology, which you have not yet purchased. So how do you handle those few orders that came in already?

For such a small number of orders, you could process their requests by hand using your company's existing laser printer. While this technology would not be an efficient solution for handling massive quantities of orders, it will suffice to satisfy those who unknowingly participated in your market research.

To be on the safe side in terms of test reliability, you might repeat the test a few more times—remember, each test is nearly free to administer. You might try the same test during different times of the day, week, or year. On one such subsequent test, you might discover that demand for customized cards skyrockets around holidays, suggesting that you should buy the equipment after all. Either way, the decision to go or not go will be rooted in something more substantial than seat-of-the-pants intuition. (If you have bosses to answer to, then this is called *covering your rear*—if your pet project fails, it's nice to have data that suggested you had been diligent and attempted to minimize uncertainty before going forward. Point to the numbers and say, "Given what we knew then, it looked like the best thing to do.")

Testing Concepts in Which the *Site* is the Product

Commercial sites are even more flexible when it comes to testing ideas for products and services for which no tangible product is related. Consider "Sound Advice" (http://www.monsoon.org/sound_advice), a Web site created to serve the interests of those using sound on the

Internet. The site was originally intended to be an online companion to the book, *Web Developer's Guide to Music and Sound*, by Anthony Helmstetter and Ron Simpson. As an online companion to a printed book, the site primarily needed to allow readers to test their browser's sound capabilities and provide hot links to resources mentioned in the book.

I was involved during the initial planning stages of this site. As we realized that a certain number of users would be visiting the site due to its mention in a book, we tried to think of other ways to add value. The subsequent brainstorming session yielded new ideas, roughly in the order presented below:

1. We could also provide unbiased reviews of new sound-related computer products (hardware and software).

2. We could let users post their own reviews in addition to just reading those we had written.

3. If enough people start coming here to learn about hardware, then why not let advertisers for such products sponsor portions of the site?

4. If people visit the site because they heard about its product reviews, what if they haven't read the book yet? Answer: make the book available for sale.

5. As long as we're selling books, why not sell royalty-free stock sounds and music clips on CD-ROM also? (Ron Simpson, the book's co-author, produces such material.)

6. If people are coming to read product reviews, maybe we should include a free classified ads section so that people can find buyers and sellers of used equipment.

7. If we have a classified section, why not also let people advertise their services, such as music writing, performance, sound engineering, voice-over, etc.? We could make the free "job board" searchable by geographic region to make it easy for a band to find a local drummer, for example.

8. This is a site about sound. Shouldn't we let professionals listed in the classified section include audio samples of their work? No, because the files would be too large. However, we could provide free classifieds with the option of paying a fee if they want to include an audio sample of their work.

Suddenly, we realized that we had a much bigger project on our hands than we had originally envisioned. But because Web sites are so flexible and scalable, we could pick and choose those features which we wanted to include immediately, while waiting to test and implement the others.

Once a site is up and running, even in an elementary form, each one of the above additions could be tested with only an incremental increase in development costs. What began as an idea for a simple, single-purpose site quickly grew into four distinct potential revenue streams:

- Book sales

- CD-ROM sales

- Advertiser sponsorship

- Classified ads' audio file fee

Perhaps testing such a site would soon find that almost nobody is interested in including audio samples with their classified ad. But then, that is why this is called an *experiment*. If the demand for this service turned out to be low, the feature could be dropped altogether with prorated refunds given to the handful of people who had actually paid for the extra service. Given that the site would still be self-sustaining from other revenue streams, it would still have been worthwhile to test this one concept. Similarly, any subsequent idea for providing some new service or information-based product can be tested with little risk beyond the development of the new features.

Keep Overhead to a Minimum

Whether or not you are able to launch your Web enterprise on the back of an existing business, always be on the lookout for ways to minimize expenses, particularly recurring expenses.

Find Ways to Automate New Content Creation

If you can license somebody else's content for a nominal fee, then you can keep changing or adding to your site without having to do a lot of work. Newspapers have been doing this for years by using syndicated columnists. Financial sites do it today by providing stock quotes that they obtain from another source.

Find Ways to Get Your Customers to Generate New Content

Product reviews, essay contests, public forums, job boards, and more can all make your site grow in size and usefulness without you having to write a word.

Outsourcing

One way to avoid hiring full-time personnel is to outsource pieces of your work. Companies of all sizes routinely outsource certain activities, but it can be particularly useful to entrepreneurial start-ups whose scale will be small at first. Many people do not realize that it is fairly simple to outsource aspects of their business such as 24-hour order-taking over 800-number phone lines; inventory stocking of your product; and fulfillment and shipping. Companies that provide this service ("fulfillment centers") often serve so-called "virtual companies" such as small businesses that are run out of an individual's home during his or her spare time. This alternative probably beats hiring an employee to sit and watch a phone throughout the night. It definitely beats having to answer the phone yourself, 24 hours a day.

For links to fulfillment services, visit http://www.monsoon.org/book. Outsourcing is a nice alternative if:

- You or your business do not possess the required skills

- You do not have scale sufficient to be able to perform the activity efficiently

- You simply don't want to do some particular type of work (such as taking phone orders at 2:00 a.m.)

If none of these is the case, then you can always consider saving money by doing the work yourself.

Doing the Work Yourself

Many commercial Web sites today are small and simple and are created and maintained by very small groups of people (in many cases, even when the site belongs to a company with hundreds of employees). The decision to outsource the following components of your Web business will be an important decision in terms of how much time and money you spend in the short and long run. The decision also depends on your short- and long-term goals for the site.

Site Structure Design

Somebody must decide for what purpose the site exists and how it should address these objectives. Should it be used to describe a company's products? If so, will it also receive orders directly? If so, will orders be taken online, channeled to customer personnel, or channeled as leads to field sales representatives? Naturally, these decisions must be made by you or someone with your company. But the best way of implementing these strategies on a Web site might not be obvious, and you might consider hiring a consultant who will help you design the best methods for meeting your objectives. In such cases, the consultant will usually wish to provide some of the services below as well, just to see that the plans are implemented correctly. If you don't expect your basic site logic or functionality to change much over the next year, then paying a one-time fee to a consultant may be the way to go. However, if you foresee frequent experimentation or changes related to company promotions (such as having your Web site activities coordinate with a company-wide, Fourth of July sale), then it makes more sense to develop this skill set within your organization.

> For smaller sites, a highly self-directed employee (or you) can read books, browse frequently, and try new things to begin this learning process. Hiring a consultant is not absolutely necessary.

However, the self-taught process will take several weeks of long hours. If you are in a hurry, consider hiring an outside individual (or firm) to help get you started. Expect to pay at least $2,000 and easily much more (on top of Web access set-up charges), depending on the site's degree of complexity, (number of pages, custom graphics, and degree of interactivity).

> **TIP:** Budgets for fancy sites can exceed $100,000, so ask your consultant to provide á la carte pricing options. Determine which items are essential and which are extravagant.

HTML Coding

If you know what you want your site to do, then you can probably find a freelancer to code your pages for about $25 per hour. Provide him or her with a flowchart depicting all of the pages and how they should link together. Provide text files to drop into each page, rather than expecting your coder to write the site's text (unless he or she is a skilled copywriter also). If you have them, provide graphics as well. If you don't already use somebody else to create graphics for your company, then look for an HTML person who can do it himself or herself or who can source it to a reliable third party.

Doing it All

Fact: According to one survey, as of early 1996, more than one-third of HTML authors also operated a server. About 80 percent of them also have some programming experience. This might be good news for Web marketers, as it suggests that many Web sites are created by computer people rather than marketing people. That's not to say that someone can't have skills in both areas, but people tend to specialize. If you browse much on the Web, you will see plenty of commercial sites that appear to have been created by people without an ounce of marketing moxie. However, the percentage of Web designers who also program and operate servers is likely to decrease. As Web development becomes more complex, the days of the one-person-show and the do-it-yourselfer entrepreneur or are becoming numbered. Even now, more serious Web projects are being developed by teams of specialists with skills ranging from database programming to consumer brand management experience.

(Survey source: GVU's Fourth WWW User Survey)

I suggest contracting with an HTML freelancer (or a firm that provides such services) only if you expect the content of your site to remain unchanged for weeks at a time. If you plan to create new pages weekly, then you really should make the investment to bring such expertise in-house. It isn't difficult to learn. You can learn HTML yourself, have an employee read a book or take a class, or hire a graduating college student who knows how to do it (and they usually don't cost much). Consider hiring a college student for a part-time job (or as an intern) if your site doesn't demand 40 hours of modifications each week.

Whether you are new to HTML or a veteran, look into off-the-shelf HTML editing software as a way of doubling productivity when it comes to creating and modifying Web sites (see sidebar, "HTML Editors").

Graphics Creation

If your existing company has a graphics department, then there's a good chance somebody there already knows most of the skills required for Web graphics (working knowledge of Adobe Photoshop is a must—anything less is

HTML Editors

New software designed to help both new and experienced users create Web pages quickly and easily is coming onto the market all the time. Here are just a few of the packages available. Many provide free trial versions.

One caveat, however, is that many HTML editors do not provide simple ways for utilizing some of the more advanced features that HTML allows. Using HTML editing software will boost productivity, but whoever is creating your site should also know (or learn) how to "hack the code," that is, manually edit HTML in order to perfect each page. See this book's online companion for links to these software companies' sites: http://www.monsoon.org/book.

Bare Bones Software, Inc.:

> BBEdit (Macintosh) $119.00

Sausage Software:

> HotDog Standard (Windows) $29.95

> HotDog Pro (Windows) $99.95

Brooklyn North Software Works:

> HTML Assistant Pro 2 (Windows) $99.95

Netscape Communications Corp.:

> Netscape Navigator Gold (Macintosh, Windows, Unix) $79

Adobe Systems, Inc.:

> PageMill (Macintosh) $149

> SiteMill (Macintosh) $595

SoftQuad, Inc.:

> HotMetal Pro (Macintosh, Windows) $195

Multimedia Systems Consulting:

> WebSucker (Macintosh, Windows, Unix) Free (shareware)

probably not professional quality. Knowledge of 3D graphics is rarer but can be very helpful, depending on the type of look you want your site to possess).

Graphics is one area where I hesitate to recommend learning to "do it yourself." To put it bluntly, many self-proclaimed professionals are not that great, let alone the dabbling hobbyists. You generally get what you pay for, and good Web graphics people are busy these days—meaning the good ones don't come cheap. If your site's graphics won't be changing often, just swallow hard and pay a great artist to make your page shine. If your business model requires new graphics to be created constantly, you can do one of two things:

1. Hire someone full-time at $25,000-50,000 per year (some really good people cost much more, but you'd probably be better off hiring them on a contract basis). If you do hire a full-time employee, knowledge of print production will make this person more useful during slow Web production times.

2. Hire a freelancer at $20-100 per hour. You can almost always negotiate lower prices from a given individual if you make a commitment for a minimum amount of work, such as a hundred hours over three months. Freelancers are almost always less expensive than comparably skilled individuals at design firms. If you can find one who is skilled and dependable, you may have begun a valuable long-term relationship.

> **TIP:** Have your freelancer sign a "Work for Hire" agreement. In the absence of a proper *written agreement*, the law clearly states that artwork copyrights belong to the individual who created it when that person is not a regular employee of your company.

As an alternative to paying somebody, consider giving your designer a piece of the action, perhaps a percentage of gross sales. This is probably the best way to get world-class graphics at no charge—if you are lucky enough to find a world-class designer who doesn't mind a little risk. If the site does well, you're both happy. If it doesn't, then you have saved a great deal of money. (See "Partnering," later in this chapter.)

Nongraphical Content Creation

Somebody must write the words that go on your site. This should be you or an employee of your company unless there is simply nobody who can write a good sentence. If there are no good writers on hand, then hire a freelance writer or Web-aware *marketing* consultant for this (*not* necessarily a Web consultant—these people are often techies who lack marketing and copywriting skills). In small companies, the task of writing the site's substantive content is too often delegated to the person in the organization who happens to know HTML. That is fine if the person also happens to be the firm's best public relations and corporate communications expert. It's not so fine if it happens to be the person who is more skilled at debugging assembly code than writing a memo. It would be better to find the gifted writer and teach him or her HTML (remember, it doesn't take long to learn, and HTML editing software makes it even easier).

Site Promotion

See Chapter 8 for a discussion of hiring outside firms to announce your new Web site to the world. Some firms will also provide ongoing, customized assistance in this area. If your Web business is important enough to continue an ongoing promotional campaign, then it is probably important enough that you or some member of your organization be charged with ownership of that process. Ideally, one person will be accountable for the success of the site, and this person will see to it that the site continues to do the following:

- Mesh with the company's strategic objectives
- Provide content pursuant to these objectives
- Be promoted and draw traffic
- Meet predetermined objectives, where possible

User Correspondence

Naturally, correspondence between the company and visitors/customers will be conducted in-house in most cases. Possible exceptions might include unusual business models, such as one in which sales leads coming into the site are routed to field rep organizations. Even so, this routing will most likely be either automated or performed by personnel within your organization. I include it here primarily to remind you to *plan on* correspondence as part of your site's ongoing operational costs. Many firms overlook this task during the planning phase and therefore do a poor job initially at responding to personalized requests.

Web Server Operation

For most, the decision between renting space on the Web server of an Internet service provider or housing their own server internally is a simple one. If your intended site is small and simple, go with a service provider. If your site is huge, complex, and highly interactive, then house your own server. However, if you are somewhere toward the middle of the complexity spectrum, then your decision may be more difficult.

Degrees of Complexity: Your Options

When you speak to different Internet sevices or network consultants, the options they present can be a little confusing at first. I've found that Figure 5.1 helps people to understand the options.

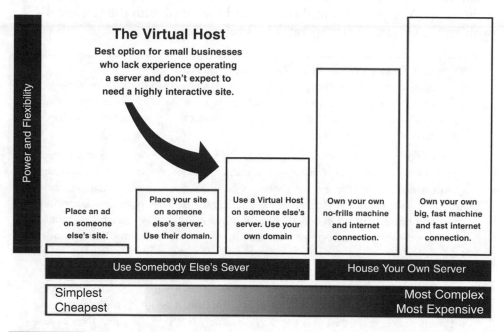

The Virtual Host

Best option for small businesses
who lack experience operating
a server and don't expect to
need a highly interactive site.

Place an ad on someone else's site.	Place your site on someone else's server. Use their domain.	Use a Virtual Host on someone else's server. Use your own domain	Own your own no-frills machine and internet connection.	Own your own big, fast machine and fast internet connection.

Power and Flexibility

Use Somebody Else's Sever — House Your Own Server

Simplest
Cheapest

Most Complex
Most Expensive

FIGURE 5.1   You have many ways to put your site on the Web, ranging from simple to complex.

Consider this chart as a general guide only. In the real world, the large variety of choices may blur the boundaries between the categories above, meaning that for nearly any financial or logistical arrangement you can imagine between yourself, full-time employees, contract labor, or outside firms to source your hardware, software, and Internet hookup, there will be somebody who can accommodate your specific needs.

While a marketer could have his or her company enter the Web at any point on this continuum, I recommend entering—at a minimum—at level three, the "virtual host." With a virtual host arrangement, your service provider essentially creates a server for you within their server (a technical name for this is "multihosting"). You get to use your own domain from their machine (remember, "domain" refers to *yourfirm.com* in the Web address, http://www.yourfirm.com). To the outside world, it is difficult for anyone to know that you don't have your own machine running in the basement.

With a virtual host, you can have a Web site ranging from the very simple to the very complex, meaning that you can grow your site without changing your degree of involvement with your service provider and server technology. You pay a monthly check and they deal with the technical problems associated with operating a Web server.

Tips on Selecting a Web Service Provider

1. Shop around—capabilities vary greatly. Make sure that it can provide you with secure transactions and usage logs (you'll specifically want access, referrer data, and agent data). Many service providers do not provide all three, even to commercial clients.

2. Ask for recommendations (specify "commercial") on your city's local Usenet newsgroup. You'll quickly hear back from people eager to tell you both glowing accolades and horror stories. For example, some service providers are notorious for having too few dial-up lines for their number of subscribers, meaning you might have difficulty getting online each day. Others are notorious for screwing up billing statements. Others are notorious for being "down" frequently, for hours (meaning customers will get an error message when attempting to visit your site—this is very bad).

3. Shop around—prices vary greatly. Keep in mind that your Web service provider could be located in another city, as long as you still maintain a local Internet account so that you can log on locally (with no long distance phone charges) and download files over the Internet to update your site.

4. If possible, physically visit your Web service provider. You will get a better feel for it as a company after you've met actual people. Some services are very small but will provide you with free technical support as though they just love doing it. Others are large and have better hardware, but they avoid answering even simple questions without billing you at their consulting rate. You might ask to look at the hardware. Rats chewing on the power cords is a bad sign.

5. It is possible to have different providers for different aspects of your service; automated e-mail (see Chapter 13), could come from a different provider than that which houses your Web site, for example. This approach complicates things (receiving multiple bills each month, for example) and may not be worth the amount of money you save.

6. Remember, you can always transfer your Web site from one service provider to another, so don't worry too much if you find out too late that your chosen company cannot meet your specific needs.

However, for sites that require a great deal of custom programming for interactivity (see "Degree of Interactivity," Chapter 3), eventually the costs of operating through a service provider can become prohibitive. Very large companies that maintain extensive, continuously updated Web sites that generate custom pages based on user input and relational databases simply become too complex and expensive to house on another firm's server without some kind of special arrangement. Special arrangements might involve long-term contracts (allowing your provider to house dedicated hardware for you) or even partnership and joint-venture relationships. While these special arrangements are an option, most owners of complex sites choose instead to house their own server and hire the necessary technical personnel to run it.

Seek Partnerships

One final way to save money is to seek partnerships. With any aspect of going into business on the Web, it may make sense to find a partner. If you are good at graphics and writing, then why not partner with a technophile who runs his or her own server out of the house? Or perhaps you are great at marketing and business in general, but have no idea where to begin with obtaining professional-caliber graphics or HTML coding. Again, seeking a partner may be the answer.

Whether it is two individuals or two companies, a lots of marriages between separate entities who possess different sets of skills are possible. The downside of partnering, of course, is that you give away a portion of profits. But going into business on the Web is inherently risky—there is no guarantee of success. If you recall, at the beginning of this chapter, I mentioned a venture capitalist who said one winner could pay for nine failures if the nine attempts were inexpensive. Partnering is one of the best ways around to make your attempts inexpensive.

No matter how simple your site or intended business model is, you will never have enough hours in the day to implement all the ideas that your

---

Sharing the Cost of Your Own Server

If you run your own server, you might be tempted to offer Internet hookup to other companies. This can work, but the business of being an Internet service provider is getting very competitive and you would compound your technical and administrative hassles, fundamentally entering a different line of work.

Perhaps a better way to offset the expenses of running your own server would be to form a small partnership arrangement with just one or two other companies that rent space on your server. If your technical personnel were available to handle your tenants' customization projects, they might be able to pay you to get such services at a very affordable rate while you would be assured that your technical staff were not idle.

---

brain will generate. Partnering not only provides you with needed skills, but it gives you access to the hours, labor, efforts, and ideas of additional individuals. Almost any idea becomes more refined when it has been bounced off a couple of listeners. When your listeners have a stake in the rewards, their efforts and contribution can help generate sales that more than compensate for the portion of the profits they take.

Projecting Costs and Revenues

The natural starting point of any project or enterprise is to gather information. At the very minimum, you will want to estimate the following as closely as possible:

- How much will it cost to go online? (See "Online Fees," below)

- How much will your product or service cost to produce?

- Who is your market, and how will you reach them?

- What should you sell, and how much should you charge?

- How much must you sell to break even?

Online Fees

Table 5.1 illustrates a sample of published prices from one Web service provider. They are provided to indicate the available options and give a ball-park estimate of start-up costs and monthly expenses. Remember, however, that prices vary greatly, and you can find bargains if you search for them. For example, the "mailbot" option below costs $25 to set up and $15 per month with this particular service provider. However, some companies provide specialized services on the Web for significant discounts, such as a "mailbot provider" that can give you essentially the same service for a flat rate of $25 per year.

Table 5.1 lists the fees for using another company's server only. None of these prices include HTML coding, CGI scripting, design, writing, or graphics produced for your site.

As you can see from this list, the "essentials" add up to $600 in set-up fees (including the annual domain registration) and ongoing expenses of $150 per month.

TABLE 5.1 A sample of Web service provider options.

Service	Set-up Fee	Ongoing Fee
Essentials:		
Commercial server leasing[1]	$200	$100 per month

> [1]This service is all you need to host a no-frills Web site on a fast, reliable server that is designed specifically for commercial customers of the service provider. This service includes secure, encrypted transmissions and provides basic Internet hookup services such as e-mail, ftp, etc.

Service	Set-up Fee	Ongoing Fee
Credit card ordering capabilities	$100	$0.50 per order
Domain registration	n/a	$50 per year
Virtual host[2]	$250	$50

> [2]This service allows your Web site to contain your own domain in the URL address, such as http://www.*yourfirm.com*. (See "Degrees of Complexity," earlier in this chapter.)

Service	Set-up Fee	Ongoing Fee
Options:		
Mailing lists[3]	$25	$15 per month
Mailbots[3]	$25	$15 per month

> [3]See Chapter 13 for in-depth descriptions of these advanced e-mail options.

Service	Set-up Fee	Ongoing Fee
Message Board[4]	$100	$50 per month

> [4]This allows your site to host public forums in which visitors can read and add messages. (See Chapter 14.)

Forecasting Sales

In a perfect world, before you commit any resources to your project, you would also want to know: How many people will visit my site? How many will buy? In the real world, however, this kind of information is not always easy to come by. One starting point for determining potential revenue is to identify the size of your target market, such as all practicing dentists who are currently Internet users. Unfortunately, this number will not be easy to determine. And even if you could know how many there were, the number would determine only an upper limit, and it is doubtful that you would ever reach most of them through normal online marketing techniques. So how is the diligent manager supposed to proceed with confidence?

> **T I P :** The Web is probably more forgiving than your boss.

The Web is fluid and flexible. You can try one thing today, see how it goes, and try something different tomorrow without incurring much cost or alienating your customers. If one idea doesn't turn a profit, no problem—try something else until you hit on a profitable formula. Many small, entre-preneurial Web ventures proceed in exactly this fashion. However, such flexibility does not always exist when creating a Web site in an existing com-pany. More than likely, the Web champion, particularly in a large company, will need to pitch an idea to somebody who will approve the expenditure. Whoever allocates the funds will expect to see projections, objectives, and periodic performance reports. In other words, accountability.

Many people start commercial Web sites with shockingly little informa-tion. They begin without ever building a solid business case for their pro-ject. By that, I mean that they proceed entirely by the seat of their pants, making decisions intuitively or reactively. They do not attempt to determine how much investment will be required or how much they predict to sell. They just start. I think these are the same people who, as children, used to start putting together a new toy without reading the directions first.

Even though the mere notion of such lack of preparation gives every self-respecting, Type-A manager a queasy feeling in his or her stomach, I hate to admit this, but proceeding without much of a plan can sometimes work. Here is why: low investment.

As described earlier, many sites don't cost very much to create, and they cost even less to maintain. As a general business rule, making mistakes is usually an acceptable price to pay if:

- The mistakes didn't cost much

- The mistakes are not expensive to correct

- The mistakes are a by-product of a process that speeds development time

A manager at Silicon Graphics once told me that his company's secret to rapid product innovation was that they do everything at breakneck pace. "Sure, that means we make more mistakes," he told me. "But when you know how to move faster, you can fix problems faster too."

> **TIP:** Do your homework, but don't fall prey to "paralysis by analysis."

Information is good, and the more the better—to a point. If gathering information makes you take too long to enter the market without substantially improving your odds of succeeding, then the extra information will not have been worth waiting for.

If you are creating a Web business channel as a separate profit-and-loss center for an existing company, you might be expected to launch a major site with full-featured functionality at the beginning.

> **TIP:** It is better to promise less than it is to underdeliver.

This is a new field. There are few experts. You will be learning as you go, and soon you will be the expert. Just remember to keep expectations modest, particularly sales expectations.

The Absolute Best Way to Predict Sales

A lot of people ask me how much a Web business makes. Not only are financial data scarce, but all businesses are different.

> **TIP:** The best way to estimate Web sales is to put up a site and see how much money it pulls in.

This is not a joke. If you put up a partly functional site and do minimal promotion, you will get a small number of visitors. The key is to find out how many visitors it takes to make a sale. If your bare-bones test site manages to make one in five visitors buy something for $10, then you have a gold mine on your hands. This is the best research you will ever find or need. From there, it becomes a numbers game. Simply add the rest of your features and then concentrate on getting as many people to the site as possible. But if 3,000 people visit your site and nobody buys anything, you might start evaluating which pieces of the puzzle aren't working. These are extreme results for the purposes of illustration. Your tests will probably yield less clear-cut answers—for example, one $10 sale per 200 visitors. This figure might not give you absolute confidence about moving forward, but it will help you either begin to plan using better projections or provide the baseline for additional experimentation.

If you are an entrepreneur who is accountable to no one, this means that you should probably begin even before you think you have enough information because you will get much more useful data once you do begin. For those of you who are spending other people's money, create this sort of test site and call it "market research." Research is meant to yield information, not profit. If no amount of modification to the test site ever produces an impressive sales-per-visitor average, then you may conclude that you should pass on this idea and begin investigating another. This attitude works well if you remember the 1-in-10 rule and keep your costs of experimentation low.

two

SITE PROMOTION:
GENERATING HITS

PLANNING A PROMOTIONAL
CAMPAIGN THAT WORKS

T he best time to begin thinking about promoting your site is *before* you build it. Fortunately for you, many of your competitors on the Web will have created their sites with little regard to a master strategy. They will get a creative blast and whip out few pages here, a few more there, a message from the President if he or she ever gets around to writing it, and maybe a major update in a few months, such as a new page that describes the company's latest product.

If you browse much on the Web, then no doubt you have seen sites that were created in such a piecemeal, haphazard fashion. Whenever you hear gloomy statistics about the number of Web sites that don't recoup their investments, keep in mind that these meager attempts are drawing down the averages.

You've probably also seen sites that were clean and crisp and flowed meaningfully from one page to the next. Every piece of information that you desired could be found somewhere on the site with very little effort. On such sites, the purpose is clear; the presentation, complete.

Incidentally, these types of sites are found most often at existing companies where a dedicated person or team spends all their time developing the site, when the site is outsourced to a good Web site developer, or when an entrepreneur or start-up creates the site as a stand-alone entity, untethered to an existing company. All of these situations have one developmental factor in common: they make a plan and follow it.

Creating Your Plan

Before you create your first page of HTML or even your masthead graphic, you should take a step back and answer a few questions: Who will be visiting this site? Why will they visit? How will they hear about it? Will most of your visitors be techies or newbies? Male or female? Teenagers or parents? Stylin' or conservative? Will they seek out your site by looking at a directory? If so, which keywords will they select to find firms like yours? Will they hear about you through a friend? Will they read about you in a magazine? Which magazines?

Once you have given serious thought to questions like these and answered them in some detail, you will have a strong starting point for designing your site. Of course, you will already know the basic purpose and audience of your site, but you will learn a great deal more about the members of your audience as you prepare a promotional plan to target them effectively. Creating a promotional plan forces you to get to know your audience thoroughly.

A not-so-obvious tip: Draft your promotional plan *before* you build your site.

First, by delaying to "build your site," I mean that you should hold off on the actual creation of text, graphics, and linked pages. You should basically know what features the site will house as you begin planning your promotion. Second, it may take you only a few days to draft your promotional plan (and this chapter will help get you started). The idea is to avoid traveling too far down one road (in terms of site creation hours) when you may later discover that another road would have been a better choice. You may even find it useful to interweave your promotion planning and site planning iteratively, making adjustments on one after thinking more about the other. Your progress may go something like this:

1. Outline basic concept of the site.

2. Figure out who would want to visit such a site.

3. Figure out how to reach these people.

4. Research competition.

5. Discover there are actually three distinct groups who would use this site for different reasons.

6. Begin planning site structure around these three interest groups.

7. Name the site and develop its theme.

8. Ask yourself, "What other groups may like a site with this theme?" (This is your secondary market.)

9. How would you reach this secondary market?

The plan itself should end up looking like a List of Things to Do that will effectively draw traffic to your site. The level of detail to include is your decision—more detail is always better when you'll be answering to bosses, spouses, bankers, or partners. But, if you are doing this alone and don't have to answer to anybody, then you'll probably want *even more detail* to be confident that you've thought through everything. In other words, regardless of your situation, this is not a time to skimp on homework. A little thinking up front can make you very efficient when you implement this plan. You have probably written enough when you could hand your promotional plan off to a bright somebody else who could implement it based on the details you've provided (which may not be a bad idea).

Once you have written the answers to the questions in the Site Promotion Plan (later in this chapter), your plan will be nearly complete. Expand areas where appropriate for your unique purposes. Remember, just complete the *writing* of the plan at this early point. Don't actually implement the steps (such as registering your site or posting to newsgroups) until your site is completed (see "When to Begin Promotion," later in this chapter).

> Exception: Register your domain as soon as you know what you want it to be.

How to Register Your Domain

A "domain" is the root part of your Internet address. For example, Reebok's Web site is called "Planet Reebok." It can be found at the URL address http://www.reebok.com.

In this address, reebok.com is the domain. Similarly, you might reach a Reebok employee at janedoe@reebok.com.

If your company does not already have a registered domain, then you will want to register it *immediately* because domain names are granted on a first-come, first-served basis. The domain might be your company's name, your site's intended name, or even a product's name, depending on your marketing objectives and whatever you think will be easiest for potential customers to remember or look up.

If you are using an Internet service provider, then it will probably be able to register your domain for you for a fee ranging from $50 to $100 per year. If you wish to save some money by doing the work yourself, you can contact InterNIC, the organization that grants domain names.

For general information, contact:
http://www.internic.net.

InterNIC Services Reference Desk
info@internic.net
800-444-4345
619-455-4600 (San Diego, California)

When you are ready to register, contact:

InterNIC Registration Services
hostmaster@rs.internic.net
703-742-4777 (Herndon, Virginia)

Once you submit your name, it can take up to eight weeks for approval, which is one reason why you should begin immediately. You can check to see if the domain name is already in use before you submit it by visiting the InterNIC Web site mentioned above. Even if there appears to be no active domain by that name, somebody could request it before you do, meaning that you still might not get the name you want. For this reason, InterNIC registration forms provide spaces for alternative names, and you should supply them, just to be safe—or risk having to go through the process again, wasting up to another eight weeks.

You should also consider doing a trademark search (see, "Conducting a Trademark Search," later in this chapter) on the domain name to avoid legal problems in the future. For example, a firm might exist with the name you've chosen as your domain, even though it may not yet have an Internet presence. Some legal precedents suggest that—under certain conditions—it might be able to force you to give up the domain, even after you've been using it for years.

Give some thought to the name you'll use—it could be with you for a long time. Once you've invested time and money getting your address out to thousands of people, you will not want to change it. Even though you may be able to add additional domains to your business, the supply of available names grows shorter every day, and InterNIC is beginning to resist granting multiple domains to one company.

Site Promotion Plan

The following steps outline everything you need to do to promote your site effectively. Steps 1 through 6 have already been covered in depth in this and the preceding chapters. Steps 7 through 16 will be described in greater detail in forthcoming chapters, so don't worry if you're not sure how to go about implementing each step at this point.

1. Describe in one sentence the primary benefit created by your site or the need that it satisfies. If you provide multiple, distinct benefits (such as unrelated product lines), then list them all and go through this process for each benefit, just as you would create a promotional plan for each distinct product group in a company.

2. Define the primary type of person who would benefit most by visiting your site.

3. List all other benefits created by your site.

4. List all other types of people who would appreciate these benefits.

5. Come up with five different names for your site (see "Trademarks," in Chapter 2). Identify the strengths and weaknesses of each. Select one based on feedback and trademark availability (see, "Conducting a Trademark Search," later in this chapter).

6. List other interests likely to be found in your primary audience, even if not directly related to your subject matter. (For example, a site about golf may appeal to retirees, who also enjoy sailing, which might suggest other avenues for reaching your audience.)

7. Come up with 15–20 keywords (see Chapter 8 for tips on selecting keywords) related to your site, your subject matter, and your audience. Rank the keywords in order of importance.

   - Later, you will use the top keywords when registering with directories and search engines (see Chapter 8).
   - You will use all 15–20 keywords (shuffled, perhaps three at a time) to conduct searches on multiple search engines to locate special-

interest sites from whom you will solicit links to your site (see Chapter 9). Set a goal for how many links you will solicit (or, better yet, actually obtain); for example, set a goal of 10 per week.

8. Identify a list of key print publications that might be interested in doing a story on your site. Compose special press releases with angles geared to appeal to these publications. Compose one to three generic press releases and distribute them to general-interest publications (see Chapter 11).

9. See that all appropriate, traditional company marketing communication materials contain your site's URL (see Chapter 11).

10. Identify the best Usenet newsgroups to which you should announce your site and develop a newsgroup posting and maintenance schedule (see Chapter 12).

11. Using your keywords, conduct a search to identify the most appropriate existing listservs (automated e-mailing lists) to receive announcements regarding your site. After checking the submission rules for each listserv, post your announcement to those that are appropriate. (See Chapter 13 for explanations of e-mail lists, finding lists, and posting to them appropriately.)

12. Determine if, and to what extent, you wish to participate in mass e-mailings (see Chapter 13). (This refers to using your own house list of people who don't mind receiving your e-mail. Sending *unsolicited* mass e-mail is *not* an acceptable practice on the internet.)

13. Determine if, and to what extent, you wish to pay for advertising to promote your site, either via traditional media or online (see Chapter 10). This step is both optional and risky—consider how you want to spend your money most carefully.

14. Always be on the lookout for opportunities to employ creative promotions such as contests, coupons, scavenger hunts, sales, or anything that will generally build word-of-mouth.

Conducting a Trademark Search

Before you invest too much money building a business around a new company, product, Web site, and domain, you should search to see whether any of your chosen names are already being used. Even if nobody has used your intended name online, someone else may have exclusive rights to the name if

---

he or she has used it (or even a *similar* name!) in any form of business. To complicate matters further, proper trademark searching must consider not only state and federally registered trademarks, but also foreign companies' trademarks. You can spend a lot of time doing the search yourself through online databases (for a fee, usually), or you can hire a company that specializes in trademark searches.

One such company, Thomson & Thomson (http://www.thomson.com/thomthom.html) has the ability to search the full database of all existing .com, .edu, .org, .mil, and .net Internet domains. For additional links to information and services about trademarks, see this book's online companion at http://www.monsoon.org/book.

Generally speaking, the more you invest in your business, the more rigorous a search you will want to conduct. Large-investment Web sites are well advised to seek professional help where this is concerned. However, smaller-budget sites should also consider hiring expert searchers because it would be a shame to grow into a large business only to be forced later to change your name or Internet address. Conducting your own search is time-consuming and very complex, given that you also have to look for phonetically similar variations of your name. If you can afford to do so, hiring a search firm will provide better protection and greater peace of mind.

When to Begin Promotion

To time promotion to coincide with the launch of your site (or a new site feature or product), think in terms of two types of promotion: active and passive.

- Active promotion—You reach somebody and tell him or her that you exist.

- Passive promotion—Somebody finds you and discovers that you exist.

It would be very unwise to actively promote a site that was not yet ready since you will usually be wasting your one chance of informing a person (see the exception, "Building Suspense," later in this chapter). It is already difficult enough to convince somebody to visit your site the first time. If he or she visits, only to find an "under construction" sign, (Figure 6.1) don't even bother re-announcing your site to that same person a week later when the site is *really* ready.

However, there is little to be lost with premature, passive promotion.

You can register your site with automated directories before your site is completely finished.

FIGURE 6.1 The infamous "Under Construction" icon.

If somebody does a search today on the words "Zuni fetish," and I have an 80 percent completed site related to southwestern Native American art, I would rather have that person visit my not-yet-perfect site than lose that visitor forever. The same person is unlikely to repeat the same search two weeks from now when my site is ready for its official opening to the public. But, if you only have one shot, don't blow it. Some smaller directories visit your site and review it before they list it on their services. In these cases, it would be better to wait until your site is ready to be evaluated.

> **T I P :** List your site *early* with non-evaluative directories to gather feedback from real people.

Most directories, however, will merely verify that the site exists, rather than evaluate the quality of the site. In these cases, it can be beneficial to list your site as soon as possible so that early traffic will provide you with some actual users to beta-test your site. Remember, no level of testing you can do will compare with a real-world test. While you don't want to miss your one shot by launching a premature idea, recognize that users will usually understand (as in the case of beta software releases) if you inform them with a disclaimer such as this one:

```
This feature of our site is still in the developmental
stage. We encourage you to try it out and let us know
what you think. If you have any ideas for improvement,
please let us know.
```

The "let us know" link connects to a mailto address. This disclaimer is very important! Without it users will just think your site is lousy. In my opinion, such a heartfelt disclaimer and plea for feedback are very different from merely placing an "under construction" graphic.

Even with a disclaimer, it would be unwise to release a new site or feature *too* early, such as when you know that it does not ever work properly. As the developer, you will have a pretty good feel as to whether you have

Under Construction

Most sites are forever changing and, therefore, are always under construction. Hipper netizens will tell you to *never* use or the words "under construction." Many see using these words as amateurish, crude, and lazy—better to make your pages inaccessible until they are ready to be seen. Personally, I shy away from such absolute statements. Try this on for size instead:

> Greg's Rule of "Under Construction" Usage
>
> Don't use it unless you have a darn good reason.

Example 1: You have an emergency change to be made in a page's content. In the next 12 hours, during which time you will make the edits, you expect a dozen new surfers to try to access the page as an entry point to your site. I think posting an "under construction" remark (including an estimated time of completion) could be better than having your visitors see the wrong information or, worse yet, a "File Not Found" error message and leaving your site forever.

Example 2: You want to do a quick experiment to see if your site visitors have any interest in a new feature you're toying with, such as making your site searchable. Instead of creating the feature and then seeing if anyone is interested in using it, do a test first. Create a "search" icon on your main menu that links to an "under construction" page. Leave this link to your bogus search feature intact just long enough to determine people's interest level. If they don't seem interested, eliminate the link. If they do show interest, build the real feature. Importantly (and this addresses those hipper netizens' complaints), *don't* leave the linked icon and "under construction" page intact during the entire time that you are building the feature. Once your little marketing test is completed, eliminate the link until the feature actually works—and nobody will have to continue visiting your "under construction" page day after day. A better way to let people know what's coming is to simply state somewhere:

> *This site will be searchable in the near future...stay tuned.*

Or, better yet:

> *This site will become searchable on March 15th. Please stop by.*

Directory Registration Lag Time

Chapter 8 explains how to register your site with hundreds of directories that will help users find your site. Many of these directories take up to a few weeks to process your registration. For those that do not actually visit your site to judge its quality, you should register your site before your site is completed so that the directory will begin displaying your site at the time of your launch.

something that is nowhere near being ready, versus something that is, for the most part, functional, even though numerous, minor improvements need to be made.

Large, well-known companies that can expect to generate heavy traffic as soon as they launch a site should generally wait until the site is in near-perfect condition before making it publicly accessible. For smaller companies that do not automatically generate a buzz of attention every time they do something new, I generally recommend releasing (that is, making your site publicly accessible in properly disclaimed, beta form) as soon as you sense that you are over the hump of your development—in other words, when your basic functionality and information are present, but before all of the small, finishing touches are made.

Planning with this schedule in mind might mean that you get a rudimentary form of each page ready before beginning any detail work, as opposed to perfecting the first page before beginning the second, and so on. Only after you have made all of the finishing touches do I recommend beginning your *active* promotion (sending out press releases, announcing to newsgroups, and so on). Because many sites never stop growing, it is important to plan your development in phases so that you will know exactly how many pages of the site should be perfected before you begin your active promotion. Once all of Phase One's pages are perfect, then the site can be actively promoted. And then you can begin creating the rudimentary forms of Phase Two's pages, if you already know how the site is to be expanded. I have seen too many sites that apparently took on too much at once, only to have a very large site, constantly growing, but with all of its pages lacking refinement. Such sites are the result of a poor development plan, with no clear point at which to announce to the world that the site is ready to be seen because it is *never* quite ready to be seen.

Building Suspense

In the section above, I stated that passive promotion (making your site publicly accessible and registering with directories) can begin before a site is fully functional. An exception to this passive promotional schedule would be when your new site or feature is so top-secret (as in the case of many larger, more well-known companies) that you dare not release it until you're ready to take the market by storm. In this case, you may want to create pre-release excitement by promoting "something big is coming" messages.

Huge pre-release promotion in the motion-picture industry often means the producer has a dog on his hands. The big promotion is meant to pack the theaters on opening weekend, in an attempt to break even before poor word-of-mouth kills attendance. Web sites, unlike movies, are expected to break even over much longer timeframes than a couple of weeks. As such, suspenseful pre-release promotion for a Web enterprise would not be as likely to indicate a loser. But if the site is a loser, then the advance promotion will fuel the fire of negative word-of-mouth once the site is made public.

> **TIP:** If you pre-promote your site with suspenseful, "It's Coming" messages, then your site *had better be good.*

If your site is simply "okay," then it might be wiser to dispense with suspense-laden, pre-promotion plans. Releasing a mediocre site and promoting it normally is not as likely to disappoint people if they do not have inflated expectations.

> **TIP:** If your site must remain a secret (not publicly accessible) until it is completely ready, then at least put up a place-holder site in the meantime, or a page with a "coming soon" message for people who might be looking for you.

Great Promotion Can't Make a Lousy Site Successful

For some reason, many Web marketers get caught up with the ongoing problem of trying to increase site hits. They get so caught up that they forget about the other two big opportunities.

1. **Increase the conversion rate**—Make adjustments so that more people who visit your site end up purchasing.

2. **Increase the average sale**—Make adjustments so that each buyer ends up buying more.

These two points are the primary reason Part III of this book exists (the "Increasing Sales" part of this book's title). For now, however, we'll concentrate on getting people to the site. But, while we cover the nitty gritty details of increasing hits, always keep in mind that hits alone will not make a successful site. Traffic is necessary but not sufficient. Generating hits is only half the battle.

A brilliantly executed site will naturally convert a percentage of its visitors into buyers. That's benefit number one. Benefit number two is that brilliant sites also get visitors to go and tell all of their friends about the site. And, of course, part of these new people buy or tell their friends as well, in a never-ending process. There was never a better example of the saying, "Success begets success."

This suggests a straightforward marketing objective: Encourage referrals. Like many other ideas presented in this book, many Web marketers simply don't bother to implement this tactic, even though it can be relatively simple. (Exception: Requesting HTML links to your site—a form of referral—is employed heavily by Web marketers. All of Chapter 9 is devoted to this topic.) Here are some ways to get people to tell their friends about your site (you may recognize some of these from non-Web businesses):

- Offer a freebie item to anybody who refers a paying customer.

- Offer a discount to anybody who refers a paying customer.

- Offer either of these to anybody who refers a visitor (or multiple visitors) who registers at your site (also a good way to help build your e-mail list).

- Create a contest in which a person's chances of winning are improved by getting his or her friends to enter (see an e-mail implementation of this tactic in chapter 13).

No amount of promotion can match the effect of getting every visitor to your site to convince two other people to visit your site. Even though this sort of exponential growth has obvious limits in practice, it illustrates that the numbers can add up fast.

So Much to Do, So Little Time

Between soliciting links, finding new directories, whipping out press releases, and dreaming up all sorts of bizarre contests and promotions, it is pretty clear why many Web marketers forget to spend time refining the site itself. With so many ways to spend one's time with promotional activities alone, it becomes more important than ever to accurately assess which of these activities are producing the best results. To do this well, you must know how many people are visiting your site and, in particular, how they found you. The next chapter tells you how to do this.

OBSESSING ON SITE TRAFFIC—WATCH THOSE NUMBERS!

Once you've built a site and begun to promote it, you will naturally want to know how many people are visiting. You have several different options for measuring traffic, ranging from quick-n-dirty to quite sophisticated. At a minimum, you can know how many cumulative visits your site has received. At the other end of the spectrum, it is possible to know much more, such as the following measurements:

- How many visits you've had, broken down by hour of day
- How many visits you've had, broken down by day of week
- Which pages within your site receive the most traffic
- Which browsers your users are viewing your site with
- Which countries your visitors are coming from
- The location of sites that are providing traffic to you via links
- Demographics of the individuals who are visiting your site

The possible uses of this information are virtually unlimited. You could use such data to do the following:

- Correlate spikes in traffic to specific promotional events
- Correlate sales increases to changes in content
- Modify content to be more appealing
- Decide which foreign languages to include

- Observe routes that users take through your site
- Charge advertisers based on how many times their ads are viewed

Quality of Hits versus Quantity of Hits

It does no good to spend time and money to draw thousands of people to your site if they do nothing once they arrive. Even if your site is advertiser-sponsored, you don't want people to hit your front page only to turn around and leave when they could be exploring multiple pages that are sponsored by multiple advertisers.

As a Web marketer, you have two concerns in life: (1) attracting hordes of people to your site and (2) having them do something once they get there; make a purchase, buy a subscription, linger curiously while being pummeled by ads, etc. If you make $100 in sales from your first hundred visits, what does that mean to you? What should you do next?

You could start making realistic sales projections, for one thing. Over time, you will discover first-hand something that direct mail marketers and casino operators have known for a long time—percentages remain remarkably consistent over time. If your first batch of 100 visits brings in $100 in sales, then your second hundred will probably do pretty close to $100 also.

> Fact: People will often visit a site more than once before purchasing, particularly for items that cost more than $20.

Your "100 visits" might be only 90 different people, 10 of whom visited your site twice. As long as your sample spans enough time to include these repeat visits, your conversion rate (the percentage of visits that turn into purchases) will usually be pretty consistent over the short term. (Over the long run, the sales rate may change. For example, an increase may be partly due to all Web users generally getting more comfortable with using credit cards for online transactions.)

Back to the question: What do you do? One obvious answer might be to attempt to get a million people to your site. If nothing about your site changes, then that should bring in $1 Million—right? Not necessarily. You would need to do something different to increase your number of visitors from a hundred to a million. Doing something different means you would be drawing different types of people for different reasons. This means they may have different buying habits once they're at your site. You must keep this in mind when planning promotions geared toward increasing traffic.

> **T I P :** Beware of the "Traffic at All Costs" attitude.

If you were to place first-run photographs of naked celebrities all over your site, which sells hats, you would undoubtedly see an increase in traffic once the word got out. You might sell more hats, but your sales-per-visit would probably plummet because most of the people visiting your site are not looking for hats.

Compared to traditional media such as direct mail, the Web does let you reach far more people for less money. But this does not mean that resources are infinite. Excessive hits at your site will clog bandwidth and make it slow or impossible for would-be hat buyers to access your site.

Lots of hits does not necessarily equate to good hits. If the above example is too extreme, the following is more subtle. Brian Wansink, Ph.D., an instructor of marketing at the Wharton School, relates an interesting story about a car that he sold with a newspaper classified ad. For the same car, he ran two different versions of the ad:

Ad 1: 1984 BMW 318i. Looks sharp. Fun to drive. White, 2-door, 5-speed, 132,000 miles. $4900. 643-8825

Ad 2: 1984 BMW 318i. White, 2-door, 5-speed, 132,000 miles. 189 hp, 10 bolt posi, 373 ratio. $4900. 646-1336

The first ad generated 19 calls and the second ad generated only 2. But here's the punch-line: Respondents to the first ad turned out to be gearheads who were only willing to pay a maximum of $2,000 for the car. Both respondents to the second ad were college students who were willing to pay $6,000 for the same car. The moral of the story:

> Different promotional tactics will draw different people. Different people are worth different amounts to you as customers.

Consider the real estate agent who must personally respond to leads or the car dealership that gives $50 to anybody that test drives a car. In both cases, there are costs associated with converting a lead into a sale.

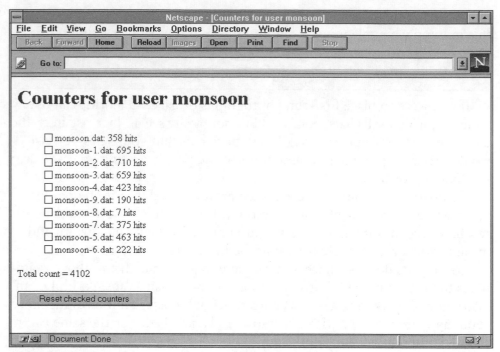

Your Web service provider can tell you how to install and monitor page counters. You can reset the counters to zero at any time by entering a password-protected region of your provider's site.

TIP: To the extent that you must personally handle leads before they can be converted into sales, use the Web to *pre-qualify* visitors as well as to attract them.

Simply put, you want more people to visit your site, but you also want them to be people who are interested in being there for the right reasons. Given the condition that your promotional effort is geared toward generating quality as well as quantity of hits, the basic truth remains the same: You will sell more with a million visitors than you will with only a thousand visitors. A lot more. So, under this condition, more hits are obviously good. There are several ways to measure traffic. We'll begin with the simplest methods.

Crude Traffic Measurement Techniques

If all you ever want to do is know how many people have accessed your site, then there are simple ways to do so. Bear in mind, however, that these methods were not designed for the interests of the serious Web marketer who needs a deeper level of data and analysis (discussed in the next section).

Page Counters

If your Web service provider has page counter capabilities, then you can ask it for its specific instructions on how to attach counters to your pages. Once this is done, the page counter increments every time the server downloads the page to somebody who is accessing it. To see how many times your pages have been accessed, you simply use your browser to visit a special page that displays your counters (see Figure 7.1).

Many people perform very little in the way of site traffic analysis, perhaps only occasionally visiting their counter page to see how many visits they've been receiving lately.

If a user visits a long page that has page counter codes at the bottom, he or she may leave the page before the codes are downloaded. In such a case, this page would not register the access. However, this counter would provide an accurate count of people who stayed long enough for the entire page to load—a measurement that might be more useful.

Using Multiple Counters

> A large Web service provider reported that *none* of its customers had ever requested more than one page counter.

This means that, shockingly, out of thousands of personal and commercial sites, not one site was measuring anything but traffic at one page, most often the site's home page. By installing counters on several (or all) pages, you can learn valuable information about the effectiveness of your promotion and site design.

Multiple Points-of-Entry

You can use page counters to discern how people are finding your site by having different promotional efforts bring visitors to different entry points of your site. For example, you might have visitors come to a "portal page" or "antechamber" that leads them into the home page or main menu of your site (see Figure 7.2).

You may have dozens of identical antechambers, with one corresponding to each ad you place, message you post to newsgroups, and so on. By placing a counter at each antechamber page, you can determine from which sources people are discovering your site (see Figure 7.3).

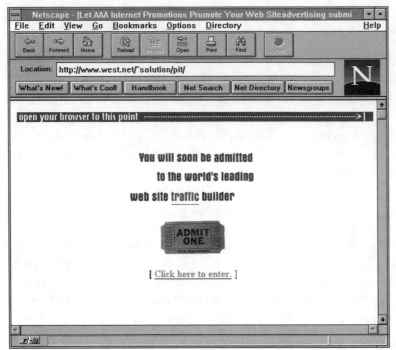

FIGURE 7.2 "Portal" or "antechamber" Pages: Users who arrive at this page must click through to arrive at the home page. This page probably exists only to count how many visitors are arriving from a certain source.

Be forewarned, however, that search engines such as WebCrawler "crawl" across the entire Net following links, listing every page they find. Some people may chance upon your antechamber pages by using a search engine, skewing your page hit statistics and giving the false appearance that they found you elsewhere. This is unavoidable. However, if your promotions are drawing significant hits, the amount of hits coming from crawlers may be relatively small; they should not muddy your statistics too much. You can also add new antechambers at any time, reducing the odds that the search engines will have found them (search engines can only find a page to which somebody has provided a link).

Interior Pages

By placing page counters on your site's interior pages, you can easily see which pages are attracting viewers and which are remaining unread; this approach can help you determine features to add or delete from your site. For example, I worked on a site that had a main menu that provided links to four separate sections. Page counters on each of these four interior

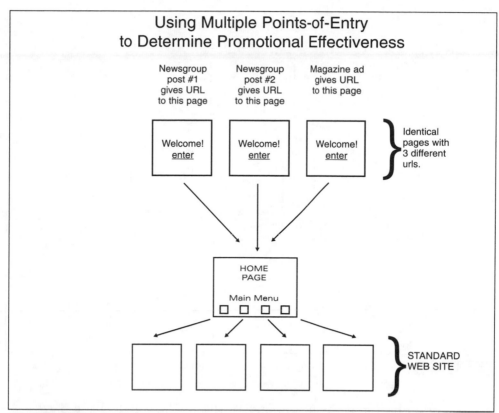

FIGURE 7.3 Placing counters at identical site entry points can help you determine how your visitors are finding you.

pages demonstrated that almost nobody was selecting the first of them, entitled "An Overview of This Site." We then replaced this button with a link pointing to a new page entitled, "What's New." Subsequent observation all of the multiple page counters showed that people visited the new page frequently, but visits to the other three sections declined—as though users will sit still only long enough to visit three sections. This prompted us to eliminate the "What's New" section altogether, and traffic to the remaining three sections returned to normal levels. By placing counters on deeper "nested pages," you can determine if visitors are actually reading the interior pages of sites they're visiting.

In Figure 7.4, it is reasonable to assume that visitors who visit Page B have looked at Page A fairly carefully, especially if the link to B is not very prominent. Not all readers of A will click on the link to B, but you can determine what percentage of them do so on average. Then you can modify something about Page A, such as the color, graphics, or its overall

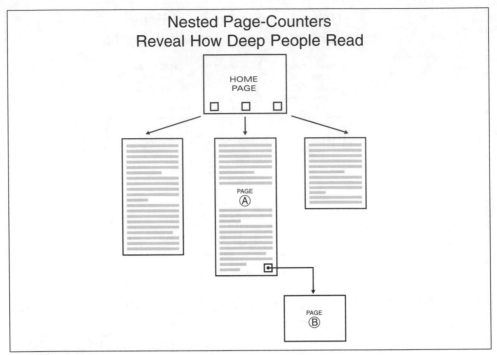

FIGURE 7.4 Counters located on pages nested within other pages can help you determine how many people are reading your content thoroughly.

length, and observe if the percentage of those who link to Page B increases or decreases. An increase would suggest that more people are reading the page thoroughly.

Variations over Time

Another simple way to observe the effects of your promotions is to watch the effects on your page counters over time. First, register your site with search engines, directories, Yellow Pages, and general listing services (see Chapter 8). After your site has appeared on these services, if your schedule permits, do no promotion for a couple of weeks and watch your page counters. At about the same time each day, or every other day, jot down the number of visits your page has received since the last time you recorded it.

Expect Cyclical Variance

The entire Internet experiences ordinary variations in traffic, such as daily "peak times." During these times, high demands are placed on the infrastructure that delivers your Web site to your customers—so it is good to know when these peak times occur.

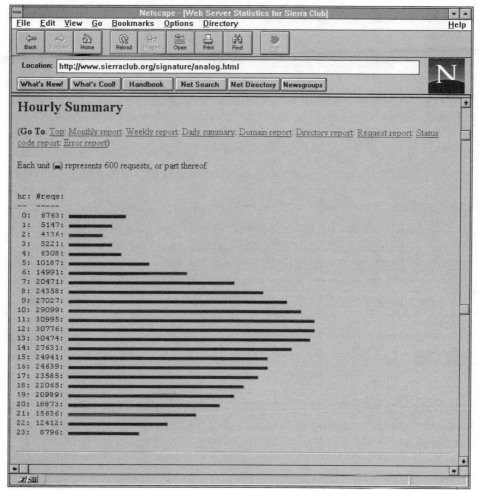

FIGURE 7.5 Throughout any given day, traffic volume consistently fluctuates in patterns similar to this one.

Of perhaps even greater importance is understanding that you must *expect* cyclical variation and not let these traffic fluctuations confound your marketing analysis. If you do no special promotion of your site, you will notice a very consistent range of traffic volume that is generated by people who discover you on search engines, and possibly by an ongoing, ambient level of word-of-mouth.

Within that baseline range, however, you will see cyclical variations that mirror Internet traffic as a whole (see Figure 7.5). For example, consider the season premiere of NBC's killer Thursday night lineup—More people watching television means fewer people on the Net, and, therefore, fewer

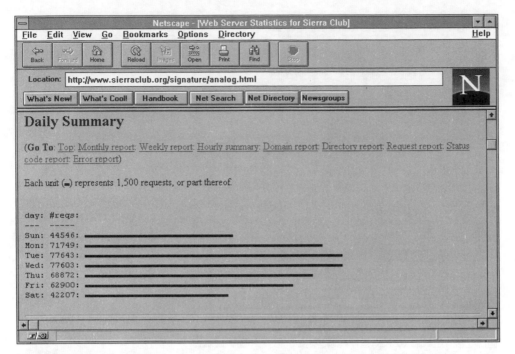

FIGURE 7.6 Weekly traffic volume consistently peaks during the middle of the week and slows during the weekend.

people hitting your site. Likewise, you'll see traffic slow on Friday and Saturday evenings and around holidays (see Figure 7.6). Don't be surprised by an almost complete halt of traffic between Christmas and New Year's.

Traffic Baseline

Incoming hits will vary day to day, but they will generally fall within a range that, you will see, remains fairly consistent over time. The standard amount of traffic your site receives while you are doing no special promotion is what I call the Traffic Baseline, which looks something like Figure 7.7.

You can take advantage of this statistical regularity by introducing new promotional activities and watching to see if they have any effect on your site's traffic (see Figure 7.8).

Over months of watching this sort of information, you will see trends emerge. For example, on one site that I monitor closely, I have discovered that most of the visitors who reach the site from directories and search engines (the baseline visitors) go no further than the home page, whereas nearly all of the visitors who find the site from newsgroup postings continue on to hit most of the site's interior pages (see Figure 7.9).

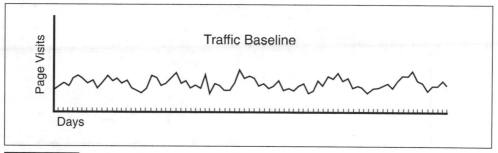

FIGURE 7.7 During short-term periods of no promotion, your site traffic will remain remarkably consistent over time.

With data and hindsight, this seems to make intuitive sense—people who are searching on Infoseek for one thing and happen across another thing (my site) are likely to check out the site briefly to see what it's about and then return to their search results page to pursue their original quest. Newsgroup readers, however, are only likely to visit an address if it appears interesting enough to make them temporarily quit reading the newsgroup or jot down the address for a later time. In both cases, they are more likely to stay longer at a site in which they are more interested or for which they have invested more effort to visit.

I stress that such explanations form only after you have looked at real data—in other words, they are not so intuitive after all. The results could be exactly reversed for another site with a different type of message and product. Only after you have gathered this sort of data, over time, will you be able to make good guesses as to the relative merits of your different promotional efforts.

Sophisticated Traffic Analysis

I know a number of people who would describe their activities as "dabbling" in Web commerce. They have constructed perhaps the first phase of a much larger Web site plan, waiting to see if there is sufficient market interest to warrant further investment. This conservative approach is appropriate for many people and businesses. The main drawback, however, is that these dabblers may not reach the theoretical investment threshold, the flashpoint where their time and money begin to pay off seriously. For example, I might spend a thousand dollars erecting a site just to wait and see what happens—only to see nothing happen at all. Meanwhile, if I had spent an additional $500 promoting the site, perhaps a torrent of traffic would have arrived.

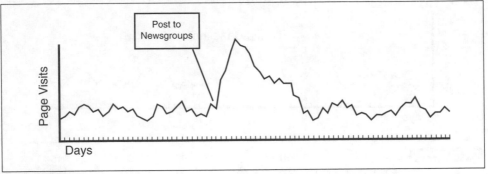

FIGURE 7.8 Introducing some unusual promotion will register as a spike on your otherwise constant traffic rate.

Other entrepreneurs or business managers know at the outset that they must do everything possible to make their projects successful. These are the people who are betting the farm—either their own personal savings, money from investors, or serious capital from their existing employers who are going online. For this group of do-or-die players, as well as the dabblers who are ready to make a serious commitment, the simple methods of gauging Web traffic mentioned earlier will not suffice. Industrial-strength traffic analysis is required.

Who Will Analyze Your Traffic?

For most Web marketers, the critical determinant of what type of serious analysis they conduct will be whether they run their own server or rent space from a Web service provider. For nearly all companies who are already running their own machines, it is a relatively small step to generate usage logs and run software that analyzes the logs and automatically generates usage reports daily, for example. Some of the log analysis software available is mentioned later in this chapter. (Also see this book's online companion (http://www.monsoon.org/book) for links to sources for this software—much of which is free.)

If you are involved with a high-budget, high-traffic site that requires customized traffic analysis and auditing, check into I/PRO (Figure 7.10) (http://www.ipro.com), one of the leaders in the field. I/PRO has forged a strategic alliance with Nielsen Media Research to integrate server log data with large-scale marketing demographics databases for customers such as AT&T WorldNet, CompuServe, Netscape, Microsoft, Starwave, USA TODAY, and Yahoo!. As an example, I/PRO's products not only distinguish visitors coming from .com domains, but also look up each .com's full

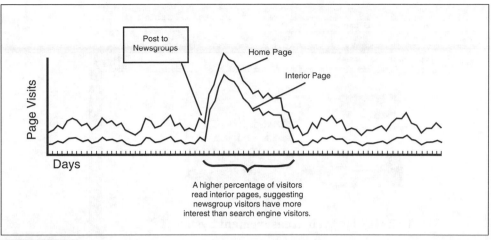

FIGURE 7.9 During a traffic spike, user habits may deviate from their normal patterns. Here, a higher percentage of visitors are exploring the site thoroughly.

company name, let you know how large it is, where it is geographically located, and in what industries it participates.

If you are not operating your own server, then you have the following options:

1. Have your Web service provider analyze your logs.

2. Use a third-party service to track and analyze your site traffic.

3. Obtain usage logs from your service provider and analyze them yourself.

Web Service Provider

If your provider is able to generate three critical usage logs, or their equivalent (all are described in detail later in this chapter)—access_log, referer_log (yes, "referer" should be spelled "referrer"), and agent_log— and it is able to analyze the logs according to your needs, then you might not need to look any further. Unfortunately, many providers don't even generate the proper logs, let alone provide analysis of the logs. Of course, it may provide such services but charge an arm and a leg, suggesting that

> **TIP:** If your provider cannot offer these logs, then either switch providers or use a third-party traffic counter service.

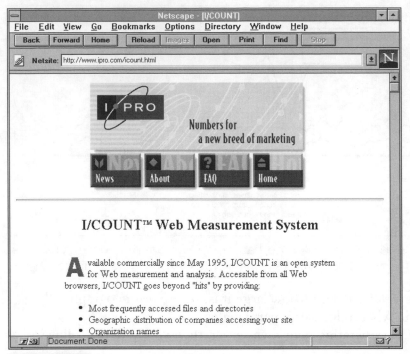

FIGURE 7.10 PRO (http://www.ipro.com) provides some of the most sophisticated site traffic analysis available.

you might look elsewhere. Needless to say, if your provider does not generate usage logs, then you will be unable to analyze them yourself.

Third-Party Traffic Counter Services

These companies operate by having you embed a piece of HTML (such as a server request for a small logo graphic) into your Web pages; the inserted HTML code accesses the counter service's server every time a visitor accesses one of your pages. Then its server analyzes the characteristics of each visitor. Not all third party services provide analysis comparable to that which you could do by analyzing your usage logs with shareware analysis tools. However, the major benefit provided by these counter services is that they work even if your Web service provider does not make usage logs available. Furthermore, these services are fairly simple to use. You just visit one of their sites, register online, insert a small piece of HTML into your pages, and then revisit the company's site periodically to access your statistics. Best of all, the prices range from free to cheap.

Not all of the companies listed below offer exactly the same services. Some provide more sophisticated analysis, security that prevents others

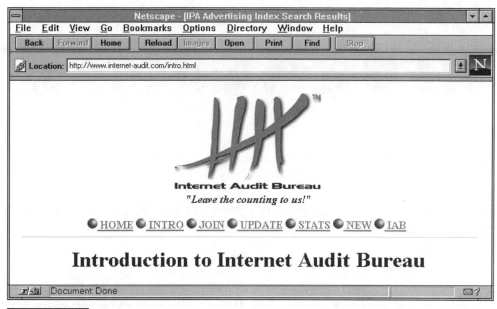

FIGURE 7.11 Internet Audit Bureau (http://www.internet-audit.com) provides a simple means of measuring your site's traffic.

from monitoring your traffic, and different bandwidths leading to their servers. If their servers gets bogged down, the delay will frustrate your visitors even if your server is working fine. These services are not the same as having an independent party certify your traffic statistics for the purposes of selling banner advertising space. See "The Future of Web Traffic Auditing?" in Chapter 10.

> **TIP:** You can receive *extremely* sophisticated—and ordinarily expensive—traffic analysis for *free* by joining one of the better banner exchange networks (see Chapter 10).

The following are some traffic-counting services you may use:

• IAB (Internet Audit Bureau) (http://www.internet-audit.com)

This service (see Figure 7.11) provides standard counter services for no charge. It also offers special services for those requiring more detailed reports of usage statistics.

• WebCounter (http://www.digits.com)

This service (see Figure 7.12) is free to sites with low traffic. It also pro-

FIGURE 7.12 Sites that use WebCounter's services display a logo such as this one (http://www.digits.com).

vides a commercial service, meaning you pay a small fee based on heavier traffic. It plans to offer advanced traffic analysis, but none is available as of this writing.

- Wishing's WebAudit (http://www.wishing.com)

This service provides a free 20-day trial and then costs $36 for six months. This seems to be an excellent value as this fee includes "plug-in CGI" that allows you to add features almost instantly to your site including e-mail snoop (see Chapter 13), an automated guest book, and reasonably sophisticated Web traffic reports (see Figure 7.13).

Confusing Traffic Terminology

Clicks—Each instance that a user clicks on a link, such as an advertising banner.

Click Ratio—The percentage of views that result in a click. For example, a successful ad might entice 2 percent of the people who see it to actually click on it for more information.

Impressions—The number of times a page or image is downloaded. Users are assumed to see each downloaded element.

Hits—A frequently misused term, real hits or "raw hits" refers to the total number of elements downloaded by the server to the client. For example, one HTML page with five graphics would count as six hits. For this reason, "hits" is technically a measure of server workload and is meaningless to marketers. However, in casual use or among laypersons, "hits" often refers to the number of visits a page receives.

Visitors—This word is usually applied to the person responsible for one visit (see "visits," below). If the same person visits a site twice in one day, he or she would be considered two visitors unless the term "unique visitors" is applied. Unique visitors are much harder to determine (see "Cookies" later in this chapter). Not all companies use these words the same way. Clarifying your terms

---

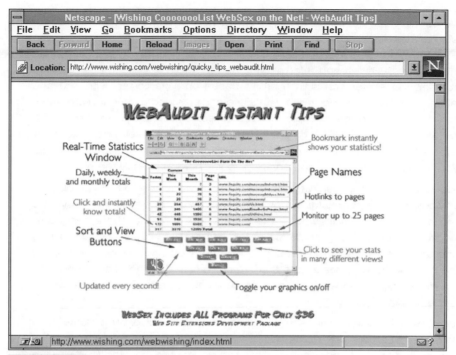

FIGURE 7.13 For a low fee, sites may use Wishing's plug-in CGI for measuring site traffic (http://www.wishing.com).

before you begin work is a good practice.

Visits—This refers to the number of times any person visits a page or a site. Because one person could generate more than one visit, a visit—or "session"—is usually defined as all of the requests from one unique user address that are not interrupted by 20 minutes (for example) of inactivity. As such, if a user were to browse through a site, go to lunch, and then resume browsing at the same site, traffic analysis software would categorize this activity as two visits if lunch took 20 minutes or longer.

Cookies

Many Web surfers usiing dial-up accounts through internet providers are randomly issued an IP address each time they log on. Therefore, when a user visits a Web site, the site's server used to have no way of knowing anything about the visitor, such as whether he or she was a first-time visitor or repeat customer. Now, however, some server software can issue an identifying tag called a "cookie" (named for no particular reason) which some browsers (such as Netscape's Navigator) store even after the online session is over and the computer is turned off. The next time this person visits that same site, the server will see the cookie and recognize this person from his or her last visit.

The cookie does not automatically allow the server to know the identity of the user (name, e-mail address, and so on). It is merely a code the server can use to match the browser with a previous session, or across multiple hits during one session. By storing information, about multiple visits made by one browser, the server can build a profile based on a particular visitor's usage habits. If the user has registered with a site and provided personal information, then the site could, for example, call this person by name the next time he or she were to visit. (Cookies only apply to the user's browser, not a particular person. If several family members are using the same computer to surf the Web, cookies would not help servers pinpoint individual family members.)

Cookie technology is useful for marketers who would like to build profiles on individuals to see, for example, how often they return to a site, what they read while there, and what they purchase. Analysis might demonstrate, for example, that frequent visitors come for certain information while infrequent visitors tend to come for a different reason. Such data would greatly help marketers and Web designers create sites that are more suited to their viewing population—including the possibility of creating customized pages in real-time, whenever a familiar visitor arrives.

Some people view cookie technology as an invasion of privacy. Software is available that allows users to be notified whenever a site they're visiting is using cookies and to block the capability if they so desire (see Chapter 10). If you are a Navigator user, you can see which companies have stamped your browser with an identifying mark by looking at the file on your system, **cookies.txt.**

Analyzing Your Own Usage Logs

T I P : For the most power and flexibility, analyze your own logs. If your Web service provider does not make the three key logs (or their equivalent) available, consider switching providers.

Usage logs are another area where you—the motivated, smart, aggressive marketer—can outflank your online rivals; at least, the small ones. Your larger rivals are often housing their own servers and, if so, are probably analyzing their logs pretty thoroughly. However, the smaller Web enterprises using Web service providers are notoriously ignorant of the availability and power of these logs.

A major Web provider reported that, out of all customers renting space on its top-of-the-line Commerce Server, only 12 percent even request to see access logs.

There are several reasons why. First, as mentioned earlier, many service providers don't generate these logs in the first place. Or they may supply some, but not all. This may be because their server software doesn't provide log capabilities; or it may be because their clients have never asked for it. And clients don't seem to ask about such things, perhaps because they are intimidated by anything related to Unix. Fortunately, these logs are just plain text files that can be opened in Microsoft Word and read, one line at a time, an approach that, believe it or not, can be useful.

The Access Log

This log, named access_log, provides the most fundamental data related to your site traffic. It is literally a time-stamped record of every file sent to every browser that has visited your site. Different servers' logs vary, but if you were to open the log in a text editor, it would look a lot like this:

```
www-f7.proxy.aol.com - -   [04/Aug/1996:00:55:49 -0700] "GET /selftalk/howto/product/product.htm HTTP/1.0" 200 1048

www-f7.proxy.aol.com - -   [04/Aug/1996:00:55:54 -0700] "GET /selftalk/graphics/3albs.gif HTTP/1.0" 200 4230

www-f7.proxy.aol.com - -   [04/Aug/1996:00:55:54 -0700] "GET /selftalk/graphics/bullet.gif HTTP/1.0" 200 3047

www-f7.proxy.aol.com - -   [04/Aug/1996:00:55:59 -0700] "GET /selftalk/graphics/phonbutn.gif HTTP/1.0" 200 5071

www-f7.proxy.aol.com - -   [04/Aug/1996:00:56:04 -0700] "GET /selftalk/graphics/ordrbutn.gif HTTP/1.0" 200 3443

www-f7.proxy.aol.com - -   [04/Aug/1996:00:56:05 -0700] "GET /selftalk/graphics/day4pers.gif HTTP/1.0" 200 4332

ip119.phx.primenet.com - - [04/Aug/1996:01:54:37 -0700] "GET /sound_advice HTTP/1.0" 302 -

ip119.phx.primenet.com - - [04/Aug/1996:01:54:38 -0700] "GET /sound_advice/ HTTP/1.0" 200 2499

ip119.phx.primenet.com - - [04/Aug/1996:01:54:41 -0700] "GET /sound_advice/sa-mast.gif HTTP/1.0" 200 6301
```

1. Who made the request? (From what domain/IP address?) For example, in the first file listed, the request was made by www-f7.proxy.aol.com.

2. When was the request made? (Date and time?) Likewise, in the first file, the request was made on [04/Aug/1996:00:55:49-0700].

3. What file was requested? Again, the following was requested in the first file: "GET/selftalk/howtoproduct/product/htmHTTP/1.0".

4. What resulted? (Codes indicating file sent, redirected, error, etc.; bytes transmitted.) The answer here is 200 1048.

We know from examining this section of the log, for example, that somebody from AOL was visiting the "Self-Talk" site around one o'clock in the morning. Then all activity stopped for about an hour, and then somebody from Primenet in Phoenix visited the "Sound Advice" page.

If you wanted to conduct a laborious but highly detailed study of the access log, you could go through the log line by line, deleting all requests for non-HTML files (graphics, etc.), which would leave you with a record of just the pages which people visited, in the order that they visited them. Because multiple visitors might have overlapping sessions, you could separate each session by the user's unique IP address (it stays the same during each user's session). This would allow you to trace the path of each individual who visits your site, including how long each person stayed on each page (except the last page—there is no way to know how long they viewed the last page because their next browser request would show up on somebody else's log).

> **TIP:** Spot analysis of access logs can be useful and interesting, but analysis software is required to aggregate thousands of lines into meaningful statistics.

Many software packages are available that analyze access logs. Some work in conjunction with the server itself and automatically generate convenient Web pages that you can access to see real-time usage statistics and graphs. Other stand-alone programs work with text-format log files output by the server, which may be more appropriate for marketers who lease server space from a Web service provider.

> **TIP:** To see an extensive list of analysis tools ranging from free and simple to pricey and exotic, visit: http://www.uu.se/Software/Analyzers.

The more expensive analysis products usually provide added benefits such as "IP address resolution," which is the process of cross-referencing the user's IP address to an existing database to learn more about the person or company visiting your site.

Intersé market focus 2 (http://www.interse.com)

The Cadillac of site traffic and usage analysis tools is Intersé market focus 2, which uses inference-based algorithms to reconstruct the usage patterns of individual visitors, allowing Web marketers to observe, for example, how long visitors are staying at different pages, which navigational routes are most commonly taken through your site, and what organizations are visiting you most frequently. Intersé market focus 2 is already used by more than a thousand Web businesses, making it the market leader. As it is the only analysis software currently approved by the Audit Bureau of Verification Services, Inc., market focus 2 is possibly situated to become a standard for independent audits for advertisers and publishers (see Chapter 10). In this example from Intersé's site (Figure 7.14), the most popular route (8.28 percent of all visitors) was for visitors to enter at the "Home" page, go to the "Evaluate" page, and then proceed to the "Our Products" page.

The most frequently used path through your site suggests a lot about the reason why users are visiting your site. If enough people come for the same purpose (such as to download software), then it will help them if you make this destination accessible via a direct link from the home page. The more steps you put between them and their goal, the more likely it is that they won't reach that goal.

Intersé market focus 2 utilizes cookie information (see the sidebar entitled "Cookies" in this chapter) and can analyze up to hundreds of gigabytes of log records daily. Free evaluation downloads are available at its site. The program comes in three varieties, depending on your needs:

- Standard edition (for log files <75 MB): $695

- Developer's edition (Microsoft Access compatible): $3,495

- Developer's edition (Microsoft SQL Server): $6,995

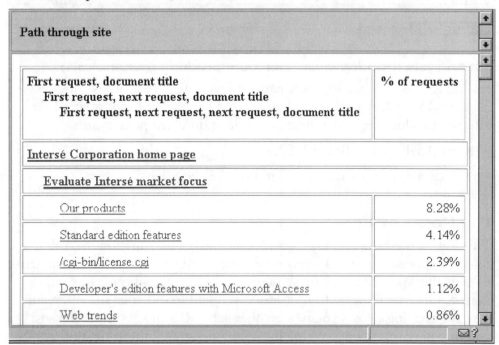

Path through site

First request, document title
    First request, next request, document title
        First request, next request, next request, document title
	% of requests

Intersé Corporation home page	
Evaluate Intersé market focus	
Our products	8.28%
Standard edition features	4.14%
/cgi-bin/license.cgi	2.39%
Developer's edition features with Microsoft Access	1.12%
Web trends	0.86%

FIGURE 7.14   Intersé market focus 2 can sift through thousands of logged visitors' records and determine the most common paths taken through the site.

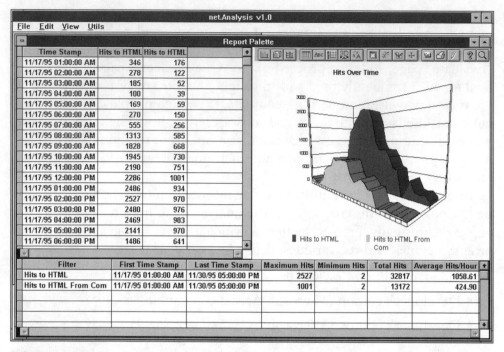

net.Analysis v1.0

File Edit View Utils

Report Palette

Time Stamp	Hits to HTML	Hits to HTML
11/17/95 01:00:00 AM	346	176
11/17/95 02:00:00 AM	278	122
11/17/95 03:00:00 AM	185	52
11/17/95 04:00:00 AM	100	39
11/17/95 05:00:00 AM	169	59
11/17/95 06:00:00 AM	270	150
11/17/95 07:00:00 AM	555	256
11/17/95 08:00:00 AM	1313	585
11/17/95 09:00:00 AM	1828	668
11/17/95 10:00:00 AM	1945	730
11/17/95 11:00:00 AM	2190	751
11/17/95 12:00:00 PM	2286	1001
11/17/95 01:00:00 PM	2486	934
11/17/95 02:00:00 PM	2527	970
11/17/95 03:00:00 PM	2480	976
11/17/95 04:00:00 PM	2469	983
11/17/95 05:00:00 PM	2141	970
11/17/95 06:00:00 PM	1486	641

Hits Over Time

■ Hits to HTML   ■ Hits to HTML From Com

Filter	First Time Stamp	Last Time Stamp	Maximum Hits	Minimum Hits	Total Hits	Average Hits/Hour
Hits to HTML	11/17/95 01:00:00 AM	11/30/95 05:00:00 PM	2527	2	32817	1058.61
Hits to HTML From Com	11/17/95 01:00:00 AM	11/30/95 05:00:00 PM	1001	2	13172	424.90

FIGURE 7.15 A display from net.Analysis (http://www.netgen.com/products/net.Analysis) site traffic analyis software.

net.Analysis (http://www.netgen.com/products/net.Analysis)

net.Analysis is another sophisticated yet less expensive analysis package (see Figure 7.15). A free evaluation kit can be downloaded from its site. Like Intersé's product, net.Analysis is available at different price points:

- net.Analysis 1.0 (Solaris): $2,995
- net.Analysis Desktop 1.1 (Windows NT/95): $495

The Referrer Log

This log, named referer_log, provides invaluable information to Web marketers. Suppose you had a hundred different links coming to your site from all over the Web. Some of these might be links you had traded or purchased. Others might be from visitors who had found your site interesting. The referrer log allows you to see the exact URLs of sites that refer visitors to you. Every time a visitor hits your site by linking from another site, that site is included as a line in your referrer log. A small CGI script can strip out internal references coming from your own server and arrange the

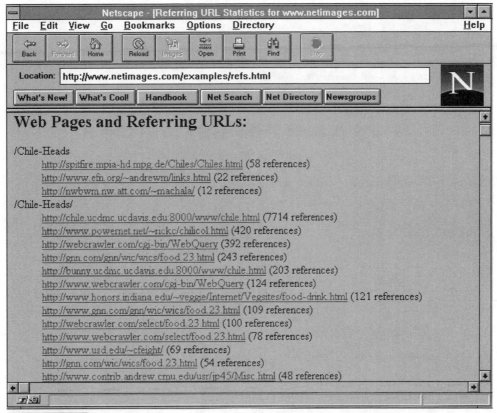

FIGURE 7.16 Sample output from Refstats 1.1, a CGI script that sorts through your referer_log and generates a report as an HTML page. According to this output, the /Chile-Heads/ page received 7,714 references from a page at the ucdavis.edu server.

referring site addresses in their order of volume—with those delivering the most visitors located at the top of the list (see Figure 7.16).

Refstats 1.1, written by Benjamin "Snowhare" Franz, is a free CGI script that is short enough that you can cut and paste it directly off its creator's page at http://www.netimages.com/~snowhare/utilities/refstats.html.

TIP: Studying your referrer log not only will tell you which of your paid links are working well, but it also will tell you about sites that you've never heard of who are sending you a lot of business. Visit these pages to see how you are represented. Consider contacting the page's owner to establish a relationship. This step will increase your chances of remaining included when this person modifies his or her site.

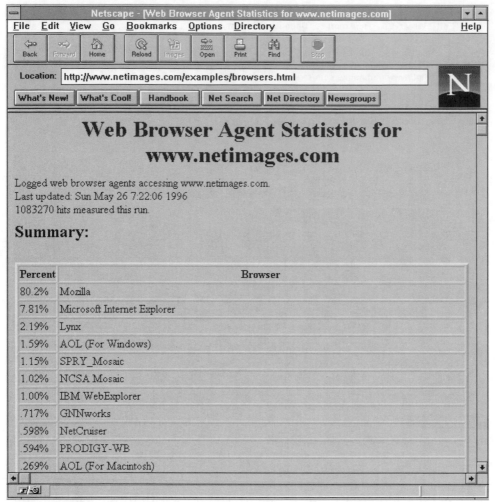

FIGURE 7.17 Sample output from BrowserCounter 1.1.1, a CGI script that sorts through your agent_log and generates a report as an HTML page.

If you use a Web service provider that generates the appropriate logs, it should be able to install this script for a reasonable fee.

The Agent Log

Of somewhat less importance is the agent_log, which lets you know what type of browser people are using when they access your site. For example, if you had enough people visiting you with text-only browsers, then you might want to create a text-only version of your site. At the time of this writing, however, over 80 percent of Web users were using Netscape's

Navigator (called "Mozilla" on agent logs). Many other browsers (including Microsoft's Internet Explorer) are capable of mimicking Mozilla so that Web servers will not withhold features intended for Netscape users.

According to the output shown in Figure 7.17, 80.2 percent of netimages.com's visitors were using Netscape or a Netscape-emulating browser. BrowserCounter 1.1.1, also written by Benjamin "Snowhare" Franz, is another free CGI script that is short enough that you can cut and paste it directly off its creator's page at http://www.netimages.com/~snowhare/ utilities/browsercounter.html. If you use a Web service provider that generates the appropriate logs, it should be able to install this script for a reasonable fee.

A Word about Visitor Registration

Even with the most sophisticated logs, analysis, and demographics databases, it is doubtful that you will know everything that you would like to know about your site visitors. However, regardless of how well-meaning your intentions are, not all visitors want you to know everything about them.

> **TIP:** Think long and hard if you are tempted to require visitors to register before they may gain access to your site.

True, this is an easier and cheaper method of obtaining better information than hiring an expensive marketing research firm. However, by requiring registration, you *will* lose a percentage of visitors who would rather not identify themselves.

> **TIP:** If you *must* have certain information, consider requiring an *anonymous* registration. Ask users their profession, for example, but don't ask them for their name or e-mail address.

This approach will alleviate some people's concerns about privacy. However, other visitors will refuse to register simply because they don't want to bother filling out the form. They consider it an expensive use of time when they don't even know what is inside the site. Imagine how difficult it would be to surf the Web if you had to register with every site you encounter. A more accurate word than "surfing" would be "drowning." The following recommendations will help:

- Make part of your site freely accessible, so that visitors can get a feel for what you've got to offer. If you've got something really worth checking out, then it might be acceptable to require people to "take a survey" before entering that page. If you don't ask them any information that could be used to contact or identify them, many people won't mind.

- Don't ask for a phone number or postal address, except in the self-evident cases when such information is absolutely required, such as for shipping a package via FedEx.

- Don't ask for any information that you won't use. Every field that you add to a survey or registration form decreases the number of people who fill it out.

- Obtain a ZIP code. This is one of the biggest bang-for-the-buck pieces of information you can ever get from a visitor. Existing marketing databases can tell you a lot with it, such as the likely size of family, household income, consumer preferences, and more. If you intend to do this sort of analysis, then ZIP code might be one question worth asking—even at the risk of alienating a few visitors. But many users don't mind giving out their ZIP code as long as they don't have to give out their address or phone number.

Requiring user registration comes at a price. If the only thing you gain for this price is a little bit of demographic information, then consider other ways of acquiring this information, such as using the techniques in Chapter 15 for soliciting feedback. In general, reserve user registration for cases where your business model depends on it, such as an online service that is available only to users who have registered and paid a fee. Under this sort of condition, users will understand why you need to have them register.

If you do require registration, you should explain *why* you require it and assure your visitors that the information will remain confidential. Say it twice and make it impossible to miss.

SUBMITTING YOUR SITE
TO EVERY DIRECTORY
IN THE WORLD

I f you've browsed on the Web for any length of time, you understand the processes by which people navigate. Either they browse aimlessly or they look for something in particular. And, of course, we're all familiar with surf sessions when we have started out looking for something in particular, only to be sidetracked by something unexpected that looked interesting. If you know the name of the company you seek, let's say it's Feral Dog, Inc., then you first might try entering the following URLs directly into your navigator: http://feraldog.com or http://www.feraldog.com.

Directories and Search Engines

If you find that neither of these URLs leads anywhere, then, if you are like most people, you will hit the Internet Search menu/option on the Netscape browser, leading you to a page that features links to several services designed to help you find your objective.

As of this writing, Netscape's Net Search page features these search engines and directories:

- Infoseek
- Excite
- Yahoo!

- Alta Vista

- Magellan

- Point

- Hotbot

- IBM Infomarket

- Lycos

- Open Text Index

- C|Net's Shareware.com

- The Electric Library

- Accufind

- Hot Websites

Although some surfers never use more than one or two of these, all of them receive some of the heaviest traffic on the Web, with daily visits in the hundreds of thousands. Much of this traffic is due to their being on Netscape's Net Search page. However, each of them promotes their sites in other ways as well. (Some even advertise on other members of the same list.)

If, rather than trying to find a site, you want somebody to be able to find your site, then it is in your best interest to be listed on as many of these services as you can. Actually, "best interest" does not make the point strong enough.

> Registering your site with directories and search engines is probably the single best use of your time in terms of creating *long-term* traffic to your site.

Some of these directories will list the URL for any Web site that you might submit to their service. Others accept nominations but then review the sites and list only their favorites or put inclusion up to a vote. Still other search engines will eventually find your site whether you submit information or not.

Many commercial Web operators register their new sites with only directories and search engines mentioned above. In fact, many don't even bother submitting an address to all of these. Instead, they just hit those five with the most prominence on the Net Search page: Yahoo!, Infoseek Guide, Lycos, Magellan, and Excite. You may recall that I stated in an earlier chapter that some Web marketers pass up opportunities to act smart. This is one of them.

Submitting to a site doesn't always guarantee that it will list you, and there are some lists to which registering would make no sense. For example, registering your site on a list of shareware sites would be pointless if you don't offer shareware. Such exceptions are pretty intuitive. What is not obvious to all Web marketers, however, is that there are literally *hundreds* of other places where sites can be registered for free.

Registering Tips: Selecting Perfect Keywords

It is not enough to register with *many* directories; you must register *intelligently*. Spend the time to do it right. One of the most important steps is to choose those keywords which will lead the most people to your site.

- Choose your keywords carefully. What words would a person use if he or she were looking for your site intentionally? What different words might he or she use if she *ought* to be looking for you, but had never heard of you before? Just because a list of keywords makes perfect sense to you doesn't mean that they're the same words somebody else would use. What words might someone use if he were not as knowledgeable about your products? Include layman's terms if you're not targeting experts.

- Ask your customers. Ask people who are unfamiliar with the details of your business how they would find you. Better yet, put someone down at the computer and tell him to "find me" and watch what he does without saying anything.

- Include your key competitor's name as a keyword. When people search for them, they'll often find you also.

If you create a personal home page with pictures of your family and a poem about sunflowers, then you might want to register this page in a few of the most popular places, just to draw an occasional visitor for the heck of it. And if you feel that filling out the online forms for each and every one of these services is a bit tedious, then there is an excellent service to automate the process called Submit-It.

Submit-It

Submit-It (http://www.submit-it.com) is a one-stop shop for registering your site with 15 of the more well-known search engines and directories. By filling out just one form, Submit-It automatically generates submissions to all 15 of its listed recipients. The best part is that it's free.

Submit-It is your best friend, but I don't suggest you use it. The reason I call it your best friend is that many of your competitors will use it, thinking they're saving valuable time. But they could do better. First, Submit-It uses one form for all 15 services, but the services themselves do not have identical forms. Some of the services allow you to enter longer descriptions of your sites or more keywords than do others. That means you miss the chance to add a few more descriptive words to some directories if you use Submit-It. But more importantly, Submit-It stops at sending your address to only 15 services, out of literally hundreds available, lulling many people into the false feeling that they have adequately registered their sites.

> Caution: I've heard of one Internet service provider suckering a new client by offering to "submit their URL with all of the major search engines" for $50. Newbies might think they were getting a great deal for something that sounds as if it might be complex. In actuality, the "service" provider was just using Submit-It and charging the client $50 for about 10 minutes of work.

Submit-It is great for sites that don't owe their existence to drawing as many hits as possible, such as personal pages. For commercial sites, I recommend a more thorough approach.

Major Directories

WebPromote is a firm that specializes in registering new commercial sites with *hundreds* of different directories. WebPromote refers to "directories" as databases that are built entirely on the information that it receives by way of people submitting URLs, keywords, and descriptions directly to the service. In other words, if you don't tell them you exist, they will never list you. The following are the most popular directories on the Internet at this time.* From the time you submit your information to the time you appear

---

* My gratitude goes out to Ken Wruk at WebPromote (http://www.webpromote.com) who provided the lists in this chapter.

on the listing will vary from service to service—ranging from very quickly to up to six weeks for Yahoo!.

- Yahoo!
- Magellan—Internet Directory
- Starting Point
- The Huge List
- TradeWave Galaxy
- Webula!
- 555-1212.com
- BizWiz
- Global On-Line Directory
- ClickIt!
- ComFind Internet Business Directory
- Comprehensive List of Sites
- LinkStar Internet Directory
- NetMall
- Pointcom.com

Search Engines

WebPromote goes on to differentiate between directories and "search engines." Although the two appear to be the same when you're using either of the services to look up something, they differ in how they acquire their information. Search engines are run by automated programs (called "spiders," "robots," or "crawlers") that go from site to site, recording and following all of the links that they find along the way. Whereas directories will only list the URLs for pages that you submit (such as your home page), search engines will eventually find and list *every* page of your site, provided it has been able to reach your site by following another link.

Because there is no way to know when a search engine would find you on its own (in fact, it would never find you if there are no links to your

> Be aware: People who find your site on a *search engine* may not enter your site through the home page. They may arrive deep in some obscure corner of your site. Make your site's navigational elements helpful so people can quickly get to your home page, regardless of their original point of entry to your site (see Chapter 16).

site), you should submit your site directly via online forms that the services provide at their sites. Keep in mind, if you submit just your home page, the spiders will have a starting point that will allow them to search your entire site. Usually, search engines use descriptions found in the body of the pages themselves, rather than allowing you to designate a special description and keywords. For this reason, it can be useful to embed your site with "spider food," or invisible words in your HTML that will show up on the search engine's radar but will not be seen by human visitors to your site.

Spider Food

In his book, *Marketing on the World Wide Web,* Jim Sterne refers to "spider food," or invisible words placed within your Web page specifically to control how the search engine ("spiders") categorizes your page once they find it.

In order to let search engines categorize your site properly, provide them with necessary words, at the very beginning of your home page's HTML. These words will not be seen on the screen by users. The tags are repeated many times to make these words rank as the most important words seen by the search engine, which, in turn, categorizes your site appropriately.

The example below is a piece of code that you might add to the HTML of a site promoting a mobile deejay service.

```
<head>
<title>Mobile DeeJay</title>
<title>party dance music live disk jockey dj</title>
<title>party dance music live disk jockey dj</title>
<title>party dance music live disk jockey dj</title>
<title>party dance music live disk jockey dj</title>
<title>party dance music live disk jockey dj</title>
<title>party dance music live disk jockey dj</title>
<title>party dance music live disk jockey dj</title>
<title>Mobile DeeJay</title>

<!-- keywords: party dance music live disk jockey dj
party dance music live disk jockey dj
party dance music live disk jockey dj
party dance music live disk jockey dj
party dance music live disk jockey dj
party dance music live disk jockey dj -->
```

```
<META name="description" content="We've got all music for all ages! Call us to guarantee your party is
the place to be!">

<META name="keywords" content="party, dance, music, live, disk, jockey, dj"> </head>
```

To make spider food for your site, you need only copy the code above and substitute an appropriate title, seven keywords and description.

My thanks go to Ryan Scott and Rosalind Resnick of NetCreations, the creators of PostMaster Direct (a site registration service found at http://www netcreations.com/postdirect), for their assistance with compiling this information.

Some of the most popular search engines are:

- Lycos
- Excite
- WebCrawler
- ALIWEB
- Alta Vista
- Apollo
- Four11.com
- Harvest
- Infoseek
- Inktomi
- Internet Sleuth
- Open Text Web Index
- The URL Tree
- WebGuide
- WWW Worm

Yellow Pages

Yellow pages are just like directories except that they are organized like actual yellow pages: alphabetically by a field, such as site title or contact name, as opposed to the category listings employed by directories. It is important to list your site with yellow pages because many users first look to the familiar format of an online yellow pages if they want to look up a company whose name they already know.

Some of the most important Web yellow pages are the following:

- BBS Yellow Pages Directory
- Brian's Revised Internet Yellow Pages
- Cybernet Yellow Pages
- IMS's Virtual Yellow Pages Additions Form
- Innovator's Network Yellow Pages
- ISP Internet Yellow Pages
- New Rider's WWW Yellow Pages
- NRP Official WWW Yellow Pages
- NYNEX Interactive Yellow Pages
- TheYellowPages.com
- Trytel's Yellow Pages
- Virtual Yellow Pages
- World Wide Yellow Pages
- World Yellow Pages Network
- WWW Business Yellow Pages
- WWW Yellow Pages
- Yellow Pages Online
- YELLOWPAGES.COM
- YelloWWWeb Yellow Pages

What's New/What's Cool Sites

Short of having your site as the subject of a cover story on *The Wall Street Journal*, getting mentioned on one of the leading Cool Site lists is probably the single biggest way to draw traffic to your site. Unfortunately, they don't list just anybody. What's New sites accept submissions for sites that they review. The best of the best are then placed prominently for all to see. It is

FIGURE 8.1 Visitors to sites displaying this logo instantly know that they have arrived at a high-quality site, and they are more likely to explore beyond the home page.

considered quite an honor to develop or own a site that has been selected by some of the more discriminating What's New sites, such as those listed below.

Web sites fortunate enough to be selected by Point Web Reviews (now owned by Lycos, Inc. and found at http://www.pointcom.com) earn the privilege of displaying this well-known icon on their site (Figure 8.1).

There was a time when What's Cool lists would mention a site that was simple and goofy. As professional Web designers and large corporations have begun to battle for Web attention, creating a Cool-worthy site on a low budget has become increasingly difficult. It still happens, particularly in the case of extremely clever or unique ideas (such as "Find the Spam," described in Chapter 2). However, don't expect to be accepted unless your site is truly outstanding in some way, such as possessing content that is unsurpassed in its usefulness, stellar design, value-added services, ingenuity, and so on. Hey, come to think of it, these are all of the things that would tend to make a site popular even if What's Cool lists didn't exist. Building a site with the intent of getting listed on a what's Cool list is tantamount to building a site with the intent of having it do well—both are worthy goals. Some popular What's Cool sites are the following:

- Cool Site of the Day
- Coolynx of the Day
- NCSA's What's New
- Net Happenings
- Netcenter's What's New Page
- What's Happening on World Wide Web
- What's New Too!

FIGURE 8.2   PC Magazine's Best 100 Sites logo.

> **TIP:**   If you have nominated yourself for a "best of" site, such as *PC Magazine's* Best 100 Web Sites (Figure 8.2) (yes, you are allowed to nominate yourself), encourage visitors to your site to second the nomination. Also provide a link to the voting booth. Notice the line at the top of this music archive site that asks visitors to second their nomination (Figure 8.3).

Minor Directories

There is an ever-growing number of directories popping up everywhere. While new directories don't receive the same degree of foot traffic as Yahoo! and the other giants, they do receive surprisingly high amounts of traffic. Some people apparently enjoy looking through smaller directories and being able to choose from a less staggering array of listings. As such, your site is likely to stand out more in a minor directory than it will in one of the larger directories. The following are examples of minor directories:

- BizWeb
- CANLink Directories
- Clearing House
- Delta Design's Business Directory
- Global Business Directory Online
- GTE Superpages: WWW Directory
- Hyper Text Addition Form
- Internet Mall
- Jump Station
- MEGA WWW LIST
- Mouse Tracks

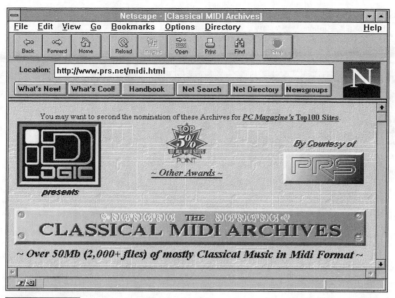

FIGURE 8.3 Notice the small line at the top of this page, encouraging visitors to second a nomination for an award.

- Nerd World
- Net Navigator
- New City Global Mall
- Open Market's Commercial Sites Index
- Pointers to Pointers
- REX
- Tarheel Mall
- The Global Directory
- The New Age Directory
- The Too Cool Awards

General Submission Sites

And then there are sites that will provide links to you but don't exactly fit into any other category described here. That doesn't mean that they aren't popular, however. As with the minor directories, your site may be much

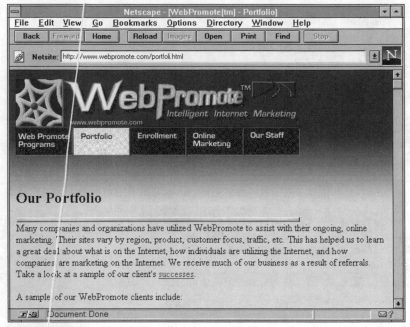

FIGURE 8.4 WebPromote (http://www.webpromote.com) will submit your site to 100 locations for $175 or to 200 sites for $235.

more prominent on many of the following than it would on the largest directories:

- Explorer
- Hotlist Dynamo!
- Jason's Add-A-Link Page
- Jumper hotlist
- Ladyhawk's Free For All Link Page
- MegaMall
- Metroscope
- The MegaMall Free For All Link Page
- AOL's Cool Site of the Day
- Bellnet
- Biz Online
- City.Net

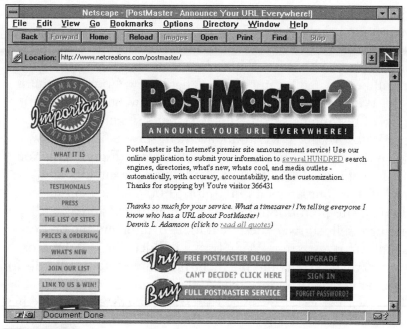

FIGURE 8.5 NetCreation's PostMaster URL announcement service will register your site at 350 locations for $500.

- Eurolink
- Funky Site of the Day
- Lexiconn
- Macmillan Web Site of the Week
- Recyclinx
- Silicon Graphic's Cool Sites of the Month
- Spider's Pick of the Day
- Tribal Voice Additions
- URouLette
- WebMall Classifieds
- World Wide Marketeers

As a way to save yourself a lot of time, some firms provide site registration services ranging from standard packages to fully targeted, custom promotional campaigns. WebPromote, which provided the lists above, submits your site to the top 100 high-quality directories, search engines, yellow pages, What's New sites, and other general submission sites (including the lists of sites mentioned above) for $175 or to the top 200 sites for $235. It also provides a detailed report listing all of the sites (and their URL addresses) to which your site was submitted. Of course, it can't guarantee that your site will be selected by any of the What's New/Cool sites, but it can't hurt to try. WebPromote's own site (http://www.webpromote.com) sports a long list of testimonials from satisfied clients (Figure 8.4).

NetCreation's PostMaster URL announcement service (http://www .netcreations.com/postmaster) provides a similar service (Figure 8.5). You can have your site submitted to 350 of the leading search engines and directories for $500 or four sites submitted for $1,000. Check out its site for some additional site promotion services not mentioned here.

At least one firm sells software designed to help automate the process for do-it-yourself site registration. Web Traffic Builder (for Windows or Macintosh) (http://www.serve.com/ephemera/promote/index.html) sells for $99.00, provides active links to more than 500 sites, and guarantees that you will get listed with at least 200 sites. *Web Traffic Builder* may be the best bet for do-it-yourselfers who want to be thorough while operating on a limited budget. My experience with this software confirms that you can reasonably expect to do in three hours what would have taken 18–24 hours to do manually. This degree of automation becomes even more important if you have multiple pages or sites to register.

Special-Interest Sites

By doing a little footwork and using some of the directories and search engines listed above, you will also be able to find special lists pertaining more specifically to your area of business or industry. There are hundreds of industry-specific directories which means there is something appropriate for every business. Here are just a few examples:

- Airlines of the Web
- All the Hotels on the Web
- Directory of Computer and Communication Companies
- The List of Internet Service Providers
- Manufacturer's Information Network
- Publishers' Catalogs Home Page

If you're unsure whether you qualify to be included in a special-interest directory, don't be shy about submitting your site.

> **T I P :** When in doubt, submit your site. Remember, they want you there.

Directories draw more traffic when they offer links to more businesses, so they usually want as many as they can get. The worst thing that can happen is that your submission will be declined. This would be very unlikely unless you are completely off-topic.

Directories can also be specific in other ways such as focusing on a hobby or geographic region. For example, if you sell fishing lures, there are directories that list only sites related to fishing. Or if you are located in Phoenix, for example, you can find all sorts of directories that will list any Phoenix area business for free.

For a local search, the Web sites of your city's Chamber of Commerce and local Internet service providers are always an excellent place to begin searching for lists of local links. Failing that, try a search on one of the major search engines, such as using the following search on Infoseek:

```
+Phoenix +business +directory
```

This particular search yielded 642 results, some of which are exactly the kind of site you would be seeking—assuming your business is in Phoenix, that is.

Once you find a good special-interest directory, you've got your work cut out for you. That is, many directories list each other. For example, one scuba diving directory might point you in the direction of a dozen more. And those might lead you even further to different ones. It is also possible that you will find more and more specialized directories the deeper you look, such as a list of underwater photography equipment manufacturers, or a list of dive trip operators that specialize in trying to find sharks.

At some point, there becomes a gray area between what is a small directory and what is just another site that also provides certain types of links. The more standardized directories allow you to submit your URL with an online form. Links, on the other hand, are not automated and usually require that you send e-mail to a real person. Soliciting links from other sites is the subject of the next chapter.

In addition to its standard services of registering you with the major directories and search engines, WebPromote, as well as many other Web

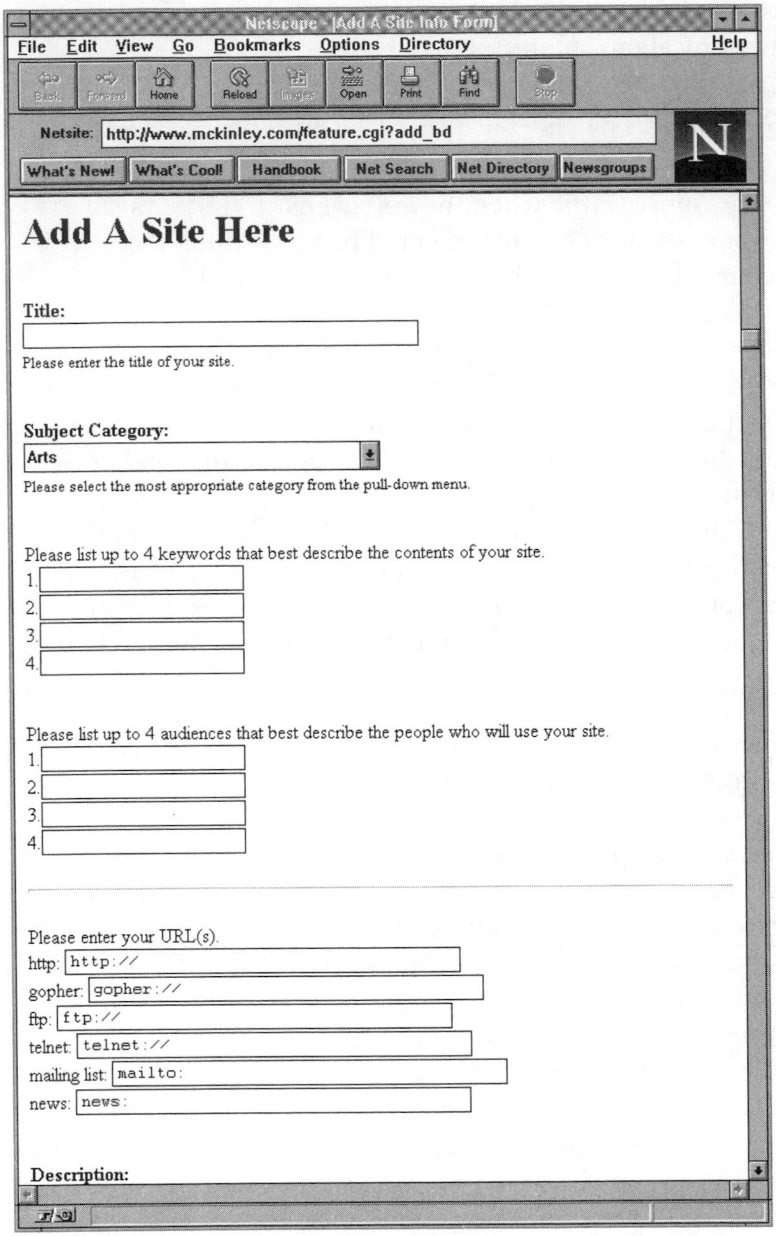

FIGURE 8.6 Most directories' online submission forms ask the same information. This is a portion of the registration form of the Magellan Internet Directory (http://www.mckinley.com/feature.cgi?add_bd).

marketing consultants, will be able to quote a price for designing and implementing a custom promotion program, targeted specifically toward your audience. This would include ferreting out the niche-related sites that cater to your subject matter and trying to get your site mentioned on those sites.

Hiring a firm to implement a customized promotional plan for your site can be an excellent way to save yourself much time. If you decide to go this route, my advice is to shop around until you find a firm that seems to ask you all the right questions. They cannot promote your site very well if they do not grasp exactly what it is that you do. Also be aware that, by hiring a firm to register and solicit links for your site, you will miss a huge (if time-consuming) opportunity to learn about your competitors and the online community clustered around your industry. A "best of both worlds" strategy might be to hire PostMaster Direct, WebPromote, or another firm to handle your registration with the 100–350 largest directories while you handle your own narrow and targeted effort with the more specialized directories.

The Registration Process

Although largely similar, different directories' registration forms allow you to enter slightly different information. After you have entered your site with several directories, you will have seen the range of differences of these online submission forms (see Figure 8.6).

> **T I P :** Print out the first couple of submission forms once you've filled them out. Refer back to them each time you submit your site to another directory to save time and avoid re-inventing the wheel.

The first two or three registration forms that you submit will take the most time because you will have to think hard and make careful decisions about which keywords to select and how to best describe your site in a few words.

Multiple Entries

Submit multiple pages of your site whenever appropriate. However, there is no need to submit multiple pages to search engines because they will automatically find these pages by following links embedded in your site. You need only submit the home page, assuming all other pages could ultimately be found from that starting point. Submitting multiple pages of your site allows you to zero in on niches within your market. For example, if your site is generally about scuba diving, then you might want to enter several of your site's separate pages such as:

- The Dive Shack (homepage)
- Underwater Photography Tips
- Caribbean Live-Aboard Scuba Trips
- Used Scuba Equipment Classifieds

By listing multiple pages, you will take up more "shelf-space" on the directories, increasing your chances of being seen. Additionally, anybody searching for one of these topics in particular will be more likely to reach your site if you separately register each page. You will be able to (and you should) include separate keywords and descriptions for each page. While this might seem like a tedious process (unless you hire a firm to do it for you), it is probably the best investment you will make for drawing traffic to your site in the long run.

ALL ROADS LEAD TO YOU: THE ART OF GETTING LINKS TO YOUR SITE

The previous chapter described how to register your site systematically with other sites that are in the business of providing links. In other words, that's about all they do. And because that's all they do, most of them will provide links to anybody who asks (excluding special interest directories and What's Cool lists). Naturally, you'll want to have your site mentioned on every relevant directory. But if your promotion stops there, you are missing an important concept:

> Surveys show that only 65 percent of Web users use directories to locate Web sites, while 95 percent use links provided by different sites.

Make Others Work for You

After you have created your Web site and listed it with about a hundred directories and search engines, you will want to begin soliciting links from other sites. Remember, if nobody finds you, how good your site is won't matter. Securing a link from a high-traffic site with a related topic is one of best ways to draw traffic to your site. Securing dozens of these links can help transform a good site into a thriving business.

Developing a Links Strategy

Ideally, every site on the Web would provide a link to you, allowing you to sit back and enjoy tremendous traffic without having to promote yourself actively. Some sites are tremendously successful at this—there are more than 16,000 links pointing Web surfers to Netscape's software download page. And the Dilbert Zone, based on the popular comic strip, has more than 1,900 links pointing to it. Of course, numbers like these are the exception. All sites that have many links to them have one thing in common—they offer something worth telling people about.

Positive Feedback

Sure, many site administrators will provide a link to your site because your topic is related to theirs or simply because you ask. In many of these cases, the administrators are not being selective, and the link to your site will probably be lost among links to many other sites. When somebody discriminates highly and provides links to only a few sites, those links are usually pointing to that person's *favorite* sites. The Master Tip applies here.

> **TIP:** Make your site something people want to visit.

Huge traffic always starts with great site content. Your passive and active promotions build some traffic, but the numbers really start taking off once your early visitors begin telling all their friends about you. The highest form of word-of-mouth is for people to provide a link to your site, particularly if their site already draws heavy traffic. Once this happens, your site will begin to be noticed by services that rate sites' popularity. If your site makes it onto any of these "What's Cool" or "What's Hot" sites, then the mere mention will cause your site hits to skyrocket in a strong positive-feedback loop. Again, success begets success; it all begins with having a good site. A site worth visiting possesses the same characteristics that make a site worth mentioning.

Do You Want to Provide Links Away from Your Site?

If your business model already suggests that your site will provide many outbound links—such as a directory—then read this section with the thought of offering a small number of special links, such as highly prominent, front-page links to select sites.

By definition, the majority of sites do not make it onto the "What's Cool" lists, which are reserved for the most exceptional sites. If your site is good enough to be listed on these, then your content is probably so compelling that providing links to other sites would not add significantly to your site's worth—unless your site is a directory, in which case your outbound links *are* the content. If your site is not likely to become a Cool site anytime soon, then you are in the same boat as almost every other site on the Net: You are all still hungry for traffic. There is a way you can help each other.

Types of Links

Outbound Links—Links that, when selected, will lead the user away from your site, as opposed to leading him or her to another page within your site.

Gift Links—Links from one Web site to another for nothing in return. These are granted more freely by non-commercial sites than by commercial sites.

Reciprocal Links—Links between two different Web sites where the Web administrators have agreed to provide a link on the condition that the other site provides a link in exchange.

Paid Links—Another term for advertising, usually consisting of a "banner" graphic rather than just underlined text (see Chapter 10).

The Theory behind Reciprocal Links

Of course, you ask, "Why would I want to provide links, thus encouraging people to leave my site?" True, if everybody linked to you and you linked to nobody, then you would make out well. However, other sites have little incentive to do this. As with most cooperative relationships between self-interested individuals, reciprocity provides both sides with an advantage over what they would have had otherwise. Theoretically, you might send away 10 visitors who would not have purchased anything, but you might receive 10 visitors, 2 of whom buy something. Of the 10 visitors who left your site to visit the reciprocating site, 2 might end up buying something from them. By swapping links, both sites gained 2 customers.

Again, in theory, this works because no two sites are identical and customers are not identical. Your particular site and products will appeal to some more than others while another site's products will appeal to those who were not as interested in your wares.

TIP: The best reciprocal links are between non-competitive sites that deal with a similar topic.

If two sites were identical, then reciprocal links between them would be useless. If two sites were identical except that one site offered lower prices, then the link exchange would be to the disadvantage of the higher-priced firm. A firm could be hurt by trading links in a number of ways.

> Warning #1: If you provide a highly prominent link but receive an obscure link, you could lose from the exchange.
>
> Warning #2: If your site receives high traffic but the other site receives low traffic, you could lose from the exchange.

Either of these conditions could lead to a situation in which you lose a hundred visitors but receive only one. In this case, a reciprocal link isn't exactly reciprocal after all. Internet purists might argue that, if everybody provided many links indiscriminately, then relative advantages and disadvantages would cancel out, on average. I suspect they would, if everybody provided enough links. If you would rather hedge your bet, follow these guidelines (these are generalizations only and exceptions to each occur later in this chapter):

- Avoid providing links to direct competitors.

- Avoid providing links to low-traffic sites.

- Avoid making your outbound links too prominent.

"Competitor" Is a Funny Word

It is not always easy to tell who is and who is not a competitor. One phone company is often a vendor, customer, and direct competitor of another phone company, making it tricky to know how to behave around each other—friendly and cooperative, or guarded and hostile? The same ambiguity can exist on the Web. If you sell herbs on your site, will a chiropractor endorse your site or see it as a competitive treatment for certain maladies? That probably depends on the chiropractor. But even if he or she sells herbal remedies directly; will your site enhance the credibility of such products overall (thus leading him or her to provide a link to you) or will it threaten to steal customers?

One possible solution to this problem would be to break your site into two basic sections: commercial and noncommercial (there are other advantages to using this model; see Chapters 12 and 14). Your quasi-competitors might feel more comfortable providing a link to the informational portion of your site if it is not obviously a competing commercial site. While it is the other site's responsibility to ascertain whether it is in its best interest to provide a link to you, in the interest of full disclosure and good business practice, I recommend that businesses volunteer the potential conflict and treat the matter frankly. In your e-mail requesting a reciprocal link, you might add a paragraph such as:

> While a different section of our site does provide related products for sale, I believe that both of our businesses might benefit by providing links to one another...

Using Links to Enhance Your Image

The Web is still heavily influenced by the give-give culture under which the Internet was born. No one will mind if you create a Web site that is, in Net parlance, "blatantly" commercial. But you might encounter problems when you go to promote such a site, particularly on newsgroups (see Chapter 12 for lots about this). One of the safest ways to avoid criticism is to offer something for free to your site's visitors, such as information. A common form of such a "gift" is a list of links to sites that your visitors might find interesting. If you provide some other sort of substantive, free information, you might not feel such a pressing need to provide outbound links.

> **TIP:** Providing even two or three links to other sites instantly conveys your willingness to participate in the give-give culture. Providing zero links may, to some, suggest unwillingness to cooperate.

I know of no studies measuring user attitudes where this distinction is concerned, but I know of cases that suggest that this attitude is prevalent in some corners of the Internet community. In particular, when some users expect to find a noncommercial site and instead find a commercial site, they might complain, for instance, that "you didn't even provide links to other sites."

This alone might be a compelling reason to provide some outbound links. But, if used properly, there is an even better reason.

> **TIP:** Hand-pick a few choice links to alter how visitors perceive your business.

This tip is possibly the best all-around reason to provide links to other sites. Remember, surveys show that concerns over the credibility of online businesses are the leading factor inhibiting people from purchasing products online. Any little thing that you can do to enhance your image will help. Not only will well-chosen links enhance your site's perceived credibility, they will provide a way to present or strengthen a bond with your customers.

For example, suppose you manufacture sandals out of old tire treads (a favorite example from Chapter 1 if you're skipping around). What should people immediately think about your products and company? Perhaps a faction of the cyberpunk subculture has come to associate your cool treaded footwear with post-apocalyptic mutants scurrying through the smoldering rubble of once-great cities searching for pieces of automobiles from which to fashion clothing.

If you intend to appeal to this niche, then you can enhance the flavor of your site and the ethos of your whole online existence by providing a couple of well-chosen links, perhaps to a site with photos from the *Wired Magazine* article depicting UV-protection fashion ensembles from the ozone-is-history, future earth.

More likely, however, you're making these unique sandals for earth-friendly customers who would prefer to avoid an apocalyptic future altogether. A couple of prominently displayed links to sites such as the Sierra Club or the Appalachian Trail Conservation Fund (to connote walking), will embed an association in the minds of your visitors. It's almost as good as if you had actually made a contribution to these causes—although, in effect, you have made a small contribution by providing a one-way link to their sites, which raise money. Of course, you could always contribute financially as well and mention that fact on your site, further bolstering your image.

If your business or industry has any negative publicity associated with it, you might consider using such *image links* to help communicate your awareness and sensitivity toward these problems. A beer brewer may wish to provide a prominent link to a non-profit organization that promotes responsible driving. Exxon may wish to provide a link to Duffey's Otter Shampoo—for oily hair (okay, maybe not).

Beware of using this technique when it may raise concerns where none had existed previously. Multi-Level Marketing organizations (MLMs) are those which not only sell products, but also recruit independent sales people who can, in turn recruit salespeople beneath themselves, and so on. There are plenty of respectable MLMs around but, by it's own admission, the industry has an image problem due largely to some people's "get rich quick" claims and percieved similarly to illegal pyramid schemes. I've seen more than one MLM site attempt to enhance its image by providing a link to the Internet Better Business Bureau (IBBB). It actually made me wonder about them because the link introduces a doubt where perhaps none existed. It's a little like running up to a police officer shouting, "I didn't do it!" His next question would be, "Do what?"

Because most industries and product categories don't have this sort of negativity to overcome, the selection of image links is more a luxury than a requirement. However, because the links you provide will make a difference as to how visitors perceive your organization, I recommend that Web marketing managers discriminate highly when granting links to other sites, particularly those that are displayed so prominently that they may seem to carry your endorsement.

> **TIP:** If you provide many links to sites that you have not visited or don't necessarily endorse, consider including a subtle disclaimer to that effect.

Image Links Could Make a Great Site Even Better

Hot Hot Hot (http://www.hothothot.com), the site that sells 450 varieties of hot sauce, provides only one outbound link at the time of this writing. It is buried fairly deep within the site and is not at all easy to find. This is an excellent Web site, but in my opinion, a small number (perhaps four or five) of high-quality, well-chosen links would improve the site. For example, it might provide a link to an anthropologist's account of a Day of the Dead festival in Oaxaca, Mexico, complete with traditional recipes using homemade varieties of sauces that Hot Hot Hot sells. Similar, noncompeting pages could be found for each region of the world that Hot Hot Hot represents with its sauces.

Even though this might be the sort of content the company would like to add to its site eventually, providing links offers a shorter-term way of expanding a site's content at no cost.

Link Prominence

When you promise to provide a link to another site, remember that you have promised only to provide a link, and no more. You have not promised to funnel half of your traffic away to another site. You have not even promised to endorse, recommend, or describe any other site. Paying advertisers will want to know how many people see their ad, but those who swap reciprocal links will generally be content to have any link somewhere on your site. Depending on how you use links to support your business model, you have some options for displaying links that will make your visitors more or less likely to click on the links.

Placement of Link

Naturally, links are more prominent when they are placed on the most popular pages of your site. Additionally, placing a link closer to the top of any given page will increase the link's prominence.

Type of Link

A link to another site can be a small word, a large word, a sentence, a small graphic, or a large graphic. It can also be one of the items in an image map (a large graphic containing multiple, embedded links that are activated when the user clicks on that area of the graphic). Visitors are more likely to click on larger links.

Editorial Prominence

With any outbound link on your site, you can affect its likelihood of being selected by adding information about it. You might give a brief description of the site to which the link points, which could either increase or decrease its hits but would tell what to expect there. You could also endorse or give a warning about the site (e.g., "...has the best selection I've seen but seems a little pricey").

I generally recommend placing Image Links (the ones that strategically convey something about your business) where people are likely to see them early or perhaps somewhere within the site that is closest to the products whose images they will support.

As for other links (particularly if there are more than eight) that don't provide significant image enhancement but are worth having to obtain a reciprocal link, I would place them on a separate "Links" page (or whatever you choose to call it) nested wherever it most appropriately fits within the overall site structure—sometimes directly accessible from the home page, sometimes not.

> **TIP:** If you have more than 12 links group them by category to make reading them more convenient for your visitors.

Do not put links to other sites directly on your home page unless there is a specific reason to do so, such as one of these reasons:

FIGURE 9.1 These icons inform users that your page works with or requires Netscape Navigator 3.0, Microsoft Internet Explorer, Macromedia Shockwave, and RealAudio's streamed audio plug-in. The icons also link to sites where users can download these browser products.

- When your site is primarily a directory service and links are the main value provided, then having them appear on the home page might make sense.

- If you receive payment for providing advertising space (which is frequently a link to your advertiser), you can charge more if the link is prominent. Home page links are usually the most prominent. (See Chapter 10, "Buying and Selling Advertising Online.")

- If your users require special software (plug-ins, for example) to access your site's features, then you should let them know this at the beginning and include a link to the site where they can obtain that software (see Figure 9.1).

> **TIP:** A small icon with no text often suffices for well-known browser products if your visitors tend to be techno-savvy. Otherwise, just to be safe, accompany the icon with text telling them what plug-in they need or simply say "Best viewed with."

Getting Links to Your Site

Take comfort in knowing that many Web site operators never make any real effort to solicit links to their site.

> **TIP:** The mere *attempt* to secure links to your site systematically gives you an advantage over the majority of your competitors because they tend to overlook this opportunity.

A few of your competitors spend a lot of time at it, however. Of those who have spent a good deal of time soliciting links, few have been systematic or thorough about their approach. Some have described the process as an adjunct to their ordinary Web surfing—whenever they go out looking around, they keep a link solicitation letter handy on the Windows clipboard, ready to make a request to any site that they serendipitously come across. Although this approach is certainly better than nothing at all (particularly if one surfs a lot), it still gives you an opportunity to be smarter than the average competitor.

If you follow these three rules, your campaign to secure links *will* succeed in dramatically increasing traffic to your site.

Soliciting Links:

1. Plan methodically.

2. Act exhaustively.

3. Never stop.

Securing Links: A Step-by-Step Plan

Before you start randomly soliciting Webmasters to provide links to your site, take some time to plan your approach. The guidelines provided here will get you started.

Step 1. Identify Other Sites

Using a few of the major directories and search engines, conduct a search on your own topic, beginning with a very narrow and specific search. To make this a thorough search, use different combinations of all the keywords you used when you registered your own site with these directories. The idea here is to find sites that are related in any strong way to yours. If your site sells a lot of different kinds of products to many diverse markets, then mentally split your site into narrow subbusinesses and repeat this entire process for each niche.

Example: If you sell exotic home furnishings and you carry a hard-to-find line of museum-replica, medieval tapestries, then conduct a search on "medieval tapestry." You can imagine the variety of results such a search would create, ranging from college students' art history projects, to real museums, to period re-enactment acting troupes—and probably some of your suppliers, customers, and competitors. As you check out each result of the search, make note of those to which you would most like to provide a link.

Provide a Link to

These sites are the ones you strategically select as being able to *enhance* your site's image by associating you with their quality, uniqueness, style, or another aspect that your target market will find appealing. If you offer few links (fewer than 10, for example), the links will be to these select sites. If you offer many links, you should make these specially selected links the most prominent, perhaps with a personal recommendation or a "What's Cool" insignia of your own. By granting such prominence to a site, you might be able to encourage that site to give you a more prominent link, but don't count on it if it receives a hundred times more traffic than you each day. If it is hot and you're not, you might consider yourself lucky to receive any link at all.

Receive a Link from

Take note of those sites you would most like to provide a link to your site. The main variable here is *traffic*—the more of it they have, the better. Sometimes they will post their traffic statistics; other times you must infer from the quality of their site whether traffic is likely to be high. Strategic fit is not so important unless they are able to, by the nature of their site, funnel your site with a high percentage of buying customers. Essentially, you want links from just about anyplace you can get them. To the extent that you spend extra time drafting custom letters soliciting these links, look for sites that provide either high-quantity or high-quality traffic to your site.

Surfing Backwards

WebCrawler (http://www.webcrawler.com/WebCrawler/Links.html) provides a very extraordinary service for finding and evaluating other sites. You can enter a known site address and WebCrawler will tell you roughly how many other sites have linked to that page. If the number is high, then you know you have a very popular site, even if traffic statistics are not available. Even better, WebCrawler provides the names to all the referring sites—which means you can "surf backwards" and obtain new sites that are related to your topic.

Once your site has been promoted, you will find it interesting to use this unique service on your own site to see who has been providing links to your site. Keep in mind, WebCrawler won't know of every site on the Web that has linked to you—only the ones that are in its huge database.

Step 2. Prioritize the Other Sites

Once you have come up with a list of sites that are related in some way to the content of your site, place at the top of your list those that most closely match the focus of your site. Of these highly relevant sites, give precedence to the noncommercial sites.

> **T I P :** Noncommercial sites are much more likely to give you a link without asking for a reciprocal link.

(Disregard this tip if your site offers many links as a service to your visitors.) Frequently, the noncommercial sites will let you know that they would like you to provide a link to them, if you're willing, but without going so far as to require a reciprocal link. (You may wish to provide one anyway—see "Using Links to Enhance Your Image," earlier in this chapter).

> **T I P :** Also give priority to sites that already provide links away from themselves. They are more likely to grant you a link because it is easier for them to add your address to their "links" page than if they do not already have such a page.

Step 3. Identify the Proper Contact at the Sites

Send somebody at that site an e-mail. Don't bother the president of a 100-employee firm to ask about providing a link. Take extra care to look for the e-mail address of the person who would actually insert the link—in many small companies this person will have the authority to decide which links to provide. This person is usually whoever created or takes care of the site, and he or she will often have a mailto link either to his or her name or to some title such as: *"Webmaster"*, *"Web Goddess"*, or *"HTML Guy."*

Often, particularly with sites owned by larger companies, there is no e-mail link that goes to the obviously correct person. In that case, send your request to any e-mail address that asks for feedback (particularly site feedback, as opposed to product feedback, etc.). These links will usually look something like:

- "Let us know what you think of this site"

- "We appreciate your input"

- "Feedback" (Sometimes this will be an online form rather than a link to an e-mail address—that's okay if there is no e-mail address. If there is a form and a separate e-mail address, don't use the form to request a link.)

Occasionally, you will get lucky and find a site that actually offers to provide links. This may be as informal as a line saying "e-mail us if you'd like us to check out your site," or as formalized as providing a form for automated submission. (Although any site with automated link submission will probably have so many links that it may to look more like a directory—the distinction is not important.)

Step 4. Ask for the Link

If your site provides many links to other sites send an e-mail such as:

```
Hi Bob,

I've been exploring your art history site and you've done
a good job with it--very informative. I've got a site that
showcases high-quality replicas of medieval tapestries
that people can learn about or buy. It seems like some-
thing your browsers might be interested in.

Would you be interested in swapping links? Please check
us out at http://www.whatever.com/tapestry. Also, I'm
always interested in hearing feedback about the site.

Thanks,

Joe

--

joe@whatever.com

http://www.whatever.com

Museum quality replicas for the eclectic decorator
```

If, for any reason, you would rather not provide a link to Bob's site, then you could substitute the second paragraph with:

```
Would you be interested in providing a link to our site?
Please check us out at http://www.whatever.com/tapestry.
Also, I'm always interested in hearing feedback about the
site.
```

If Bob runs a noncommercial site, he may very well write back with:

```
Joe,

Nice looking tapestries. I'd be happy to provide a link.

Bob
```

Well done, you've secured a link. And he's given no indication that he expects a reciprocal link, so it's up to you to decide if you'd like to provide one.

If Bob runs a commercial site, he may or may not be interested in providing links at all. If he doesn't mind giving you a link, and if he's smart, he will ask for you to provide a reciprocal link. People will frequently assume this is what you meant and reply with something like:

```
Joe,

Hey, great tapestries. Sure, we'd be happy to provide a
link. Please make your link to us go to:
```

```
http://www.bobspage.com.
Thanks,
Bob
```

If he or she assumes you are going to provide a reciprocal link, then you should probably just go ahead and provide it—even if you tend to not provide links to other sites. Otherwise, you'll have to write an embarrassing e-mail explaining how you want a link but don't want to give one in return—not very cool.

> **TIP:** If you say you'll provide a link, then be sure to implement it promptly, such as within 48 hours. That's just good business.

Step 5. Follow Up

When you have agreed to provide reciprocal links with another site, check back in a week to verify that it has added the promised link from its site. You will often find that the link has not been added. The other site's failure to do so is more likely due to being too busy or simply forgetting rather than dishonesty. In most cases, it simply hasn't gotten around to it yet. In the case of a reciprocal link, a very polite and gentle "nudge e-mail" is appropriate. Remember, you have both agreed to provide something in exchange for something, so you have a right to see that the other side follows through, just as you have a responsibility to follow through.

> Nudge e-mail—any e-mail sent as a gentle reminder to someone who has probably forgotten to do something he or she agreed to do. The softest nudges remind people without it seeming like your intent is to remind them. Firm nudges are more direct but still polite.

> **TIP:** When reminding someone to provide a link remember to include your site's URL address in your signature.

This not only ensures that the other site's administrator remembers who you are, but it adds a measure of convenience by keeping them from having to look up prior e-mails. A gentle nudge might look like this:

```
Hi Susan,

I've included your URL to our list of links. I included
a brief description of your site that you might want to
see. Please let me know if you like it.
```

```
Bye,

Greg

--

The Self-Talk Solution

http://www.monsoon.org/selftalk
```

In fact, it is a good practice to send this type of letter as soon as you have provided your link to the other site, even if it has already provided your link. It is a good way to strengthen the relationship after the agreement has been made. Again, provide your link to the other site quickly—I've seen people include a link to my site and notify me within a day. As you might imagine, I was impressed by their diligence.

If you check the other person's site and he or she still has not provided a link to you, wait another week. Make a note in your Day Planner or calendar or you *will* forget to follow up.

TIP: Save all e-mails related to exchanging links for a record of who said what and when. This will help you make sure everyone (including you) is covering his or her commitments.

If you have heard nothing and the other person has still not provided the link, a firm nudge e-mail is appropriate. For example:

```
Hi Susan,

I was surfing on your site and I didn't see the link to
us anywhere. Did I miss it? Sorry if I just didn't see
it. If it's not added yet, do you know when it will be?

Bye,

Greg

--

The Self-Talk Solution

http://www.monsoon.org/selftalk
```

Remember, these recommendations apply to *reciprocal* links, not gift links, which require a softer approach. Wait two weeks. If the other site still has not provided a link, give it one more try—and continue being pleasant. I wouldn't, for example, threaten to drop its link if it didn't immediately comply. I would just wait a little longer, and if it still didn't provide the link, I would probably forget about it.

Step 6. Maintain Your Links

> **TIP:** Keep your outgoing links fresh.

At least once a month, hit all of the links away from your site and make sure they are still operative. Don't expect anyone to notify you if they become obsolete. Eliminating obsolete links is beneficial to visitors to your site because it saves them time. It is beneficial to you because it provides fewer ways for people to leave your site and fewer options to distract your visitors. If you find that a link is not working, don't immediately erase it— it could just be temporarily unavailable for technical reasons. Try the link a few more times over the course of a couple of days. If it never works, then it's probably safe to erase it from your site.

> **TIP:** Check up on incoming links to your site.

You will never be able to know about *all* of the links that other people have made to your site (though you can know about many of them—see the sidebar, "Surfing Backwards"). You should keep track of the ones of which you are aware, such as reciprocal links or links that you have solicited. Periodically check to see whether these other sites still provide links to your site. Make certain that they are in the case of reciprocal links. If you find that you've been dropped from a list of links, inquire why. You may discover that a complaint about your site has been sent to the person who referred you rather than directly to you. If so, you will want to know about it. Remember the Cockroach Theory—for every one you see, there are hundreds you don't see. If anybody out there has a complaint about you, you'll want to know about it so that you can address it immediately.

> **TIP:** Make sure that links to your site function properly.

Imagine you've gone through all the effort to secure a link from a wonderful site that draws thousands of hits every week from people interested in your products. Better still, assume that the link provider has checked out your site and liked it. He writes a glowing review, "Whatever you do, visit this site! We personally use their products every day." And, if that weren't enough, imagine that a good percentage of their visitors actually did click on that link to visit your site. And then imagine they saw Figure 9.2:

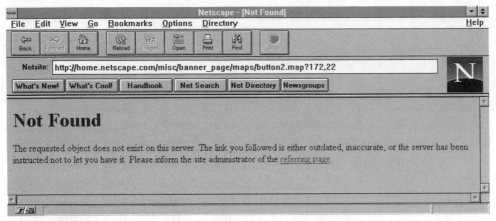

FIGURE 9.2 When a user clicks on on link to your site, you hope he or she is not greeted by this message.

How unfortunate. All of those people won't visit you after all. What went wrong? Your browser requested a page that was not available or not accessible. This could have been caused by several things:

- You gave an incorrect URL to the link provider.
- The link provider made a mistake when he or she added the link into the to his or her site.
- Your pages have moved since the other site made the link.

All of these reasons involve an error on somebody's part. Miscommunication between you and the link provider could happen easily enough, such as missing a "/" when e-mailing your site's address. This is the reason to check back later to verify that everything works properly. If you find an error, notify the link provider right away, and he or she will usually fix it quickly. Site operators don't want to provide links to nowhere.

A common practice among Web marketers who do not have access to server usage logs is to have different links point to unique entry points within the site. By counting the hits on these alternate entry pages, marketers can know from where the hits are coming, that is, how surfers are finding the site.

In the case of paid links (advertisements—covered in depth in Chapter 10), marketers often create a customized site entry point (rather than funneling all visitors to the home page) that corresponds to the advertisement that brought the visitor to the site. This practice is similar to direct mail marketers sending out mail with a phone number that includes an extension number. In many cases, regardless of which extension you enter, the same phone rings. The telemarketing operator may follow a different phone script (or access different prices, for example) depending on which ad you've seen.

If you have multiple providers of paid links, free links, reciprocal links, as well as newsgroup and traditional media promotions going on all at once, keeping track of all of the different entry points could become an administrative nightmare, particularly if content varies from one page to the next, and even more so if pages change frequently. Software developers are working to create and improve specialized site-maintenance and hit-tracking software to help Web marketers keep up with the challenge.

Despite complex Web site-management systems in place, "Not Found" errors are more likely to occur when you have large numbers of multiple entry point pages, some of which may even be updated on the fly by automated processes. If you have a bad link out there somewhere, people might notify you somehow, but don't count on it. Verifing for yourself that links to your site are working properly is the safest course.

Step 7. Never Stop Soliciting Links

Regardless of how good or not-good your site is, and regardless of how good your solicitation letters are, you must remember this tip.

> **TIP:** The number of links you get will primarily be determined by your persistence.

Unless they hire a company to handle ongoing site promotion, many site owners fail to continue the practice of soliciting links thoroughly after the site has been up and running for a while. As with registering with directories, the task appears to many to be a one-time chore, and then site managers get caught up doing other things, such as making ongoing modifications to the site. Don't let this happen to you. Even if the world stayed exactly as it is, it might take you months to contact every site that may be appropriate for providing a link to you. When you factor in that the number of Web sites is growing exponentially, you quickly see that you will never contact all of them.

Keep in mind the value of time spent performing this task. You could spend your life sending e-mail to every site administrator on the planet, but that would be a poor use of your time. Periodically reconduct steps 1 and 2 of this plan for selecting and prioritizing sites by their appropriateness, and concentrate on those at the top of the list. New sites will have popped up each time you do this. They should keep you busy without your wasting time going after low-traffic sites that relate only marginally to your subject matter.

> **TIP:** You shouldn't try to contact *all* sites who might provide a link. Just the *best*.

Extra Tips for Securing Links

Somewhere, perhaps on your home page, you might provide a very small text link that says,

`Would you like to provide a link to this site?`

Have this sentence link to a page where you provide the exact HTML address to which they should link and provide a thumbnail graphic of your logo or masthead, in several sizes. Including the file size of each.

> **TIP:** Make it easy for visitors to provide a link to your site if they wish to do so.

Giving the file size of each graphic lets savvy Web designers link to you using a larger thumbnail without fearing that the file size will slow down the transfer time of their pages. You want them to use a larger thumbnail to make your link more prominent on their pages.

> **Thumbnail Graphic**—A small version of your site masthead or logo that the link provider may drop into his or her site, providing a more attractive link to you than underlined text.

> **TIP:** Offer a freebie to people who provide you with a link.

If you have a product that does not cost much for you to produce, then consider giving away a sample to "qualifying" sites. You can make these qualifications be anything you want, such as sites with a certain amount of traffic, nonprofit organizations, or any other category. If you use this technique, place a line on your home page such as the following:

`Your organization may qualify`

`for a free Excalibur Widget.`

Have this link to a page that explains the conditions and lets visitors e-mail you if they are interested in providing a link. This works very well and will even qualify your site to be placed on some "Free Stuff" directories! In other words, you get more promotion because you give people the chance to promote you. Gotta love the Web.

BUYING AND SELLING
....
ADVERTISING ONLINE
....

Surveys have shown that most Web users do not mind if the sites they visit devote some space to advertiser sponsorship. People seem to realize that advertiser dollars are the only reason that some sites can continue to provide free services, and they would rather wait an a little longer for these advertising graphics to download than have to pay directly for access to the Web sites.

As stated earlier, estimates put total advertising revenue for 1996 at about $74 million, which equates to an average of well under $1,000 per commercial site. I also stated earlier that averages are a lousy way to look at a lot of things—this is a good example. In actuality, according to WebTrack, a whopping 75 percent of total ad revenues went to the *top 10 sites*! Not the top 10 *percent*, but the actual 10 highest ad revenue-earning *sites*.

What does this mean for most of us? It probably means, at least for anytime soon, that getting *rich* from selling online advertising is doubtful. Covering costs and even making a decent profit are possible, but it's hard to strike gold using this business model without combining it with some other revenue maker at your site. (This chapter is written from the point of view of a person who is *selling* ad space on his or her Web sites, but the flip side of the same information applies to those of you who are considering *buying* online ad space. Additionally, specific tips for buying ad space are located at the end of the chapter.)

How Are People Advertising Online?

First, recognize that there are different types of online ads.

- **Classified Ads**—Some people place free ads in classified-like sections of large, multipurpose sites in order to sell personal items such as used textbooks at the end of a school year. Sometimes sites charge a nominal fee for classified ads like these, but the term "classified" generally connotes small, one-time sales between private individuals, as opposed to the ongoing advertising activities of businesses.

- **Paid Listings**—Companies (or individuals in business for themselves) often pay a one-time or annual fee to have their name and URL (and possibly a brief description) listed on a page of links, such as one listing all dentists in a geographic region. Frequently, these advertisers will not even have their own Web sites and the listing provides only an e-mail address or phone number.

- **Banner Ads**—The most visible of all Web advertisements are the long, skinny "banner" ads, often running along the top of a site's page. The banner (usually about 600 pixels wide by 40 pixels high) may have the advertiser's logo, a catchy slogan, or a cryptic message enticing the user to click on it to find out the answer. Banner ads are also frequently accompanied by a nearby line of text, such as "This site brought to you by" or "Our sponsor." It is not uncommon for a site to have a page of paid listings (text only) with a prominent banner ad at the top of the same page for advertisers with larger budgets.

- **Genuine Sponsorships**—Technically, all advertisements are sponsorships, but I use the word "genuine" somewhat arbitrarily to distinguish between most banner ads and those sites that have a long-term relationship with one or several companies that are investing money in hopes that the site will succeed, such as joint-venture partners or charity sponsorships.

While, admittedly, the boundaries between genuine sponsorships and ordinary banner ads can be fuzzy, I make the distinction due to the different sales processes employed for each. Most sites with banner spots available have some form of rate card that anybody can ask to see. The advertisers may commit for only a month; they come and go. Genuine Sponsorships are typically sought out by the site developer, often before the site has gone public. Or the sponsor may even have come up with the site's original concept. Commitments tend to be longer term, and the sponsor may have a strategic connection with the site; perhaps the site is using donated database technology by Oracle, and Oracle would like to let the world know about it. For these reasons, sponsorships sometimes consist of donations other than money, such as hardware, software, technical support, server space, managerial talent, co-promotion, and so on.

> **TIP:** To some Web users, the term, "advertising" invites contempt and reminds them of overt commercialism on the Web. However, use of the word "sponsorship" is often viewed as acceptable or even positive. Semantics perhaps, but—if it works—use it.

Who Is Advertising Online?

With little effort you can find plenty of examples of any sort of business, of any size, advertising on the Web. According to WebTrack, as of January 1996, the companies spending the most money advertising on the Web were the ones listed in Table 10.1.

TABLE 10.1 Companies Spending the Most Advertising on the Web, January 1996

Web Advertiser	Spending
1. IBM Corp.	$460,900
2. Microsoft Corp.	248,200
3. AT&T Corp.	245,700
4. Netscape	227,400
5. Nynex Corp.	198,500
6. MCI Communications	187,300
7. clnet	177,800
8. Internet Shopping Network	172,900
9. Excite Inc.	165,900
10. Saturn Corp.	158,400

Source: WebTrack (http://www.webtrack.com)

This list demonstrates what prevails today—many Web advertisers are companies involved directly with (as opposed to just marketing via) the Internet, such as communications, computers, software, and Web-only

Case Study, *Year 2000*: The Clock Is Ticking...

What will happen to your checking account when the millennial clock rolls over on December 31, 1999? Many of the world's largest, most complex computer systems are running on legacy software that was written before anybody thought to make the date/year variables capable of holding four digits. For many companies' databases and operations, it's anybody's guess what will happen when 99 changes to 00. Fixing all of the world's software before this event occurs promises to be one of the most challenging and expensive information technology tasks in history.

"Year 2000" (http://www.year2000.com) (Figure 10.1) is a notable Web site not only because it is devoted exclusively to this highly focused and crucial issue, but also because it is almost entirely advertiser-sponsored ... *and* profitable. Year 2000 has managed beautifully to combine the sponsor volume of paid listings with the character of genuine sponsorship. A staggering 55 companies have signed on to support the cause—and promote their businesses, which can help their customers fix the impending mm/dd/yy disaster. The site's mission is kept tight and on topic throughout the site. For example, clicking on sponsor Ernst & Young's link doesn't take you to E&Y's company home page—it takes you to the E&Y Year 2000 page contained within the Year 2000 site. Only then can users leave the site and go to E&Y's home page.

This site is successful because a good execution was built upon a good business model. Think about this model's unique characteristics:

- It targets a very specific topic.
- It targets a topic with mass-media newsworthiness.
- It appeals to a specific type of highly targetable sponsor.
- It appeals to specific potential customers of the sponsors.
- It appeals to technical sponsors (the easiest kind to reach on the Web).

As for execution, the site is fully congruent with the model, capitalizing on the Doomsday flavor with a black background, "spread the word, it's not too late" paraphernalia, and a CGI-scripted "count down" clock, in its own omnipresent frame, that tells you exactly how many years, days, hours, minutes, and seconds you have until the year 2000.

businesses. The only exception on this list is automobile-maker Saturn. But as more advertisers begin to recognize the Web's marketing potential and as more mainstream (less techie) users proliferate on the Web, we will see more mainstream businesses begin to advertise heavily for diverse products, such as theme parks, beer, and shoes.

How Much Money Can You Charge For Ad Space?

The exact amount that you can reasonably charge for advertising on your Web site depends on such factors as the following:

- Quantity of traffic you receive
- Nature of your site
- Nature of your viewers
- Type of ad
- Frequency of impressions
- Duration of the advertiser's commitment.

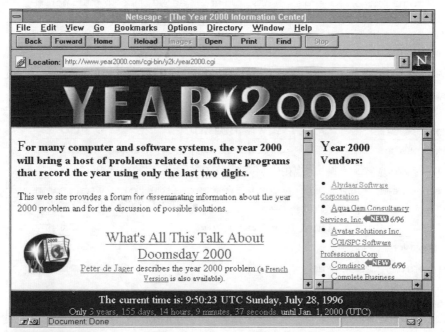

FIGURE 10.1 Year 2000 (http://www.year2000.com) is a profitable site funded almost exclusively by niche-related sponsorship.

Most heavy-traffic sites seem to zero in on a magic number of about $30 per thousand impressions (meaning 1,000 views of your ad), but consider this only as a rough starting point. If you look at several sites' rate cards (which can usually be obtained on the site directly or via automated e-mail) you quickly begin to see a complexity that makes side-by-side comparisons difficult.

Infoseek's Published Rate Card, May 1, 1996

Banner ads on Search Results pages—search banner rotations

Advertisements that rotate through Infoseek on Search Results pages, 4-week period.

Impressions	Cost Per Thousand	Cost
Up to 99,000	variable	$2,500 minimum cost
100,000–399,000	$25	$5,000 @200,000
400,000–499,000	$23	$9,200 @400,000
500,000–999,000	$20	$10,000 @500,000
1,000,000–2,999,999	$18	$18,000 @1,000,000
3,000,000 or more	$13	$39,000 @3,000,000

Note: MegaPression schedules can be run at the above rates so that impressions are concentrated in shorter time frames to add heavy message pressure and exposure for special events and launches. Infoseek can deliver 1, 2, and 3 million impressions in a given week.

Banner ads on topic pages—topic banner rotations

Ads appearing when people click on Guide Directory Topic pages, 4-week period.

Impressions	Cost Per Thousand	Cost
All Impressions	$32	$2,000 minimum

Banner ads on selected Key Word Search pages—key word banners

Advertisements that appear only with the results of a specific key word search. All costs are per word, 4-week period.

	Cost Per Thousand	Cost
Any key word	$50	$1,000 Minimum

Frequency Discounts	% Discount
3 consecutive months	2%
6 consecutive months	5%
12 consecutive months	10%

Combination Volume Discounts	
2 million impressions per month total from a combination buy	10%
3 million impressions per month total from a combination buy	5%

Comparing different sites' rates is difficult because they all have different things to offer. Infoseek, for example, gives advertisers the option of having their ads appear only when users search on specific words, in order to target the audience more narrowly. Advertisers can save money by declining this option and having their ads cycled randomly with other ads.

Owners of smaller sites often report successfully charging anywhere between $5 and $30 per 1,000 impressions (or "CPM" for "cost per thousand"). Sometimes the prices are reported as $.02 per impression, particularly on smaller sites that cannot deliver tens of thousands of impressions each month. Five to thirty dollars is quite a large range. Occasionally, a small site that is extremely well targeted at a special demographic group will fetch a much greater rate. The owner of a Web site that caters to healthcare professionals in South Africa reportedly receives a flat rate of about $636 per month, on site traffic of only 600 to 700 visits per month. That's roughly $1 per impression!

TIP: For the most frank and honest accounts of real rates and Web marketing war stories by veterans and newcomers alike, subscribe to the Online Advertising Discussion List listserv. Pose any question to this list of more than 1,000 people and you will get plenty of responses. You can subscribe using an online form at http://www.tenagra.com/online-ads.

The best way to get a feel for what your Web site can successfully charge (and for seeing what options you might provide), is to find a site that is similar in scope and scale to your own site, and then find out how that site charges for advertising. The best way to do this is to search the IPA Advertising Index at:

http://www.netcreations.com/ipa/adindex/#search

The search form provides an option (select "list names only" and leave the other fields blank) that lets you see IPA's entire database of sites that sell ad space. Click on the site name to view fundamental data (traffic statistics, ad rates, and advertising clients) for any of the sites listed on the database. (Caution: beware of statistics that have not been updated recently—check the dates.)

By selecting various sites on the IPA database, you will be able to scan the various pricing methods of hundreds of sites of all shapes and sizes, both famous and obscure. Observe the search results for an extremely high-traffic site, The Dilbert Zone, in Figure 10.2.

To view the statistics for a less well-known site, you might select Alaska Guide (http://www.alaskaguide.com), a forum for Alaskan businesses

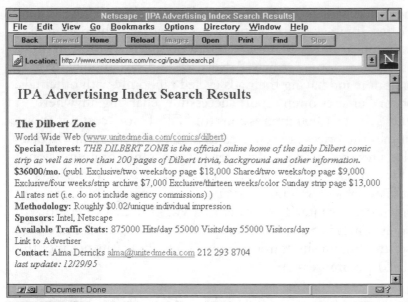

FIGURE 10.2 IPA Advertising Index displays fundamental data for the highly popular Dilbert Zone, based on the popular comic strip (http://www.unitedmedia.com/comics/dilbert).

to showcase their products and services to Alaskans and visitors from around the world.

According to the IPA Advertising Index, Alaska Guide receives about 20 visitors per day. In addition to providing all kinds of information on the state of Alaska, the site sells ad placements to businesses such as Alaskan hotels, car rental agencies, and charter fishing and hunting trips. The guide uses a paid listing advertising model, charging businesses a one-time registration fee and monthly fees that vary depending on the length of the commitment. For this fee, advertisers receive links to a page of their own, which is provided and designed by Alaska Guide.

To get an idea of the rates you might charge, you can do the following:

1. Scan the list for sites that sound similar to your own until you find a few that are comparable.

2. Visit the sites to verify that they are comparable to yours.

3. Check to see if the sites provide current rate cards in case those given on the IPA database are outdated.

4. Check to see how many advertisers appear to be currently buying ad space. If they don't have any advertisers, then you don't want to copy

their approach too closely. (However, it is possible that their rates are appropriate but they just haven't aggressively sought sponsors.)

5. If you find a noncompeting site that is comparable to your own, you may even wish to e-mail the proprietor (if it's a small business) and start a dialogue, tell him or her what you are doing, ask for advice, and so on.

Problems with Measuring Ad Effectiveness

In nearly all cases, advertisers will want to know how much traffic your site receives before they spend money advertising with you. Others will want assurances of how many times their specific ad is viewed. Still others are interested only in paying based on how many people actually click on the ad, visiting the sponsor's own page or site. To make matters even more complicated, auditing standards for verifying the accuracy of sites' traffic have not yet emerged. These problems have several causes (also see Chapter 7).

Confusing Terminology

Some people use the word "hits" to refer to how many visits a site or page receives, while others use the word in reference to "raw hit count" (a much higher number), which includes the total number of server requests made by the user's browser, with every graphic file being downloaded, for example, counting as a "hit." Raw hits are a good measure of how hard the server is working, but it is useless information to advertisers because the raw hit count can be inflated simply by adding more graphics to each page.

Tradition

Media buyers have operated for decades under the CPM (cost per thousand impressions) framework. When magazine publishers issue rate cards, they assume that every reader views every ad in the magazine and determine a price from there. Of course, in reality, not every reader sees every page of a magazine, but there is no way to measure how many actual impressions are made, so the method has remained as a best-guess. As long as all publishers use the same method, media buyers can compare rates and make their purchasing decisions. The Web enables publishers and advertisers to get a much better idea of how many times a page has been viewed, meaning each metered "impression" is a *real* impression. This makes a thousand impressions on the Web much more valuable than a thousand estimated impressions in a magazine. Comparing CPM between traditional media and the Web is therefore meaningless, comparing apples to oranges.

Traffic Measurement and Auditing

Unlike the case with magazine subscribers, Web advertisers often do not know who is viewing their ads or visiting their sites. It is also sometimes difficult to determine how long a visitor has viewed a page. Additional difficulties with measuring traffic arise when an ad that is placed on a publisher's server points to a page on the advertiser's own server and when large networks such as AOL "cache" frequently request Web pages to reduce bandwidth usage. And finally, the owners of sites that sell ad space can gauge their own traffic by studying their server logs, but advertisers need confidence that these published statistics are accurate. They need protection against inconsistent methodologies, honest errors, and fraud—any of which could lead to overstatement of site traffic. Independent, third-party audit services have emerged, attempting to fill this role, but technical aspects of the Internet that limit measurement accuracy and a lack of agreed-upon procedures mean that it may be a while before any standards become widely adopted.

The Future of Web Traffic Auditing?

Established in 1914, the Audit Bureau of Circulations (ABC) is the first and largest organization that audits the readership claims of printed publications. A division of ABC (established in January 1996) called the Audit Bureau of Verification Services (http://www.accessabvs.com) "provides independent third-party auditing of Web sites to advertising and publishing standards."

As of July 15, 1996, Interusé market focus (http://www.interse.com) was the only "Web analysis software product to meet the measurement and auditing standards set by the Audit Bureau of Verification Services." More than 1,000 customers including Microsoft, Dow Jones/Wall Street Journal, and Federal Express use Interusé market focus, making it the most frequently used Web analysis software on the market.

However, an entirely different approach is being taken to help advertisers understand Web site traffic and viewer habits. PC-Meter, a subsidiary of The NPD Group, Inc., uses a traffic-measuring methodology similar to that which Nielsen uses for determining its famous television viewership ratings. PC-Meter selects a cross-section of representative households (no businesses yet) and installs its own software in these homes that allows PC-Meter to monitor the families' exact Web usage habits. While critics argue that no sample of the population is large enough to estimate traffic at niche-oriented, low-traffic sites, the service does provide data that Web server logs cannot. By measuring usage from the home, PC-Meter provides much richer demographic information of ad viewers, is not affected by log inaccuracies caused by caching, can determine the duration of sessions and page views, and—importantly—is able to measure "interdomain usage" (recording all the different companies' sites that a viewer visits in a given session). The PC-Meter sample was to comprise 10,000 homes as of July 1996, and nine of the leading U.S. advertising agencies have already subscribed to the service.

Using Click Rates

Partly because advertisers lack confidence with unaudited traffic claims, and partly because the Web is more capable than traditional media of measuring viewer behavior, some advertisers have argued that they should pay based only on the "click rate" (or "click-through rate") for the number of viewers that actually click on their ads to visit the sponsor's own site.

Sellers of ad space argue against this method because the sellers have no control over the sort of ad the advertiser produces. The publisher would be assuming a risk that the advertiser will produce a bad ad. Meanwhile, the advertiser pays only when the ad works. This would be like placing a full-page ad in *USA Today* and saying, "I'll pay based on the number of people that call my 800 number."

Before adopting a policy regarding click rates, consider the following points:

- The exact ad used makes a difference. On the *San Jose Mercury News* Web site, certain ads have produced five times more responses than other ads with identical placement.

- If you really want the business of an advertiser who insists on paying based on a click rate, try breaking the rate into two parts, such as a flat placement fee plus an extra fee for each click. This risk/reward compromise keeps the advertiser from recklessly experimenting with untested ads while still encouraging the publisher to provide good placement for the ad on the Web site or page.

- An even more extreme concession is to accept payment on a "pay-per-lead" basis, such as $5 for every customer who clicks-through the ad and actually fills out an online questionnaire at the advertiser's site. This offer is highly risk-free for the advertiser and could make selling ad spots much easier if you're willing to take a risk in hope that the advertiser will create a compelling ad.

Selling Your Own Ad Space

The methods that you employ for selling ad space will depend on your choice of business model.

> If your site has ad space for sale or if you routinely trade links with other sites, you can register your site with WebTrack's Adspace Locator at: http://www.webtrack.com/sponsors/sponsors.html.
>
> In exchange for providing information about yourself, you will make your site available to advertisers who search the databases looking for particular types of sites on which to advertise.

Passive Sales

If your site is funded primarily by nonadvertising revenue, then selling ads will probably not be your first priority. On the other hand, every visitor to your site who does not see an ad because none is present is a wasted income opportunity. Here is a procedure that you might try:

- Following the steps outlined earlier in this chapter, find a site that is similar to yours.

- Create a rate card similar to its and make this rate information available at your site. If you happen to catch somebody who's interested in placing an ad, great—they'll e-mail you or call. If not, that's okay, too.

- At first, you will have no sponsors. Consider granting a free trial ad to somebody. If this lucky firm gets good results, it may be willing to pay you to continue placing the ad. It also may serve to "salt the tip jar"—other potential advertisers will be more interested in your site if they see that somebody else is already placing an ad.

If your site is small and new, you will not have a consistent site-traffic history on which to base your rates. You might be able to charge a low, long-term (such as six months), flat rate for running an ad. This limits the risk to the advertiser and offers the incentive that it may end up with a great bargain if and when your site traffic explodes. Many small sites do not offer even token traffic reports, much less independently audited statistics. You should attempt to provide information if you can, but you may be limited in what you can provide by your service provider's usage log capabilities. A good solution to this traffic auditing problem is to out source your media sales by participating in a banner exchange network (described later in this chapter below).

Active Sales

Rather than merely posting a rate card and waiting for interested advertisers to drop by, you may choose to go out and sell to them. If you have a small site serving a narrow market niche, then your niche will suggest which advertisers you should go after—those that are most interested in being exposed to your viewership. If your site is not directed to a particular type of audience, then you might go knocking on the doors of companies whom you know advertise on the Web.

> **TIP:**
> To search a database of major U.S. advertisers that advertise online, see WebTrack's Advertiser Index at: http://www.webtrack.com/adverts/adverts.html.

If you are a small business operating a site that is exclusively advertiser-sponsored, then you should seriously consider hiring somebody with media sales experience unless you possess this experience yourself. Because many media buyers come from the world of traditional advertising, they will be most comfortable dealing with somebody familiar with the jargon and practices of traditional media sales. Also, I sometimes feel that the world has two kinds of people, those who can sell and those who can't—with not much in between. Web media sales may be a novelty today, but it is likely to become as competitive and specialized as any other media sales, suggesting that you'll want somebody on your team who is polished and aggressive.

If your site is big and exclusively advertiser-sponsored, then relevant sales experience is almost a must. One possible exception would be if your site is extremely narrowly niched. In such a case, you or your personnel may know the ins and outs of a particular industry that requires its own experience and jargon, such as dealing with small companies in a highly specialized high-tech field. This type of background would probably be more productive than generic media sales experience. Ideally, you might find somebody with both the specialized knowledge and sales experience.

If you are a small site, with nonadvertising revenue sources, the best active approach to selling ad space might be to seek out an ideal, noncompetitive, strategic link—and exchange banner ads with one another. Even though this is actually a reciprocal link (see Chapter 9), the banner makes you look advertiser-sponsored and will help get you noticed by paying advertisers that visit your site.

Selling Mailing List Sponsorships

If you publish an e-mail mailing list (see Chapter 13) with as few as 500 subscribers, you might be able to sell advertiser sponsorship. Because this is a relatively new form of advertising, industry-wide rates are not yet established and should be negotiated on a case-by-case basis. According to Dr. Cliff Kurtzman, moderator of the Online Advertising Discussion list, "One thing to keep in mind is that a mailing list subscriber is likely to be significantly more qualified than a Web site browser. The fact that someone gives you permission to put mailings into their mailboxes tells you they are very interested in the subject matter being discussed." For this reason, some online advertisers would be willing to pay 10 times more per mailing list viewer than they would be willing to pay to place an ad on a Web site related to the same subject matter.

Dr. Kurtzman also administers a monthly electronic tennis magazine (e-zine) with 14,000 subscribers. He charges sponsors $400 per month for an insert in his newsletter, which equates to about three cents per reader. Sponsors are granted 35 lines of text, and their ads must be related to tennis. To send their own longer, special mailing to the list one time, sponsors must pay 10 cents per subscriber ($1,400).

Use a Rep Organization

Many sites owners neither possess the experience nor wish to deal with the hassle of selling ad space. If you fall into either of these groups, consider outsourcing your media sales to an independent rep organization, such as CyberSalesOne at: http://www.cybersalesone.com.

They have experience repping major print publications to advertisers, and they have expanded their operations to include Web advertising venues. You, as the publisher (the company with ad space to sell), agree to let them handle your media sales for one year. You pay a monthly consulting fee to cover operating expenses, and you pay them a 20 percent commission on net sales (up to $25,000 per month, 15 percent on net sales over $25,000 per month). You also reimburse pre-approved travel, entertainment, research costs, and expenses related to special sales presentations. Although CyberSalesOne handles sites that are likely to appeal to national advertisers with large media budgets, other firms provide similar services for smaller or industry-specific publishers.

Ad Space Consolidators

A slightly different service is provided by Burst Media: http://www
.nerdworld.com/burst. Instead of representing a few, select clients, Burst
Media consolidates many member Web sites and sells ad spaces, while paying you a commission ranging from 50 to 80 percent, depending on the
length of the exclusive agreement you sign.

Banner Exchange Networks

Banner exchange networks operate in a similar way to ad space consolidators such as Burst Media, with a few extra bonuses. In total, the benefits
provided by these exchange services possibly make them one of the best
resources available to Web marketers.

As I said earlier, 75 percent of Web advertising expenditures went to the
top 10 sites in 1996. The top 97 percent of 1995 ad dollars went to the top
150 sites. This concentration of budgets borders on the obscene when you
consider that there are over 80,000 commercial Web sites. Part of the reason for this concentration is that no advertiser—large or small—has the
resources to search the entire Web to locate every tiny Web site that caters
to a moderate flow of users with unique demographics and preferences.

This is where consolidators like Burst Media come in. By lumping
thousands of sites together, they can provide a sort of "syndication" for
advertisers. Banner exchanges take this a step further. When you register
with one of the better exchange services, you must first qualify (meaning
your site has to be of high quality). Next, you insert a piece of HTML
code onto whichever of your pages provides ad space. Every time a visitor
accesses your page, a banner ad also appears, but unlike the rest of your
page's content, this graphic does not come from your server; it comes from
the exchange's server. The person visiting your site—without knowing it—
accesses the server of the exchange service, where sophisticated, high-end
analysis software is used to record traffic and user-behavior of people visiting your site.

By classifying your site according to many criteria (including user habits
through cookie technology), the exchange service provides a way for advertisers to target, for example, a hundred thousand female doctors during the
morning hours only. Because not all Web sites will be called on at all times
for these highly targeted ad campaigns, the exchange services avoid wasting
your ad space by "exchanging" ads between Web sites. This means that if
there is no paying advertiser who needs your space, the exchange places a

banner on your site advertising another member site of the exchange. For every visitor who comes to your site and views one of these banners, you receive a credit that allows *your ad* to appear on another member's site—this is why it's called a banner exchange network.

Every time somebody visits your site, he or she sees an ad, either promoting a paying advertiser or another site that is a member of the exchange. Regardless of whose banner appears, you benefit. When another member site's banner appears on your page, then your banner appears someplace else providing, in essence, a reciprocal link—free publicity for your site. When a paying advertiser's banner appears on your page, you receive a commission in actual money.

The Benefits

The beauty of this system is that it allows you to spend all your time focusing on running a great Web site rather than worrying about selling ad space; somebody else does that for you. Professional media sales representatives go around visiting the media buyers at leading national advertisers and sell thousands of Web pages of ad space contained on their members' sites. Banner exchanges essentially allow you to outsource some or all of your media sales. You never waste unused space. If you still wish to sell your own space, that's not a problem—banner exchanges can be used only to sell your unsold spots if you choose.

In addition to providing you with free exposure and extra revenue, banner exchanges handle the traffic analysis of your site—for free—and provide you with reports detailing statistics such as the following (specifics vary from one service to another):

- Number of page visits
- Number of ads shown
- Revenue earned by each Web page
- Number of times your site's banner was displayed by another site
- Paths visitors take through your site
- Average session duration

The deal is attractive to advertisers as well. Advertisers receive detailed reports showing what sort of people saw their ads, how many people saw their ads, and how often people clicked on the ads.

Advertisers can target audiences based on many demographic factors. IMGIS AdForce*, for example, states that it can customize a direct-marketing program based on any combination of the following variables:

- Geographic location (city, state, zip, address)
- Gender
- Age
- Product affinity (Web site independent)
- Established product preference
- Marital status
- Income
- Country
- Occupation
- Home ownership
- Persons in household
- Adults in household
- Number of automobiles
- Body size of newest car
- Web site category
- Browser type
- Operating system
- Internet/online service provider
- Day and hour of ad placement
- Advertisement frequency
- Sequence of ads

---

*IMGIS states that it can target individuals based on these attributes using a proprietary database that does not depend on "user registration, cookie technology, or IP address inferences." That's quite a trick.

Choosing a Banner Exchange

Shop around before you select an exchange service since they are not identical. They differ in ways such as these:

- Some require fees for affiliates to join, some don't.
- Some are more selective than others about who can become a member.
- The commission structures they offer to their affiliated Web sites are not the same.
- Their advertising rate cards are not the same.
- Their respective abilities to attract paying advertisers may vary.

Consider shopping these services as though you were a paying advertiser rather than an affiliated site. You will probably make more money as a member of the service that is most successful selling to advertisers.

> **TIP:** Look for server reliability and high bandwidth (such as a T3 line) in a banner exchange. Visitors to your site will be accessing the exchange's site as well, meaning the opportunities for page-delivery delay or failure are twice what they used to be.

There are several exchanges currently operating, and more are likely to emerge as advertisers and publishers become aware of the tremendous benefits they provide. Don't assume that the following list of exchanges is exhaustive.

- Double Click—http://www.doubleclick.net
- IMGIS Network—http://www.imgis.com
- WWIN (World Wide Internet Network)—http://www.wwinet.com
- IBN (Internet Banner Network)—http://www.banner-net.com

Buying Online Advertising

While buying ads on the big sites like Yahoo! and ESPNET SportsZone are out of the budget for most small companies, plenty of smaller sites offer more reasonable prices. Their cost-per-thousand views may be about

> **What About the Internet Link Exchange?**
>
> The Internet Link Exchange (or ILE, http://www.linkexchange.com) operates much like the banner exchange networks described above, but it is more appropriate for private individuals' pages than for commercial sites. ILE's concept of centralizing the sharing of links remains a good one. However, other services will have more appeal to commercial site owners for several reasons.
>
> 1. Anybody can join the ILE, meaning that your site could easily end up displaying badly produced banners to pages with names like "Jesse's Cockroach Recipes."
>
> 2. Exchanged banners are not matched to connect sites with similar topics or viewerships.
>
> 3. While the ILE funds the service by selling banner spots to advertisers, the affiliated sites that display these ads do not earn a commission. Thus, the ILE provides free exposure, but no revenue.
>
> 4. Because your banner will be placed randomly on (most likely) unrelated sites, and because ILE reserves a large portion of banner placements to promote itself, some users report that they have received very low traffic from the service (such as receiving only 20 ILE-generated hits while displaying somebody else's ugly banner 2,000 times).

the same as the big sites, but you'll have the option of buying far fewer impressions, making your bill smaller. Before you spend money to advertise your site, do the following:

- Make sure your site is working perfectly. Solicit feedback and work out the bugs using your free visitors before you start paying for visitors.

- Spend time identifying the most ideal site—one for which every visitor should have some reason to want to visit your site. Remember to focus on your niche.

- Before you pay money for an ad, explore the less risky options like trading links.

- Negotiate, negotiate, negotiate.

Once you decide where to place your ad, make your first purchase commitment small. Talk the salesperson down from the stated "minimum" by insisting on running a trial before committing to spend more.

Create an Ad That Works

Most banner ads will be required in a particular format for each Web site. A relatively standard format is a .gif file under a size of 10K (although 7K is better for speedy downloads), with the dimensions 468 pixels wide by 60 pixels high.

The banner ad's mission is not to make a sale; it is to generate a click. Banners must make potential customers *want* to click. Merely showing your company's name is a terrible underuse of the medium in most cases. Tempt visitors. Tease them. Promise them something they want. If you use your banner to make them curious, then try to make them *desperately* curious.

Always test different banners on real Web sites. You might be surprised by which one works the best. And remember, your real goal is sales, not just clicks. Measure which banners lead to the highest sales, as opposed to the most clicks.

Animated banners (such as spinning logos and transition effects) might make your ad get noticed, but look for more clever ways to tie the animation to your company or product so that the animation reinforces viewers' memory of what your site is about. Examples: an animated "WebCrawler" logo could have a tiny spider crawling around on a web, or a thundercloud logo for "Monsoon Media" could have subtle lightning flashes deep inside the cloud.

Depending on the nature of your product, banner ads might be more effectively used to promote a feature of your site, rather than directly promoting your company or product. You might place ads describing one of the interesting aspects that your site provides free of charge. Use the banner to get visiters to the freebie, then use the freebie to get them to your commercial message. Just make sure you hold their attention.

CHAPTER 11

THE MOST OVERLOOKED OPPORTUNITY TO PROMOTE YOUR SITE

Many Web marketers are short on time, money, experience, or all three. They all have a list of things they must do, such as creating their sites, registering with search engines, and so on. There are so many free and relatively simple ways to promote their sites online that they completely neglect to use traditional methods of marketing communications to get the word out, including these:

- Inclusion of their URL in printed company information
- Direct mail
- Magazine, trade publication, and newspaper advertising
- Broadcast advertising
- Promotional events
- Free media publicity

Myopic Web Marketers: The Bias Against Traditional Methods

Clearly, not every medium is appropriate for every business. And there may be one or two media ideally suited for any given business. However, there may also be additional routes for increasing exposure that would be worth whatever time and money it took to utilize them.

> **TIP:** One of the best ways to outsmart your competition is to use the conventional weapons of marketing that they have forgotten.

On the Web, marketers rely on search engines, directories, and word of mouth to route traffic to their sites automatically while they concentrate heavily on using e-mail and newsgroups to promote their sites actively. Pursuing these methods alone can take a lot of time and can generate a lot of traffic. But it's not enough. A site that is appealing to users in your niche who are reading newsgroups will also be appealing to those users if they are reading a magazine. In general, your site will either be inherently interesting to people in your target market, or it won't. If it is (and it needs to be in order to be successful), then it is going to sound interesting to the right audience no matter where they hear about it.

Businesses that have been in existence for a while who are adding a Web site as a new marketing tool are the most likely to use traditional media for promoting their sites. They already use these media, and adding their URL to their message requires little effort. However, some fail to get this extra bonus out of their advertising budgets.

> **Missed Opportunities**
>
> The June 1996 issue of *Worth* magazine—technology-oriented enough to feature Bill Gates on the cover—demonstrated how slow many companies are to promote their Web sites, if, in fact, they even *have* a Web site. Fewer than half of the ads in the issue featured URLS despite encouraging readers to contact the advertiser using some other means. Some advertisers, such as Fidelity Investments and T. Rowe Price, included their URLS in one ad but left them out of other ads *in the same issue* of the magazine.

If existing companies sometimes miss opportunities to build their Web traffic, then new, Web-only companies are notoriously blind to the opportunities provided by traditional media. What causes this tunnel vision on the Web as the only way to promote one's business?

Limited Time

There are only so many hours in a day. A small business operating a commercial Web site has got a lot of opportunities to chase and not enough time to chase them all. In fact, a person could spend all of his or her time doing nothing but soliciting links from other sites. If you suggest to a busy Web marketer that he might also send out press releases to print newspaper editors, he would very likely respond with something like, "Great idea. I'll do it just as soon as I've done registering with a hundred search engines, secured dozens of links from key sites, announced to newsgroups, contacted mailing list moderators, refined our existing pages, added a new interactive feature, and responded to user feedback". Of course, these tasks are never completely done. If you think you're over the hump of your promotional efforts, then it's probably time to add a new feature to your site and begin all over again. The work is never done.

Limited Money

Some small companies that are running a Web-only business would never consider paying money to advertise their sites in traditional media. I mean this literally—it would *never even cross their minds*. Of those who did at least briefly consider the idea, most would quickly dismiss it as being a poor use of money. They would probably conclude that—if they were going to spend money on advertising—any money should be spent placing banner ads on other sites, for example.

On one hand, they might be right—they would at least know for sure that every impression their ad made was on a person who had Web-browsing capabilities. No such guarantees exist when advertising in a gourmet magazine, where perhaps fewer than a third of the people may be regular Web browsers. On the other hand—who knows?—maybe you could find a way to target an otherwise hard-to-reach niche. For a site that sells nothing but hot sauce, it at least seems plausible that advertising in a magazine devoted exclusively to spicy food might be worth considering. It might be worth running a test. If you do, try these tips:

- First watch a couple of issues to see what other advertisers do. If somebody places a Web-centric ad one month but doesn't do it the second month, this might be a sign that the magazine's readers are not big Web users.

- Negotiate down from the publisher's rate card. Explain that you must run a test before you commit to advertising for a long duration.

- Attempt to appeal secondarily to non-Web customers if your situation permits. Provide another way for customers to contact you, such as an 800 phone number.

- First try to obtain free publicity in the publication (discussed later in this chapter). When seeking publicity, make no mention of whether you are considering buying advertising from the publication.

Limited Perspective/Experience

I suspect that this is the primary reason why most small Web businesses overlook traditional media to promote their sites. By its very nature, the Web seems to draw entrepreneurs who are looking for different ways of doing things. In business, as in biology, evolution and innovation occur at the fringes, where people have nothing to lose by trying a new method of making a living. The firmly entrenched incumbents have everything to lose, which is why big businesses tend to cling so fervently to the old way of doing things.

If colonial America—by its nature—disproportionally attracted rugged individualists to its untamed shores, then the Web—by its nature—attracts entrepreneurs with a fondness for technology and a predisposition for doing things differently. Both of these inclinations create people who are more interested in figuring out the newest untried Web tactic than trying something that has worked well for many decades; they are people who would rather spend days learning Java than five minutes picking up the phone to call the editor of a metropolitan newspaper.

I'm guilty of possessing this bias myself; I expect you may be too. But while it has been said that greatness was never achieved by doing the same thing that everybody else does, the following has also been said: "Whatever works."

Add to this bias for using new technology the sheer inexperience of many online marketers. Many Web start-ups today are being put together by a handful of *very* young people or people who have worked only in very small companies. These individuals are the least likely to even think about how to proceed with traditional methods of reaching people. Think about this; doesn't it seem beyond crazy to use direct mail to promote your Web address? What a waste of trees—right? The idea gets shut out at the front gate of your mind's party. No consideration whatsoever. But what about this question: For a million dollars, could you think of a way to get your URL listed for free on a mailing that somebody else was already going to send out? (You might not get a million dollars, but there is an answer—see the "Tag-Along Advertising" sidebar, earlier in this chapter, and apply the same concept to small companies that frequently send direct mail.)

The point is that our frothy embrace of the new paradigm is causing many of us to completely forget the powerful, conventional weapons in our arsenals. The trick to unleashing these weapons is simply to remember that they are there. Who can forget the classic scene in *Raiders of the Lost Ark* when the black-robed swordsman in the market began twirling his sword menacingly in front of Jones? And then Jones, looking mildly annoyed, pulled out his gun and shot the swordsman. Everybody in the theater laughed because the problem seemed so exotic that an ordinary solution did not even cross our minds.

> **TIP:** Web marketing is an exotic problem. Don't overlook ordinary solutions.

Ordinary Solutions

This section is made up of a handful of the best tips related to marketing your Web business with traditional media. The bang-for-the-buck power of all of these combined, however, is dwarfed by the results to be had by obtaining free publicity, a discussion of which follows this section.

Company Printed Materials

Sound too simple to need mentioning? Good—that's exactly why people forget to use this technique.

> **TIP:** Every single piece of paper on which your company prints its phone number should also display your URL.

Okay, there are possible exceptions. Phones tied to special promotions requiring live discussion or revenue-generating 900 lines shouldn't be printed next to the url if your specific goal is to get someone to pick up the phone. In these rare cases, however, think of ways to broaden the promotion or revenue stream to include the Net and then display the URL.

> There will always be people who will access your site but who will never call you. If you don't provide a URL, you lose these people.

Ignoring exotic exceptions, the truth remains that many companies simply—negligently—forget to include their Web address. This happens all the time in companies where the Web business is its own division, one that probably hasn't proved that it can pay for itself. Other divisions don't take it seriously as a legitimate marketing tool (or worse yet, they *don't even know* that their own company has a Web site!). This tip may be for one of those rare, decidedly undiplomatic, "memo from the President" situations.

```
TO:        All personnel
FROM:      Mr. Peabody, CEO
RE:        Web Site Address
All new printing of company communications that display
our phone number will also include our company's Web site
address, which is:

http://www.becauseIsaidso.com

This includes all new printings of business cards, let-
terhead, envelopes, forms, packaging materials, brochures,
catalogs, fliers, etc.

Please visit our site and familiarize yourself with its
features. Direct any feedback on the site or questions
about this memo to...
```

Your company may print pieces that are not designed to generate communications. You may also prepare "image" ads that are intended only to enhance your brand identity. The test for determining whether to include your URL is whether you include a phone number. In this regard, think of your Web site address as simply another phone number, and always present them together.

Print Advertising

Generally speaking, use the same rule mentioned above for deciding whether to include your URL in print ads: Include it if you include a phone number. One possible exception: Companies sometimes run ads that direct callers to third parties, such as customer-service contractors or product distributors and dealers. Your corporate URL should accompany your corporate phone number almost always. However, whether it accompanies a special-purpose phone number will depend on the situation. I recommend building special purpose sites to parallel any special-purpose phone use. Again, remember that there will always be a category of people who don't want to talk on the phone but who will eagerly visit a Web site. Expect this percentage to grow as the populace becomes more accustomed to getting everyday information over the Web.

If you sell directly as well as through distributors, be careful about how you promote your URL in advertisements. Your distributors may see this as an attempt to circumvent them depending on the wording of your ad and the content of your site. Depending on the nature of your product, a good balance might be to accept small orders directly while channeling all large orders to your distributors. If your distributors feel that your site is helping them, they will be supportive of your efforts to promote it.

> **TIP:** *Do not* allow people to visit your site without offering some way for them to ultimately buy—even if it means directing them someplace else.

If you choose not to sell directly online (many firms don't), at least help people find your products. For example, visitors ideally should be able to quickly locate the nearest retail location that sells your wares. Exception: Naturally, this rule does not apply to company Intranets and sites designed to facilitate communication between your company and suppliers or distributors. In other words, if your site is geared to your customers, then it should tell your customers what they need to know.

Even if your Web site does not sell directly, you can use it to measure the effectiveness of your print ads. For example, run two different ads (or the same ad in two publications) directing people to separate URLs for more information. By measuring these pages' respective traffic, you will have an idea which magazine ads generate more interest.

As mentioned earlier, many companies still do not include URLs in their print advertisements. In many of these cases, it is because the companies do not have Web sites. Until the day when URLs are used as frequently as phone numbers in ads, I recommend making the URL at least as prominent as your phone number if, in fact, you would rather have people visit your site than call. Making either your phone number or your URL more prominent than the other suggests the method by which you would prefer to have people contact you.

It has become common to dispense with "http://" when including your url in print, at least when your address begins with "www." For example,

(800) 555-1234

www.kangaroo.com

is sufficient to let readers know how to find your site. However, if your site address does not begin with "www," then include the full URL:

(800) 555-1234

http://kangaroo.com

Broadcast

Deciding whether to attempt to relay your URL over the airwaves requires a bit more discretion.

> **T I P :** Don't try to mention your URL on the radio unless it is simple to convey verbally.

Have you ever noticed how difficult it is to give certain e-mail addresses over the telephone? You have to spell certain words one letter at a time, including niceties like "P as in 'Paul'" or "M as in 'Mary.'" Imagine trying to tell somebody this URL over the phone: http://www.smartz.com/welcom/~ad_rep/free.html.

Forget it. No wonder so many people just say "I'll send you an e-mail with the address." Nobody would attempt to convey this monster over the airwaves, particularly when paying by the second. The same goes for using the address on television. It must be simple enough to be easily and correctly remembered, verbally or visually. If your domain contains a hyphen or an oddly spelled word, I wouldn't risk using it; your time on the air is expensive, and the audience's attention is short. There are better ways to use this expensive medium than to give out a Web address that people won't be able to remember.

If your business plan calls for heavy broadcast advertising, choose a domain based on simplicity first, relevance second. For example, if you provide home loans, "www.money.com" would be better than "www .homeloan.com" because people hearing your address would not know if "homeloan" was hyphenated.

With both radio and television, for the near future, don't expect everyone to know what a Web address is. It is okay to simply show your address in a television spot without mentioning it. But if you verbally mention your address in either a television or radio spot, I recommend always saying something like

"Visit our Web site at..." or "You can find us on the World Wide Web at..."

Free Publicity

Publicity is perhaps the most potent, least understood, and least used of all marketing communications by small businesses. In my years working at a marketing communications firm, I was consistently amazed by how many experienced business owners had never even considered trying to get free exposure in the form of publicity. The reasons varied:

- They had never heard of small businesses seeking publicity.
- They didn't really understand how publicity works.
- They didn't think their product or service was newsworthy.
- They assumed hiring a publicist was prohibitively expensive.
- They assumed publicity wouldn't do much for them.
- There are no guarantees of getting press.

How Publicity Works

For those unfamiliar with the process, publicity is relatively simple. Either you, an employee, or a publicity specialist writes one or more press releases featuring your company. The press release might center around your company, product, or service, or it may simply embed a mention of your company into any piece of information that editors are likely to find newsworthy. Whoever is handling your publicity will send the press release to an appropriate list of editors at newspapers, magazines, trade publications, and broadcasters.

Most of these editors will disregard the release (unless you've discovered life on Mars). Some may pull a fact out of your release and mention it in a related story, citing you as the source. Others may closely paraphrase and relay most of your release. Still others may contact you directly, interview you, and do a feature story on your company. But there are no guarantees that anyone will say anything about you. The best way to gauge the success of your campaign is to enlist a clipping service to keep an eye out for any mention of your company in the press. When you hire a public relations firm to handle your publicity, clipping services—which aren't cheap—are typically included in the fee.

Is It Really Worth It?

Magazines seem to promote sites more than word-of-mouth does. According to the GVU's Fifth WWW User Survey, an impressive 65 percent of respondents reported visiting sites that they had read about in magazines, compared to only 59 percent who reported visiting sites that their friends had told them about. Indeed, some sites report having their traffic go from almost zero hits to thousands of hits per week after receiving a mention in just one national publication.

Initially, magazine and newspaper editors were eager to publicize the URL of nearly any Web site they heard about. They remain eager to publicize Web addresses, but now, with so many sites competing for attention, the editors must discriminate more heavily between those they think will be of interest to their readership and those that won't. It remains true that a site must have an interesting reason that makes people want to visit.

> **TIP:** Even if your *site* isn't particularly interesting, it might get mentioned if you can come up with some interesting *fact* or *story* that would appeal to an editor.

Work hard to get some media exposure, and the process may become easier. Success begets success. Some editors and writers first learn about a Web site by reading about it in another publication. The editors may then investigate further, choosing to mention the company in their own publications. This positive-feedback spiral also leads to higher traffic and greater odds of making it on one of the more prestigious "What's Cool" lists (see Chapter 8).

Online Publicity Resources

There is no shortage of places online to help you write or submit press releases. A few of them are mentioned here. For more, see Marcia Yudkin's *Small Business Publicity FAQ*, reprinted at the end of this chapter.

E-mail Lists for Media Outlets

At the following addresses you will find a list of e-mail addresses for newspaper, magazine, broadcast, and other media outlets that accept online submissions.

> **T I P :** Do your homework before blindly sending mass-mailed press releases! Study the process, learn how to write a good release (or hire someone to do it for you), and target your audience. Start by studying the FAQ at the end of this chapter.

- Peter Gugerell's e-mail: MEDIA (an enormous collection of e-mail addresses for media outlets)
  http://www.gugerell.co.at/gugerell/media/index.htm

- WWW Links to Various Media Sites
  http://www.intex.net/intex/media.html

- John Hewitt's Trade Magazine List (Figure 11.1)
  Links to trade magazines organized by category
  http://www.azstarnet.com/~poewar/writer/pg/trade.html

> **T I P :** When sending e-mail to editors, do not include a long list of other e-mail address at the top of the e-mailed press release. An e-mail that does not look like mass mail is more likely to be read.

Remember that editors are constantly looking for words to fill their pages. Many publications will publish entire articles written by you if they feel the content is consistent with their editorial objectives. Space will generally be provided to give information about how readers may contact the author of the article. Readers usually perceive much higher credibility from contributors than advertisers in print publications.

WebStep Release It!

http://www.mmgco.com/release.htm

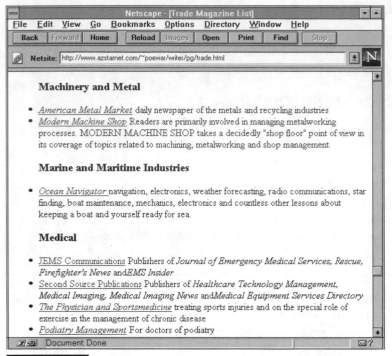

Netscape - [Trade Magazine List]

File   Edit   View   Go   Bookmarks   Options   Directory   Window   Help

Back   Forward   Home   Reload   Images   Open   Print   Find   Stop

Netsite: http://www.azstarnet.com/~poewar/writer/pg/trade.html

Machinery and Metal

- *American Metal Market* daily newspaper of the metals and recycling industries
- *Modern Machine Shop* Readers are primarily involved in managing metalworking processes. MODERN MACHINE SHOP takes a decidedly "shop floor" point of view in its coverage of topics related to machining, metalworking and shop management.

Marine and Maritime Industries

- *Ocean Navigator* navigation, electronics, weather forecasting, radio communications, star finding, boat maintenance, mechanics, electronics and countless other lessons about keeping a boat and yourself ready for sea.

Medical

- JEMS Communications Publishers of *Journal of Emergency Medical Services, Rescue, Firefighter's News* and *EMS Insider*
- Second Source Publications Publishers of *Healthcare Technology Management, Medical Imaging, Medical Imaging News* and *Medical Equipment Services Directory*
- *The Physician and Sportsmedicine* treating sports injuries and on the special role of exercise in the management of chronic disease
- *Podiatry Management* For doctors of podiatry

Document Done

FIGURE 11.1   John Hewitt's links to trade publications.

This is an online service that will send your press release out to its nurtured list of more than 800 media professionals (at over 400 organizations) for just $150 (see Figure 11.2).

You can enter your release directly onto WebStep's online form. Releases should be 750 words or less and well written. WebStep will review your release and send it out within 24 hours if it passes the company's quality check. WebStep's site offers advice for writing effective press releases, including several examples. If you would like help, it will write your press release for an additional $100. The submission fee of $150 is far less than you might pay by hiring a PR firm, but WebStep admits that it does not yet offer integrated clipping services for tracking the success of your press releases.

Here is a partial list of the publications to which WebStep will send your announcement:

AdAge	*Atlanta Journal*
Anchorage Press	*AudioNet*
Asia Week	*Big Issue (Scotland)*

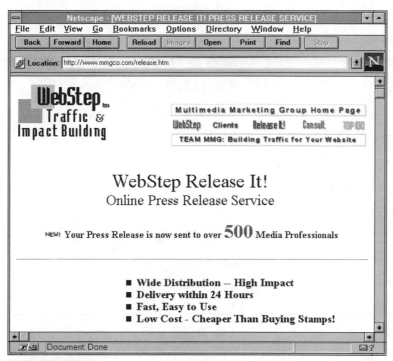

FIGURE 11.2 WebStep Release It! will distribute your 750-word press release to more than 800 media professionals for $150.

Boardwatch	*Daily*
Boston Globe	*CyberWire Dispatch*
Business Week	*Dallas Morning News*
Byte Magazine	Denver KDVR TV
CINET	*Denver Post*
CBS	*Digital Media*
Chicago Sun Times	*Digital News and Review*
Chicago Tribune	*Direct Magazine*
CIO	*Discover*
CNN Computer Connect	*Electronic Marketing*
Computer Life	*Electronic Info Report*
Computerworld	*Entrepreneur*
Cowles/SIMBA Media	*Entrepreneurial Edge*

Family PC

Florida Today

Forbes ASAP

Fortune

Herald Sun (Australia)

HCI Communications

Home Office Computing

Home Office Show

HomeWorker Magazine

Home PC

Homeworker

HotWired

Houston Chronicle

Huntsville News

Huntsville Times

Hurwitz Consulting Group

I+Way

Inc.

Information Highways

InfoWorld

Interactive Age Daily

Inter@ctive Week

Interactive PR

InteractiveGames

InterFace Magazine

Internet Consulting

Internet Life

Internet on CD

Internet Week

Internet World

INTERPRESS Japan

KDVR TV (Denver)

Knight Ridder Newspapers

KTVI TV (St. Louis)

LA Weekly

LAN Magazine

LAN Times

Life

London Daily Telegraph

Los Angeles Times

Mac Home Journal

Mac User

Mac Week

Macworld

Minneapolis/St. Paul StarTribune

Money Magazine

Money & Investing

Morph's Outpost

Mother Jones

Multimedia Daily

Multimedia Merchandising

Nation's Business

NBC

NetGuide

Netguide Now!

NetSurfer Digest

New Haven Advocate

New Media

New York Times Online

New York Times

New Yorker Magazine

Newsbytes

Newsday

Newsweek

NL

PC Home & Education

PC Home Office & Executive

P.C. Letter

PC Laptop

PC Magazine

PC Shopper

PC Week

PC World

PC/Computing

Playboy

Portable Computing

Presentations

Publish

Release 1.0

San Diego Daily Transcript

San Diego News-Tribune

San Francisco Beacon

San Francisco Chronicle

San Francisco Examiner

San Jose Mercury News

Savetz Publications

Scientific American

Scout Report

Seattle Times

Seybold Publications

Sharing Ideas for Professional
    Speakers

Shift

Smithsonian

Soft-Letter

Sunexpert

Tales from the Bitstream

Tampa Tribune

Telecommunications Magazine

Teleconnect Magazine

Texas Business

The Business Computer

The Cobb Group

The Computer Paper

the net

Time

Time Daily

Tucson Weekly

United Press International

Unix Review

USA Today

U.S. News & World Report

VAR Business

Video Store

Virtual City

WAGA TV (Atlanta)

Wall Street Journal	*Weigand Report*
WSJ Personal Technology	*Windows Magazine*
Washington Post	*Windows Sources*
Washington Technology	*Windows Tech Journal*
Washington Times	*Windows Watcher Newsletter*
WebMaster	*WinUser Magazine*
Web Review	*Wired*
Websight	*WWWiz*
WEBster	*Yahoo! Interactive Life*
Web Track	Ziff-Davis
WebWeek	

The Small Business Publicity FAQ by Marcia Yudkin

I. The what and why of media publicity

1. Media publicity—you mean free advertising?

No. Publicity and advertising are two very distinct methods of marketing. With advertising, you pay for a specific space or time to get your message across a predetermined number of times. With publicity, you pay only the minimal costs of getting your message out to the media by phone, mail, or fax. The media then may choose to disseminate your message, at their expense and at whatever time, setting, and length they choose. Once you've pitched your story to the media, whether you receive a blizzard of publicity or none whatsoever is largely out of your hands.

2. Why would the media want to publicize my business?

If you know how to answer a key question—Why would our readers/listeners/viewers be interested in learning about you now?—they will be happy to use your story to fill up their airtime or column space.

As a reporter once told a friend of mine, "The media are a hungry animal that needs to be constantly fed." So the trick is to feed them an angle on your business that their particular audience will perceive as news, entertainment, or useful information.

3. What do you mean by an "angle" and why is that important for publicity?

The angle is the aspect of your product, service, or event that makes your business qualify as news and hence worthy of publicity. For example:

- What's new about your business?

- What's distinctive about your business?

- How does your business solve a prevalent problem?

- How does your business relate to a current trend?

etc.

One way to understand angles is to examine the coverage in a newspaper, magazine or radio or TV broadcast, asking yourself precisely what about the businesses that were featured appear to have earned them attention.

4. Don't you need a PR firm to make contacts for you?

If you have a controversial product or need a constant stream of publicity instead of a jump start or occasional boost, you may be better off hiring a PR firm to handle publicity. But the basic principles and effective execution are not difficult to master. Sheer beginners whom I've coached on catching the attention of the media have ended up being featured in the *Wall Street Journal* or other prestigious media outlets, where they knew absolutely nobody. Pre-existing contacts aren't essential. A catchy angle on your business and effective communication of a newsworthy message often do the trick.

II. How to Get Media Publicity

1. What's a press release and how do I write one?

A press release is a brief document in a specific format that sets forth for media gatekeepers the newsworthy angle on your business. The top two lines identify the source of the release (your company, with its address) and the name and phone number of the person the media should contact for further information. "For immediate release" usually belongs on the next line, signifying that the story need not be embargoed until a specific date. Then comes the headline, which sets forth the main point of the release in big, bold letters.

The first paragraph of the release begins with the place and date of the release, as in a news article, followed by the journalist's who-what-when-where-and-why with respect to the angle announced in the headline. Subsequent paragraphs expand on the main point, usually with quotes from you, industry leaders, or other authoritative figures. The release often closes with the practical details about the event, service, or product, such as price and ordering or contact information. It's best to keep the whole release to one page.

After making copies of your release, send them to the media representatives most likely to take an interest in your message.

2. Can you give us a sample release?

Here goes...

For: Creative Ways, P.O. Box 1310, Boston, MA 02117.

Contact: Marcia Yudkin (617)871-1577 or marcia@yudkin.com.

FOR IMMEDIATE RELEASE

NEW INTERNET "MAILBOT" FROM VETERAN FREELANCER OFFERS 24-HOUR
ANSWERS FOR FREQUENTLY ASKED QUESTIONS

Boston, MA, November 10, 1995 - Beginning writers searching for guidance when all the libraries are closed and other writers are asleep now have a unique reference available online. By sending any E-mail message to "fl@yudkin.com," flummoxed freelancers can receive a collection of answers in a matter in minutes to pesky questions like, "How do I prevent people from stealing my ideas?" "What's a kill fee?" and "Are multiple submissions OK?"

Marcia Yudkin, the creator of the new Freelance Writing Frequently Asked Questions (FAQ) file, says that she included the questions she's heard most often in the seven years she's been teaching and consulting for freelancers. "The FAQ format makes a perfect reference for beginners," Yudkin says, "and putting the file on a mailbot, or automatic E-mail robot, makes the information available almost instantly, day or night, to anyone with access to the Internet."

Yudkin, the author of *Freelance Writing for Magazines and Newspapers* from HarperCollins, learned about FAQs and mailbots in the course of research for her most recent book, *Marketing Online,* from Plume/Penguin. In 15 years as a professional writer, she has published hundreds of articles in magazines and newspapers ranging from the *New York Times Magazine* and *Psychology Today* to *New Age Journal* and *Cosmopolitan.*

In addition to being available by E-mail from "fl@yudkin.com," the Freelance Writing FAQ is posted regularly to the alt.journalism.freelance newsgroup. Anyone in the U.S. not wired for E-mail can receive a printed copy of the Freelance Writing FAQ by sending an SASE with 78 cents postage to: Marcia Yudkin/Freelance FAQ, P.O. Box 1310, Boston, MA 02117.

3. What's a pitch letter?

If you have only one or a few specially selected media outlets to target, instead of sending a press release, you can put the information in the form of a personalized business letter. Begin by establishing some special connection with the editor or producer to whom you're writing (e.g., you're a devoted listener or reader—but don't say this if you're not). Then explain straightforwardly what you have to offer and close the way you would any business letter.

4. Can I phone in my news?

For an effective phone pitch, you must have a curiosity-provoking opening line and be able to say in a sentence or two what's newsworthy about your business. Don't get insulted if media people are brusque. When they're on deadline, they can't chat with you. But if you have a story that sparks their interest, they will get back to you. When you're contacting radio or TV, the person you need to speak with is the producer of a show, not the on-air host.

5. Can I contact the media by E-mail or fax?

Unless a media outlet has specifically put the word out that they welcome press releases and pitches by E-mail, stick to the other methods of contact. For faxes, keep in mind that a large newspaper or broadcast station might have half a dozen or more different fax numbers. Make sure any fax number you use for press releases was designated (for instance, in a computerized or printed media list) for that purpose.

6. How about posting press releases on the Internet and online services?

If you post press releases on the World Wide Web, you then face the problem of having to publicize the press release, since the right media people won't normally stumble across it there. Specific forums or bulletin boards on the online services, or Internet newsgroups, may allow the posting of relevant press releases. Check the guidelines or FAQs (Frequently Asked Questions file) where possible, or ask first.

Two publicity wire services, PRWire and BusinessWire, make their offerings available on some online services and to their online subscribers. See information in III below.

7. Does it pay to schmooze with reporters?

I've gotten a significant amount of media coverage from writers who personally knew me. But this didn't transpire because I wanted to get media coverage and then in a calculated fashion called up to invite them out to lunch. If you're already a good networker, it wouldn't hurt to pay special attention to media folks you run across. Remember, though, that you still must have a newsworthy story for them. No one will give you media coverage merely because they like you.

8. Do I need a press kit?

A press kit, or media kit, usually consists of one or more press releases, a photo of you or the product, background sheets on the company, bios of the principal people involved, your company brochure and prior press clippings, all packaged in a nice colored folder. If budget allows, you can send these out in place of a simple press release—or you can send out just the press release and wait until someone asks for more information. I've never routinely sent out press kits and am asked for one only a few times a year.

9. Will I need to hype my business to win media publicity?

To get publicity you will need to toot your own horn, but extravagant claims and blatant boasting hurt your chances. A survey of more than 100 newspaper editors found their most common criticism of press releases was "Sounds like advertising." You need to use the same objective tone about your business that a journalist would use.

10. If I send something in, should I call to follow up?

Although many professional publicists swear by followup calls, I interviewed numerous businesspeople who get a good deal of media coverage without ever making follow-up phone calls. If you're especially effective on the phone and have the time, followup calls might be worth a try.

11. How will I know when and where my information was used?

Although some editors will print your story almost exactly as you wrote it, most will contact you for additional information so that they can write it up in the way that most meets the needs of their audience. At that time, you should ask when they think they'll run the story. Similarly, radio and TV stations will call because they prefer to have you show or tell about your news.

In addition, if you include an offer for a free booklet or brochure in the last paragraph of your press release, many media outlets will include your 800-number and/or your address when they publicize you. Then it's easier to track where and when the story appeared. One Sunday morning my 800-number began receiving an onslaught of what turned out to be 200 phone calls from the area surrounding Dallas. Obviously an article that had been making the rounds of the newswires landed in the Dallas paper that day.

12. What if I do all the above and nothing happens?

Don't assume you've failed if you just don't hear anything. One client of mine experienced utter silence about her press release for eight months, then received a full-length photo feature in the *Boston Herald.* My coauthor for the book *Smart Speaking* got called to appear on the Oprah Winfrey Show three years after our publisher sent a copy of the book and a press kit! Besides patience, remember the old saying, "If at first you don't succeed, try, try again" —with a fresh angle.

III. Publicity Resources

1. Listings at your library

Many public libraries carry one or more of the following, which contain media contact information. Make sure you're using an up-to-date edition. In addition, there are regional directories, such as one for Southern California or New England media. Ask your reference librarian.

- Bacon's Newspaper-Magazine Directory. 2 volumes.

- Bacon's Radio-TV-Cable Directory. 2 volumes.

- Broadcasting and Cable Yearbook.

- Editor and Publisher International Yearbook.

- Gale Directory of Publications and Broadcast Media.

- Newsletters in Print.

- Oxbridge Directory of Newsletters.

- Standard Rate & Data Service.

- Ulrich's International Periodicals Directory.

- Working Press of the Nation.

- Writer's Market.

2. Newswires

- Business Wire. For a few hundred dollars, this newswire service can bring your press release to thousands of business-oriented newsrooms around the U.S. and several online databases. For more information: 800-227-0845 or check the white pages in the nearest large city for a regional office; E-mail: newsroom@bizwire.com.

- PR Newswire. Functions like Business Wire, but not limited to business press. For more information: 800-832-5522 or 212-832-9400; World Wide Web: http:/www.prnewswire.com.

3. PRSIG forum on CompuServe

Get friendly, free publicity and marketing advice from the pros on this long-established electronic bulletin board frequented by marketing pros on the international online service, CompuServe. For a one-month trial membership on CompuServe, call 800-848-8990 or E-mail sales@cis.compuserve.com.

4. PR-Profitcenter

The most inexpensive computerized media list available, in a format that imports into your existing database program. In the fall of 1996 it cost $200 plus $5.00 shipping to the U.S. or Canada for unlimited use of contact information on approximately 4,900 magazine editors, 6,500 newspaper editors, 2,700 radio producers, 1,800 TV producers, and 701 syndicated columnists, searchable by topic, geography, and medium. E-mail marcia@yudkin.com for ordering information.

5. Six Steps to Free Publicity

This paperback book by Marcia Yudkin from Plume/Penguin Books offers practical tips for making your business newsworthy and attracting print or broadcasting publicity on a limited budget. Look for it at your local bookstore, or send for an electronic brochure from info@yudkin.com.

6. PR Firms

If you decide to hand over responsibility for publicity to public relations professionals, ask business colleagues for references and check your yellow pages under "Public Relations." You'll get the best service and appropriate pricing if you match the size of your company to the size of the PR firm. Expect to pay a monthly retainer plus all out-of-pocket expenses such as copying, printing, and postage or fax charges.

7. Publicity Coaching

This is an appropriate, cost-effective option if you're prepared to do the detailed work yourself but want professional feedback and guidance. For more information, send any E-mail message to info@yudkin.com or call Marcia Yudkin at 1-617-266-1613.

CHAPTER 12

PROMOTING YOUR SITE TO NEWSGROUPS WITHOUT GETTING NAPALMED

If the entire Internet were a small town, then Usenet would be that town's central square—the most public and visible of venues, whether the day's events are centered around a carnival and parade or the courthouse and gallows. With a few exceptions, almost nobody cares what you do on your own little corner of the Web—your site. That's your property and your business. But doing something that is generally considered inappropriate by the masses in a place like Usenet can create problems for you.

Usenet is the Internet's public forum, comprising thousands of newsgroups, each of which is devoted to the public discussion of a narrow, chartered topic such as microbrews, baseball cards, arthritis research, or traveling in Africa. In fact, it is safe to say that for any topic you might think of, there are probably a couple of groups that directly relate. Depending on which study you read, somewhere between a third and half of the people on the Internet access these newsgroups, well over 10 million people.

A single newsgroup may be read regularly by as few as a dozen or as many as 200,000 people. While these large groups might seem like a great place to announce your new Web site, they are probably among the worst. The largest newsgroups are those that pertain to topics with the broadest appeal—such as presidential elections. This means that any announcement you make to this group had better be closely related to elections, or you risk seriously offending 200,000 Internet users—something you *don't* want to do. A much better option is to find the newsgroup with just a couple of hundred readers who are all very interested in your site's subject. You give up quantity in exchange for quality of readers. Because success on the Web almost always depends on a firm's ability to target unfilled niches, Usenet can be a powerful tool. That's the good news. The bad news is that there are more ways to screw up and tarnish your firm's or site's reputation than there are ways to promote it positively. Proceed with great care.

The Perils of Posting

People make several mistakes when they first start promoting themselves on Usenet. Most errors fall into one of three categories:

- Ignoring Usenet netiquette

- Ignoring Usenet's conventions regarding commercial announcements

- Failing to handle flames (criticisms) properly

I have listed them in this sequence intentionally because this is the order in which you must learn how to behave on Usenet, if you are not already experienced. I will address each of these individually, but first I must implore you to do one thing:

If you are going to promote your site to newsgroups, you *must* read the following documents. Although Usenet is not governed by any authority, these documents cover the defacto cultural standards that will dictate whether your behavior is appropriate and well received.

The following required reading material is regularly posted to news.announce.newusers. Below, you will find some of the key points made in these "Usenet manuals," which are too long to reprint here. Still, you must read these source documents to avoid the pitfalls that may await you in Usenet. You should be able to read all of these in an hour or two. Doing so will be an excellent use of your time, condensing what would otherwise take many months of learning by watching, participating, and making mistakes in newsgroups.

See news.announce.newusers:

- A Primer on How to Work with the Usenet Community

- Rules for Posting to Usenet

- Answers to Frequently Asked Questions about Usenet

and, in particular,

- Advertising on Usenet: How to Do It, How Not to Do It

The penalties for violating Netiquette range from "just some friendly advice" e-mail to full-blown electronic warfare. Perpetrators who behave badly enough have literally had their Internet service providers shut down due to receiving mass quantities of automated hate e-mail. These perpetrators often lose their Internet accounts. They get listed on public "blacklists" for all to see. They start receiving C.O.D. packages that they didn't order. Their fax machines start printing pages of gibberish throughout the night until the paper runs out. They even find out that the Post Office has been delivering their mail someplace else by mistake.

I find that the majority of people looking to get into a Web-oriented business are good, ethical, hard-working people. Most of their mistakes come from ignorance rather than disregard for others. Most mistakes, fortunately, are narrow enough in scope that they are quickly forgotten by the world. However, certain actions cross a line that the Internet is not as likely to forget:

1. *Spamming*—If somebody sends essentially identical messages to enough groups, the posts will eventually be targeted for cancellation from Usenet before anybody ever gets a chance to read them. Spamming is considered one of the rudest of all netiquette breaches.

2. *Forging Identity, Return Address, etc.*—Fortunately, most forgeries are easy to spot by looking at full header information. People who get caught doing this can kiss any hope of future credibility good-bye.

3. *Less Exotic Misrepresentation*— Also known as "Hey everyone, I just found this really great site which you must see!" Of course, the same person posts the same message to a dozen groups and is instantly recognized as the owner of the site. A much more dignified alternative is to clearly state one's association with the site and simply ask— as the developer—for feedback that will be used to improve the site.

4. *Mass E-mailing*—The act of sending unsolicited e-mail goes against most Internet service providers' agreements, meaning violation can easily get you kicked off the Net. The appropriateness or inappropriateness of mass e-mail is covered in Chapter 13.

Usenet Netiquette

Evolved from a medium designed to allow efficient communication between academic institutions and other research facilities, the Internet has a form of etiquette as strong as that of any other culture.

> Sociological Truism: Cultural norms evolve to facilitate efficient social interactions. The rules are almost never arbitrary.

When you are next in line to use the automatic teller, have you ever noticed that there is an appropriate distance which you must place between yourself and the person currently conducting a transaction? Or maybe you've been at the machine and felt uncomfortable because the person behind you stood too close. In a few short years of using cash machines, a stable cultural norm has been established with no help from the banks, Congress, or Emily Post. We all know the unwritten rule even though nobody taught it to us. The required standing distance, about eight feet, evolved out of the circumstances—any closer and you might see the person enter his or her PIN number; any further and somebody else walking up would not know you were next in line. Born out of its own unique set of circumstances, Netiquette also exists for a reason and serves a special set of purposes.

Bandwidth Conservation

The majority of generally accepted Net customs can be related to conserving scarce network bandwidth and data storage resources. Some of these customs are very prevalent in Usenet:

- Don't spam (sending the same or essentially the same message to many different newsgroups).

- When following up a long post, don't quote the entire original post only to contribute a sentence or two. Only quote relevant sections of the original message.

- Don't post replies that add nothing to the conversation (such as "I agree" and "me too" messages).

- Limit your signature to four lines or less.

- Be concise.

- Avoid participating in flame wars (arguments in which more insults or comments *about the arguing* are traded than actual substantive points related to the original issue).

- Follow up unrelated or personal threads with e-mail.

Efficient Communication

In a text-based medium, making information easy for people to find, particularly when there are many options from which to choose takes effort. Usenet users typically refer to the "signal-to-noise ratio," meaning the degree to which useful, appropriate information is obscured by unwanted and irrelevant information.

- Again, don't spam. Posting the same message to many groups virtually guarantees that the message is off-topic in most of those groups because each group is supposed to cover a different topic.

- Don't post off-topic at all. This simply means you should keep your discussion within the confines of the group's stated purpose. It also means not posting things that nobody wants to read—such as advertisements, in many cases.

- Use clear subject headers. Ideally, users know what your post is about without having to read the whole thing. Vague subject names like "An Idea" help nobody sift through all the available information efficiently.

Give Freely

The Internet started as a way to share information. Shareware, helpful technical advice, and knowledge of every sort were (and remain) free for the asking from people who were glad to help. The system works as long as enough people are willing to contribute. You give something for free, and because everyone else does, you receive thousands of free things in return. Everybody recognizes that this sort of reciprocal-altruism model breaks down when enough people exploit the goodwill of others without contributing themselves. Fear of this breakdown is what has led many veteran Net users to resist commercialization of the Internet. An almost ritualistic gift-culture now exists by which individuals or companies signal their willingness to pay their dues in the tacit social contract. This gift-culture manifests itself in several ways.

- *General* aversion to advertising on Usenet (there are exceptions, fortunately, or this would be a very short chapter)

- The custom of offering something useful and free to people "just for stopping by"

- The practice of providing links away from one's Web site

- On Usenet, willingness to answer people's questions without expecting remuneration

Advertising on Usenet

Very generally speaking, advertising is *not welcome* on Usenet. In the free give-and-take exchange of ideas of a discussion group, the arrival of someone announcing something for sale has the same appeal as would one person selling food at a pot-luck—while sampling everybody else's dishes for free. Tacky.

This person's intrusion would also likely violate one of the other causes that drove the evolution of Net culture and Netiquette: efficient communication. Imagine, for example, you were having a class discussion about the chemistry of nitrogen-based fertilizers and someone with a bullhorn and an obnoxious suit bursts into the room shouting, "Fertilizer? Did somebody mention fertilizer? I have got some of the best darn fertilizer in the world—yeeeew won't believe how big your corn will grow when you sprinkle just one tablespoon of my..." Rude.

This example demonstrates how *selling* fertilizer is *not* on-topic with every topic *related* to fertilizer. The intrusion interrupts the flow of the discussion. On Usenet, it means readers have to sift through noise (unwanted posts) to find the signal (wanted posts). It means bandwidth is wasted by messages that nobody—at least, nobody in this group—wants to hear.

> **T I P :** The general, guiding principle for advertising on Usenet is that it's okay *when people want to hear it.* In practice, this is difficult to know, and rules vary greatly from group to group.

Advertisements are acceptable on Usenet in several circumstances. The specifics of building a promotional plan upon these considerations are discussed later in this chapter.

Sigverts

Usenet and mailing lists (Chapter 13) universally accept the use of brief "signatures" at the end of legitimate contributions that you make to newsgroups or lists. Many people include in their signatures a political remark, a favorite quote, a graphic made out of ASCII characters, or information on how to contact them. For example:

```
Dan Wade
"A day is not wasted if a friend is made or a building is
demolished."
Wade Demolition
(602) 555-5540
http://www.kaboom.com
```

> **TIP:** Netiquette dictates that you keep your signature to four lines or less. Many people use more, but by doing so they walk closer to the line of upsetting newsgroup readers, particularly if the signature is used for advertising.

"Sigvertising" is the practice of using your signature as a marketing tool. The word sometimes has a negative connotation, particularly in the case of "sigvert spamming," when advertisers transparently pretend to contribute to newsgroup conversations only to get their signatures in front of as many eyes as possible.

Because brief signatures with marketing content are broadly approved, deciding whether somebody is sigvert spamming becomes a subjective judgement. That is, somebody who posts a follow-up to every thread in a widely read group might be legitimately attempting to contribute, or he may be doing as little as possible to get his name read. Unfortunately, lack of a well-written, insightful post cannot suffice as a test of intent because there are many responses (with no signatures) that add little to Usenet discussions. Unless the sigvertiser is guilty of true spamming (sending the same message to many groups), then Netiquette watch dogs would be hard-pressed to accuse this person of any violation of protocol. Many other Web marketers, however, employ sigvertising that annoys nobody. They post only when they have something that is unambiguously thoughtful, original, and useful to the group or current conversational thread. When somebody offers real insight to a conversation, nobody cares whether the signature is an advertisement because the individual has contributed something worthwhile.

> **TIP:** Use sigverts, but don't post unless you have something truly useful to say.

A good self-test that you might use when deciding whether to post a follow-up or new topic is this: If the conversation were taking place in a classroom, would you raise your hand? If so, then you probably have something worth saying—at least by your own standards of what you hope will be useful. If you wouldn't stand up in a crowded room to make your point, then it probably isn't worth wasting people's time or bandwidth to make it either.

> **TIP:** Customize your signatures for different newsgroups. Appeal to niches wherever appropriate.

Commerce-Oriented Groups

Newsgroups with "marketplace," "forsale," and "biz" in the names exist specifically for selling or announcing products. However, each group has its own rules, and you should not assume that any group with one of these words in its name is appropriate for you. Forsale groups, for example, are geared more toward classified-style ads selling single items between private individuals who are not using the medium to fuel an ongoing enterprise. Naturally, a group named rec.arts.books.marketplace is not going to want to hear about the motorcycles you're selling. But even if you are selling a book, you would need to check with that group to verify that its topic is related to your specific product.

On-Topic Announcements

Depending on a group's charter, it may generally discourage advertising while allowing or even welcoming a one-time post pertaining to a commercial site that is very closely related to the nature of the group. As you can imagine, interpreting this exception could become a huge gray area. And the level of acceptance will be affected by more than just the subject of your site.

The Demeanor of Your Post

If you are loud or hypish, you will not be well regarded. If you are modest, understated, and matter-of-factly sharing information, then you will be appreciated more. Think of this not as an ad, but as an announcement letting people know you exist—just as if somebody else had found your site and wanted to inform the other members of the group about its existence.

Never use ALL UPPERCASE in either posts or subject headers. Technically, according to the rules of Netiquette, it means you are yelling. In practice, it gives you away as an uninformed outsider, an advertiser who is "here to hawk and not to talk." Messages with uppercase subject headers will go largely unread.

Good Subject Header:

```
Announcement: Site offering primitive world art
```

Good Body:

```
We have just completed the Africa Room of Terra
Incognita, a site devoted to providing unique col-
lectibles and primitive art from around the world.

Those interested in outdoor photography or climbing
Kilimanjaro will enjoy this month's photo album on loan
from Pauley Blass of the International Wildlife
Federation.

http://www.incognita.com

Your feedback is greatly appreciated.
```

Bad Subject Header:

```
!!! BONGOS-SPEARS-TRIBAL MASKS !!! GREAT DEALS
```

Bad Body:

```
You won't believe the incredible collection we've pulled
together of the most exotic primitive artwork and handi-
crafts from around the globe. We've literally scoured the
earth finding the coolest handmade treasures sure to be
the centerpiece of any collection.

Tell a friend about our site and you'll DOUBLE YOUR ODDS
of winning a trip-of-a-lifetime to Tanzania!!!
```

The Blatantness of Commercialism at Your Site

The degree to which a gray-area, on-topic post is appreciated will also be affected by what people see once they arrive at your site. If your site is loud, obnoxious, splashing mostly prices, an order form, and little else of value, then there is a good chance somebody will publicly slap your hand for advertising on a group "that prohibits advertisements."

On the other hand, if your site offers rich, non commercial content in addition to a commercial facet, then visitors may be pleased. Here is where the gift-culture comes into play—offer something for free that makes them glad they visited your site. With a little bit of work and creativity, this can be done for any subject matter. People who feel that you have provided a real benefit will possibly report glowing remarks to others on the news-group. Sometimes they will say for you the things you are not allowed to say:

```
>Those interested in outdoor photography or
>climbing Kilimanjaro will enjoy this month's
>photo album on loan from Pauley Blass of the
>International Wildlife Federation.

>http://www.incognita.com

I just checked out these guys' site and it's awesome!
I've never seen anything like it. Don't need to look any
further next time you decorate a room. There's also a
contest to win a free trip to Africa.
```

One way to avoid overt commercialism is to break your site into two basic sections, commercial and noncommercial. There are other advantages to using this model—see Chapter 14.

Individual Preferences

Some people accept newsgroup advertisements as inevitable and simply ignore them. Others react violently to any commercial statement—even those that are considered appropriate by most readers of the group or even by the group's charter. I once witnessed a company defending what had been a noncommercial post promoting a charity event on phx.general, which, at that time, allowed advertisements with few restrictions. Repeat: a *charity* event was announced on a group that *allowed ads*. And somebody still got upset enough to flood the company's e-mail server with lengthy copies of a Netiquette FAQ. When the company publicly asked this person why he had flamed them, the individual simply replied:

```
I just hate anything that sounds like an ad.
```

> No matter how careful you are, you will inevitably upset somebody. Accept this and learn how to handle flames appropriately.

Be sensitive to complaints. Is it possible that you've crossed the line? Overstepped the bounds of generally accepted behavior? Even if you don't think you have, it's what the majority of news readers think that matters.

Responding to Flames Appropriately

As stated above, just about anything goes if you keep your reach limited to your own Web site. Your product may be ridiculously overpriced, your graphics may have been created by a small child, and you probably won't suffer much detrimental word-of-mouth if you limit your marketing promotions to registering with search engines.

> People tell their friends about good sites frequently. People rarely bother to tell their friends about lousy sites.

There are some exceptions to this. You might offend a site visitor to such extreme that he or she actively publicized a gripe. But this would probably require a pretty bad offense, such as defrauding somebody, failing miserably at customer service, or creating a site with unambiguously offensive content such as the "Torturing Puppies for Fun" site. (No, there is no such thing as far as I know.)

An individual who doesn't like something about your site ordinarily has no place to talk about it where anybody will care. However, once you step out into the public light of day that is Usenet, the whole game changes. Anything you say at your site or in a post is up for grabs in a public forum that—depending on the group—can be anything but polite. Even if you post an on-topic (relevant to the particular group) message to a group that allows the announcement of commercial sites, you have still exposed yourself for the first time to real public scrutiny. Some of the readers are very likely to visit your site and report back if they saw anything they didn't like. They will post a follow-up directly to your announcement—creating what's called a threaded conversation or "thread"—with comments potentially more bare-knuckled than these:

```
[blatant commercial hype snipped here]
>visit our site at http://www.ourfirm.com and please
>let me know what you think.
Yeah, I'll tell you what I think. I checked out
this bozo's so-called site and nearly puked a lung
when I saw how much he was charging for the same crap
I can get cheaper elsewhere. Don't waste your time.
```

Because this glowing remark was posted as a follow-up to your announcement, many of the people who read your announcement will also see the follow-up. The critic's remarks may be totally unfounded. You may choose to defend your prices in the public arena or simply walk away, hoping some people will still visit your site and decide for themselves.

Many site managers would simply let this drop and either move on to a different newsgroup for a while or contribute to the same group without making any reference to the criticism. Others might respond to the critic via e-mail, which is Netiquettely the most appropriate response because a discussion of your pricing methods is no longer on topic with the group's charter. Still others would engage this criticism in the public arena, perhaps inviting others to visit the site and see if they agree.

In most cases, just walk away from a public brawl and it will soon be forgotten. If your reputation has been tarnished so badly that you must reply publicly, then ignore the attacking individual and address the relevant criticism with utmost professionalism. Do not get defensive or take any of it personally.

```
>>visit our site at http://www.ourfirm.com and please
>>let me know what you think.

>Yeah, I'll tell you what I think. I checked out
>this bozo's so-called site and nearly puked a lung
>when I saw how much he was charging for the same crap
>I can get cheaper elsewhere. Don't waste your time.

I have conducted a thorough search and have been unable
to find our items available online for prices lower than
those that we offer, with the exception of one model that
we have now marked down. If anybody knows of other excep-
tions, please contact me directly at jdoe@ourfirm.com, so
that I may remedy the situation immediately.
```

Notice how the manager here, with the last sentence, has attempted to pull the price discussion over to e-mail where it belongs. He has projected an interest in providing first-rate customer service by quickly investigating the claims and correcting any instances where the criticisms were accurate. He has not become defensive—in fact, he is emotionally unfazed by the critic's remarks. He has avoided making any remarks about the critic, and he has ignored the critic's name-calling remarks altogether ("blatant commercial hype," "bozo," and "crap").

By keeping his cool while including the critic's remarks in his own follow-up, the manager actually makes the critic appear to be the offensive party. New visitors may still think the prices are high, but at least they cannot criticize his professional handling of a delicate situation. At worst, this manager has probably salvaged the site's reputation with this group. At best, he has improved its image by demonstrating his ability to solve grievances quickly while getting the chance to suggest that they have the "lowest prices available" without being blatantly commercial.

Developing Your Usenet Strategy

If the potential for upsetting millions of people hasn't scared you away from the idea of marketing on Usenet, then you will come to know what an extraordinary medium it is for reaching finely targeted niches. If you follow these steps closely, you should make it through with nothing more than a few minor nicks and cuts. This list of action items assumes you have no knowledge of Usenet. If you already know a lot about it, just skim for ideas that may be new to you.

Learn the Ropes

At the moment your site is up, running well, and buffed to a high sheen, *do not* make an announcement to the most perfectly suited newsgroup on Usenet. An honest mistake made out of ignorance can mess up your one shot at attracting people. In fact, don't start by making any announcements—not even noncommercial ones.

1. First, go back to the part of this chapter that told you to read the Usenet FAQs about posting and advertising. If you have not done so already, read them. Adhere to them.

2. Pick out a dozen or so newsgroups about any topics that interest you. A couple of them should be related to your product so you can begin to get a feel for the subculture that spends its time on that group.

Culture from group to group can vary tremendously. On some groups, people swear enough to make a sailor blush. On others, people are sickeningly sweet and begin every post with an apology for posting. One thing is for sure, you don't want to use one of these temperaments when posting to the other group.

> **TIP:** Lurk before you leap. You "lurk" when you watch a group but don't participate in the discussion. It is always wise to do this for a while, until you become familiar with the idiosyncrasies of each newsgroup.

Spend at least two weeks lurking before you post. Watch both big groups and small. Follow threads. Familiarize yourself with different people's styles. Particularly on those groups related to your business, jot down any acronym that you are not familiar with. Watch the group until you do know what all of these acronyms stand for.

For keystroke economy, every newsgroup has its own acronyms and specialized jargon. A good way to look like a beginner is to post a note asking what these stand for. Don't do it. If you cannot figure it out, e-mail somebody who used one of them and ask him or her what it means. You will usually receive a prompt, friendly response. If you happen to get the occasional grumpy ogre, well ... welcome to Usenet.

Usenet Acronyms

Many acronyms are common to all of Usenet. Most of the popular expressions can be found in the Usenet FAQs.

    IMHO   In my humble/honest opinion...

    BTW   By the way...

    RTF   Read the FAQ (or RTFM, "Read the F* Manual")

"RTF" is one acronym that you don't want to have directed at you. It is told to people who ask a question that has already been answered in the group's FAQ. In the interest of improving signal-to-noise, experienced newsgroup users hate seeing the same questions asked and answered over and over. This is why FAQs were invented. Read them before asking and you will avoid most of the pitfalls of Usenet.

Post a message once you feel comfortable with the vernacular of a given group and have something valuable to contribute. If you post a follow-up, take care to respond to the appropriate person in the thread. If you are responding to somebody else's follow-up, for example, then reply to that person, not to the original poster who started the thread.

Meanwhile, as you master newsgroup Netiquette and procedures by practicing on fun topics, you can be identifying those groups that relate most closely to your business.

Research Your Market(s)

You could scan the entire list of thousands of newsgroups to see which might appeal to you, but it would take a long time and you wouldn't know what many of the groups were about just from looking at their names. There is a better way.

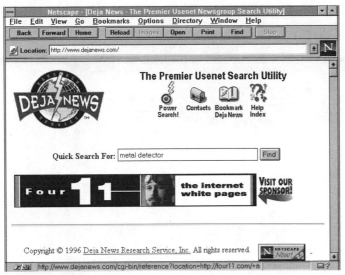

FIGURE 12.1   Deja News allows you to search a vast archive of Usenet posts.

Think back to Chapter 8, where you developed a list of keywords that would draw people to your site. Using this list as a starting point, conduct a search of Usenet for articles in which people have used these words. Conduct your search at the great, free service, Deja News, the Premier Usenet Newsgroup Search Utility (http://www.dejanews.com)(see Figure 12.1).

For example, if you wanted to find groups in which people discuss metal detectors, you would conduct a search on these words, just as you might search for Web sites using the major search engines.

A search on "metal detectors" (see Figure 12.2) has produced a long list of resulting posts in newsgroups such as rec.woodworking, rec.collecting. coin, and rec.scuba.equipment. Because the articles are displayed in reverse chronological order, those at the top of the list are timely. You could click on the subject name to read the text of the post, or you could visit the newsgroup to see what other topics are currently being discussed.

Once you have compiled a list of potential newsgroups (there could be dozens that apply to your business), visit another online resource, the Usenet Info Center Launch Pad (http://sunsite.unc.edu/usenet-i/home .html)(see Figure 12.3).

From the Usenet Info Center Launch Pad you can look up the newsgroups on your list to find out vital information, such as the whereabouts of each group's FAQ and approximately how many people read each group. In Figure 12.4 below, 46,000 people read the group alt.beer. Numbers such as these are more meaningful when you begin to compare one group to

FIGURE 12.2 The words "metal detector" have produced a long list of resulting newsgroup posts.

another. You may find that one group, while not quite as closely related to your topic as another group, boasts 20 times the number of readers.

The next step is to read the FAQ of each of your best newsgroups. If the FAQ mentions nothing about the group's stance on commercial announcements, go back to Deja News and conduct a search made up of the group's name and the word "charter." For example, enter:

```
rec.boats.cruising charter
```

This kind of search will provide a list of rec.boats.cruising posts that contain the word "charter." Some of the posts have to do with chartering

FIGURE 12.3 At the Usenet Info Center Launch Pad, you can look up vital statistics on any newsgroup.

boats. This one, however, has the subject title "Newsgroup Charter" (see Figure 12.5).

This group's charter specifically states:

```
Note the second-to-last paragraph, barring for-sale
postings, and rc-directing them to rec.boats.marketplace.
```

There you have it. Not only have you learned that this group permits no for-sale postings, but it has also told you where they should go. This charter is quite clear about not advertising—no gray area here. Other than sigverts on genuine, on-topic posts, I would forget about commercial activity on this group.

Not all charters are so discouraging, however. The range is quite broad, as seen in these two charters for two currently proposed Usenet groups:

Charter: rec.collecting.coin-operated

"The newsgroup rec.collecting.coin-operated will be for the discussion of collecting, trading, buying, selling, and general use of coin-operated devices such as, but not limited to: Jukeboxes, Slot Machines, Pay Telephones, Soda & Vending Machines, Trade Stimulators, Peanut and

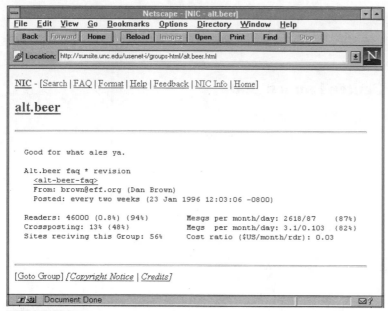

According to the Usenet Info Center, 46,000 people read alt.beer.

Gum Machines, and Fruit Machines. All posts pertinent to gameroom collectibles that relate to coin-operated devices would be welcome."

Charter: sci.space.history (portions of charter only)

"The sci.space.history newsgroup will be directed toward discussion and informational exchange concerning the history of all manned and unmanned spaceflight and spacecraft..."

"...Advertising is specifically prohibited within the sci.space.history group. Reviews and announcements of products or services appropriate to the group (i.e., spaceflight memorabilia auction, books, etc.) may be posted if it is felt that the overwhelming majority of group members will benefit from the information. These should be kept brief and not be formatted as 'advertisements.'"

The first charter for coin-operated devices specifically allows selling on the group. The second charter, for discussing the history of spaceflight, takes a position leaving the decision whether to advertise wide open to interpretation: Advertising is specifically prohibited ... unless the members will benefit, in which case, make it quick and don't look like an ad.

So ... is advertising permitted or not? Even though this seems hopelessly vague, it is really just codifying my statement at the beginning of this

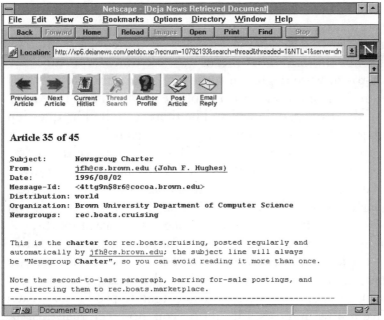

Netscape - [Deja News Retrieved Document]

File Edit View Go Bookmarks Options Directory Window Help

Back Forward Home | Reload Images Open Print Find | Stop

Location: http://xp6.dejanews.com/getdoc.xp?recnum=10792193&search=thread&threaded=1&NTL=1&server=dn

Previous   Next   Current   Thread   Author   Post   Email
Article   Article   Hitlist   Search   Profile   Article   Reply

Article 35 of 45

Subject: **Newsgroup Charter**
From: jfh@cs.brown.edu (John F. Hughes)
Date: 1996/08/02
Message-Id: <4ttg9n$8r6@cocoa.brown.edu>
Distribution: world
Organization: Brown University Department of Computer Science
Newsgroups: rec.boats.cruising

This is the **charter** for rec.boats.cruising, posted regularly and
automatically by jfh@cs.brown.edu; the subject line will always
be "Newsgroup **Charter**", so you can avoid reading it more than once.

Note the second-to-last paragraph, barring for-sale postings, and
re-directing them to rec.boats.marketplace.

Document Done

FIGURE 12.5 Deja News is useful for locating a newsgroup's charter, which usually describes the group's stance on advertising.

chapter—it's okay when people want to hear it. As a marketer, you must use your best judgment. I recommend erring on the side of conservatism—don't post unless you are pretty confident it will be appreciated.

Begin Announcing—Cautiously

Once you are familiar with the rules of Usenet and have selected your target newsgroups, watch these groups for a while. You may see that, even though a group's charter explicitly prohibits commercial announcements, the members actually seem to harbor no animosity toward on-topic ads. If the regular users frequently begin nonflaming, threaded discussions based on previous commercial posts, then it's probably safe to assume that the group is okay with the idea. Watch, learn, and act judiciously.

When you begin making commercial announcements, go very slowly at first. Make one and then do nothing for 10 days except watch who—if anybody—responds to the announcement. If nothing happens, then all you know is that you probably didn't infuriate anybody. Occasionally, you'll get some useful feedback about unclear wording in your post or ways that your site could be improved. These bits of feedback are gems (see Chapter 15) and you should pay close attention to them.

I personally tend toward conservatism when it comes to posting on Usenet. There is one area, however, where I break slightly from the prevailing "Net-correct" attitudes. That is, on-topic posts are seen as appropriate by many groups *one time*. That means *only* one time. Unfortunately, there is a difficult-to-measure degree of turnover among any given group's readership. Six months from now, a portion of the group will be new people. True, some of the same people will still be there as well. The question I find myself asking is, "How soon is it okay to post again?"

As I said, the prevailing answer is "never." But then, some of the more obnoxious Usenet advertisers post to the same groups almost constantly. I've concluded that once about every few weeks does not seem to irritate anybody, particularly if your subject matter is a perfect, on-topic fit. If you are just a "somewhat close fit," then perhaps once every three months. Even though I've never received a single flame for posting too frequently, I do feel that these (or longer) intervals are justified. That is, the longer you wait, the more like "news" it is for people to hear the message, even a second time. Longer intervals, from my experience, tend to produce a greater number of positive follow-up posts. I'll caution you, however, that this, like everything else on Usenet, can vary greatly from one group to the next. Again, proceed cautiously and see what works.

Become Involved

If being able to post periodic, appropriate, and stylish Usenet announcements that draw praise and no fire is the level to which most Web marketers aspire, then the next level—the Zen Buddhist of Usenet marketing—is to become a Genuine Respected Contributor.

First, you find yourself looking for obscure newsgroups to which you might put some strange spin on your concept and force a fit between the group and your business. It's natural to try to look for these—even if you don't act on the urge, and I advise that you don't. Remember the fertilizer story? Usenet readers are notoriously smart—they'll have an easier time spotting your forced fit than you had thinking of it.

The next plane of Marketing Consciousness is to quit looking for these loose associations and focus instead on keeping to a regular plan, such as making new, on-topic announcements when a new feature is added to your site, for example—or perhaps, even when you've created *a new site* that caters more directly to some new niche. Either way, at this level of enlightenment, you are modifying the reality of your site rather than just the face of your message. You are one step closer to the Gift Ideal in that you are more concerned with making your site something that people want than simply drawing more people by waving your arms madly.

If you read a few of your favorite newsgroups long enough, however, a special thing starts to happen. You forget about marketing. You become *involved* with the conversations. You discuss anything *but* your site. You find yourself posing thought-provoking questions that generate long-lived threads (the sure sign of a successful post is to have begun a worthwhile conversation that lasts for many weeks, drawing many participants). Perhaps you have begun corresponding with some of the other regulars by e-mail. Maybe people ask you what you think about this or that. And then one day, it happens. You are explaining your point-of-view on a complex topic and you hastily grab an example from the back of your mind to make your point. And then you realize you've briefly mentioned some aspect of your site or business. The inadvertent plug. A flagrant self-serving pitch? Or a good example to illustrate your point? Should you send it or not?

You do. And the thread continues as usual. Nobody accuses you of commercialism and people respond to the substance of your remarks, perhaps referring to your business, perhaps not. The point is, you have reached Usenet marketing Nirvana—the point of Ultimate Relevance. That is, the mention of your site was so appropriate at that moment and in that context that there was nothing commercial about it, yet people were exposed to it just the same. This is where you want to be.

Usenet Factoid

According to the GVU's Fifth WWW User Survey, half of the male respondents said they learned about Web sites from Usenet as opposed to only a third of the female respondents.

CHAPTER 13

HARD-CORE
E-MAIL TECHNIQUES

here are few things that you can take for granted when it comes to Internet users. Some have fast connections, others have slow. Most are using Netscape's Navigator, but not all of them are. Some people on the Internet browse the Web frequently, and others almost never do. You can no longer even assume that they are highly computer literate. But there is one thing you can count on.

> At least we know one thing for certain—everybody on the Internet uses e-mail.

According to the GVU's Fifth WWW User Survey, over 98 percent of the respondents use e-mail, compared to only 83 percent who use search engines and 44 percent who read newsgroups. In fact, many people maintain Internet accounts to use e-mail and for no other purpose.

Given e-mail's ubiquity among Net users and its inherent ability to target individuals directly, online marketers should be aware of several ways for using e-mail to reach their audience.

Autoresponders

E-mail autoresponders (also called "mailbots" and "mail-reflectors") provide an automatic, one-time, e-mail response to anybody who requests information. For example, you might have an interesting or persuasive message that you'd like to share with the world, such as, hypothetically, why eating organically grown produce leads to a lower incidence of colon/rectal cancer. If somebody were to ask you about this, adequately explaining your position may require several hundred words. In many cases, you would rather just have somebody read a good article about the topic, perhaps one that you have written.

Autoresponders allow you to make such an article conveniently accessible to anybody who would like to read it.

> **TIP:** It is often more convenient for people to obtain information through your autoresponder than through your Web site.

To receive your e-mailed article, all the reader has to do (depending on the service you use) is send a blank e-mail to, for example,

```
organic@yourfirm.com
```

Some autoresponders require that the requester place certain words into the subject line or body of the message; others ignore these fields. Once the autoresponder has received e-mail from the requester, that person's return e-mail address is read and used to deliver the article, often within just a few seconds—instant gratification!

The person who has requested your information then receives your e-mail article, which can be as short or long as any other e-mail. You have just received permission to fill somebody's mailbox with your material. Your article could comprise purely academic research findings. It could be a long article containing a small ad for your organically grown product. Or it could only list a few research findings and spend the rest of its pages explaining why your product is great and providing ordering information. What you include is up to you. An e-mail autoresponse might contain a press release, a catalog, a price list, technical specifications, a brief pitch encouraging people to visit your Web site, something humorous, or a free sample of your subscription-based e-mail newsletter. Here are some e-mail tips to keep in mind:

- People are more likely to keep e-mail than they are to bookmark your site.

- People are more likely to forward e-mail to their friends than they are to pass along a site's URL.

- There are many people who almost never browse the Web but read and send e-mail many times each day.

- E-mail can deliver a more persuasive, single, linear message than Web sites, which are better suited for providing nonlinear exploration of a network of associated ideas.

Autoresponders are easy to set up. If you use an Internet service provider, it can probably provide this functionality within a couple of days for about $10-15 per month and a $25 one-time set up fee. If you shop around, you can find services around the country that will give you a year of service for as little as $75, with no limit on the number of requests it receives or fills. Once your autoresponder is set up, it operates 24-hours per day, and you can change the outgoing message for a small administrative fee. Some services that require the requesters to type predetermined words into the subject or body of the message will allow you to reply with as many as 10 different messages—depending on the words in the message line—for no extra charge. While this requires the requester to take an extra step in order to receive the correct file, it also allows you to target multiple markets or promote multiple products.

TIP: One of the best ways to promote your autoresponse message is to mention it in the signature at the end of all e-mail you send out, including posts to newsgroups and public mailing lists (see sigvertising, later in this chapter).

Encouraging Word of Mouth

This wine seller has done a good job of letting other people do the marketing for it. Imagine how getting this e-mail into just one person's hands might quickly lead to reaching many others.

"You and a friend may win your choice of matching trips for two to either Bordeaux, France or Napa Valley, California.

All you need to do is visit The Chateau Select Wines & Gifts WWW site (URL below) and enter The Wines Of The World Sweepstakes.

http://www.chateau-select-wines.com

Now, to greatly increase your odds of winning, simply forward this E-mail message to your friends, request they enter the same as you did and include your name on the entry. If either of you are selected in our sweepstakes drawing, you both win matching prizes!"

Public Mailing Lists

There are over 50,000 publicly accessible mailing lists that you can use to reach narrowly targeted markets. These lists are very similar to Usenet newsgroups in that they are dedicated to specific topics of discussion and are read by groups ranging from as few as a dozen people to over 10,000 subscribers. Lists typically appeal to smaller groups of people with more specialized interests than do typical newsgroups.

Public mailing lists allow their readers to post e-mails to every other member on the list. Some of these groups are moderated, meaning that the list owner filters through the submissions and decides which messages will be sent out to the list. Some lists are also available in a "digest" version, which periodically distributes recent submissions in one long e-mail rather than multiple, one-message e-mails. Public mailing lists should not be confused with private or "house" lists, such as a list of all the e-mail addresses of people who have purchased a company's products (discussed below).

Promoting Your Site to Mailing Lists

> **TIP:** *Always* find out a list's rules about commercial announcements before you do anything.

A word of caution—one of the few things more risky or potentially inappropriate than advertising on Usenet (see Chapter 12) is breaking the rules when advertising on public mailing lists. Many lists expressly forbid such uses of the list, and these guidelines should always be respected. Each mailing list carries with it a community composed of the list's recipients and its administrator or moderator. This community is similar to that which exists for a Usenet newsgroup, with one key distinction. With any newsgroup, there are infrequent readers as well as the "regulars." However, because everybody on a mailing list receives every submission (though they may not read them all), every person on the list is more like a regular. This gives mailing lists a more "private party" atmosphere than many newsgroups of the same size. The feeling of anonymity is diminished on a mailing list, suggesting that certain offensive behaviors—such as sending flames or using profanity—will be tolerated less on lists than they might be on a newsgroup.

Any discussion of marketing to mailing lists would probably begin with a thorough coverage of marketing to newsgroups due to the two media's similarity. If you are considering this as a way to promote your site, you should first read Chapter 12 (which covers posting to Usenet) and the FAQs that it mentions; most of the rules of Usenet Netiquette apply to public mailing lists. For example, blatant commercialism is not appreciated on most lists, yet some will allow certain appropriate types of announcements.

On-topic Messages

Like Usenet, some lists allow all sorts of advertising while others expressly prohibit all forms. And like Usenet, most lists fall somewhere in between these extremes—generally allowing one, nonhyped announcement if your subject matter is on topic with the list's focus. Be very judicious about what you consider to be on topic; as with Usenet readers, list readers are smart enough to know when you are grasping to make a loose association between your product and their discussion.

Generally speaking, list subscribers (and Usenet readers) do not want to hear announcements from "outsiders" because this opens the door to every unrelated advertiser on the Net. You should be a regular reader or active participant of a group before you make any commercial announcement. Assuming the list allows commercial announcements, it's a good idea to begin with something like,

```
I've been a subscriber to this list for a few weeks now
and I thought some of you might have an interest in...
```

Because public mailing lists' audiences remain made up of mostly the same people over long periods of time, *one announcement* is all that is necessary, if indeed such one-time announcements are allowed.

Sigvertising

As with newsgroups that allow no commercial announcements, mailing lists that prohibit commercial announcements will generally permit you to include a brief signature at the end of your message. This is an excellent way to let people know about your Web site, e-mail autoresponder, or your own mailing list, as in this example from a mailing list owner (although Netiquette suggests that this signature is a little too long):

```
^^^^^^^^^^^^^^^^^^^^^^^^^^^^^^^^^^^^^^^^^^^^^^^^^^^^^^^^^^^^^^^
Owner of online mailing list that gives access to name
brand merchandise at up to 70% off retail. Part of prof-
its benefit children with learning and attention prob-
lems. For info, e-mail ot@sprynet.com or subscribe TO:
majordomo@databack.com with Message: Subscribe savemoney
```

Avoid "Velveeta," the derogatory name given to submitting many short messages when one message should have contained all the points. Unfortunately, some online marketers abuse sigvertising by posting frequently rather than substantively. This type of behavior is fairly transparent and is not appreciated on mailing lists or newsgroups.

Always be cautious about abusing sigvertising by contributing fluff or nonsubstantive remarks. Apply this test to yourself: Would you still post if you were not going to include your signature? If so, then you are probably contributing something worthwhile to the discussion.

Locating the Right Lists

Several excellent online resources allow you to search databases of public mailing lists by their name, topic, or keywords. Search to find mailing lists using the keywords you used to register your site with directories and search engines (Chapter 8).

Visit *each* of the three following directories to look for lists. Their records overlap somewhat, but not as closely as you might think. You will always be able to find a list on one of these directories that is not listed with the other two.

- Liszt Directory:

    http://www.liszt.com

- Tile.Net/lists:

    http://www.tile.net/tile/listserv/index.html

- Internet Publicly Accessible Mailing Lists

    http://www.neosoft.com/internet/paml

Contacting the List

The above directories will provide you with specific instructions for getting information or subscribing to any list that you find. Upon subscribing to a list, you will usually receive an automated message explaining how to use the list. This includes administrative issues (such as unsubscribing and accessing archives) as well as instructions on how to contribute to the list and what types of messages are appropriate. There will often be a specific mention of the list's rules for making commercial announcements.

If the information message does not mention advertising, *do not* assume it is okay to advertise. It probably isn't okay. Instead, look for an e-mail

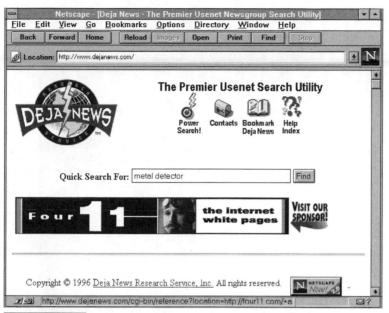

FIGURE 13.1 Liszt allows you to search over 54,000 mailing lists.

address for a real person, such as the list owner. Contact this person directly and find out the rules. It will help if you describe who you are and how your topic is relevant—but avoid any trace of hype. To do a good job of explaining how your site is relevant to the group, it will help if you have been reading the list for a while before you make your first contact.

Filtering Your Own E-mail

If you subscribe to even one mailing list (and certainly if you subscribe to many), you will begin receiving a great volume of e-mail. Buying more sophisticated e-mail management software, if you do not already own it, is worth the investment. Qualcomm's Eudora Pro (as opposed to it's entry-level product, Eudora Light) allows you to define rules-based filters that separate your incoming mail into different mailboxes based on factors such as who sent the mail, words in the subject line, and so on (see Figure 13.2).

Host Your Own Public List

One of the strongest online marketing assets you can build is to host your own public mailing list, one that becomes popular. For very little money, you can control the daily messages that are sent to thousands of people within a very specific niche. Because receiving e-mail is a passive procedure

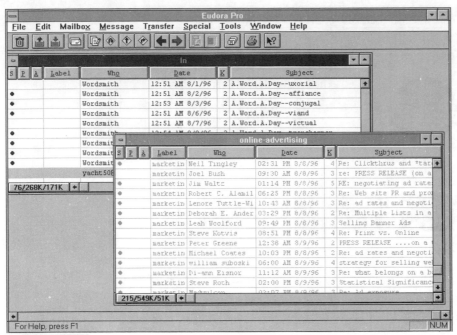

FIGURE 13.2 Eudora Pro e-mail software can sort your mail before you read it.

once people subscribe, you will contact your audience far more frequently than you ever could with a Web site. As the list's owner, it is up to you what—if any—advertising you wish to allow. You could promote your own site but allow no others to do so.

> **TIP:** Sell sponsorships to your mailing list.

The practice of providing advertiser sponsorship opportunities on lists—even small lists (500 subscribers)—is becoming very popular among list owners and sponsors alike. Some list owners have reported receiving 10 cents per name for including a brief message from their sponsors. A sponsorship might take the form of several lines attached to each e-mail message distributed to the entire list, such as this one from the Online Advertising Discussion List (http://www.tenagra.com/online-ads):

```
This week's Online Advertising Discussion List sponsor:
WEB ADVERTISING '96 How to Bring the World to Your Web
Site.
Oct. 31-Nov. 1, New York. $1,000 in Free Web Advertising
for each company sending attendees. For more info:
www.thunderlizard.com/WebAdv.html.
```

Your Internet service provider will probably be able to set up a mailing list for you. It is basically a separate e-mail account that includes a list of all the people who will receive your messages. Anybody with an e-mail account can automatically subscribe, unsubscribe, or contribute to the list. If you choose, you can assign somebody as a moderator to control which messages are distributed to the list. Mailing lists cost in the neighborhood of $15 per month plus a one-time $25 set-up fee. As always, prices will vary so shop around.

Everybody thinks to register their site with search engines, but many list owners forget to register their mailing lists so that people will be able to find them. If you host your own list, be sure to register it with as many directories of lists as you can find.

House Lists

Unlike a public list, a private list does not allow others to send messages to other people on the list. In fact, your personal e-mail software might allow you to keep a list of "nicknames" that makes it easy to send e-mail to your friends. This is an example of a small house list. For your business, the possible uses are many. You could use a house list frequently or infrequently to send your customers:

- Price updates
- News of site updates
- "What's New" industry announcements
- Noncommercial but related information
- Newsletters (both free or subscription-based)
- E-mail catalogs that sell directly, circumventing your site

Building a House List

The most important thing to remember about building your own in-house, private mailing list is to include only the names of people who have asked to be included. Some sites that require each user to register (and therefore have the person's e-mail address) may send out periodic announcements or surveys to their registered users, but this edges closer to the edge of a somewhat gray area: "What is and what is not considered unsolicited?"

Some site owners feel that any visitor who gives out his or her e-mail address is giving implied permission to send e-mail. While I can understand this logic, I recommend that site owners avoid ambiguity by stating their intent anywhere that users are asked to provide their e-mail addresses. To avoid any confusion, simply state on your forms that you periodically send out announcements to your customers and site visitors. When this statement is included on the form, the user's consent is more than just implied. By submitting the form (with the required e-mail address field filled in) the user gives consent.

To diminish users' fears and increase the number of people who fill in your forms, tell them that you will not release their names or e-mail addresses to anybody. This does not prevent you from including sponsors' messages in e-mail that you send to your private list.

The best way to build a house list is to offer something valuable to people who give you their address. This could be a newsletter, jokes, tips, or anything related to your target market and your site. Some Web businesses have no immediate plans for using their house list, yet they collect names for future use. These sites tend to take a very passive approach, such as including a field on their feedback and order forms that allows people to check a box if they would like to be added to the mailing list.

A more proactive approach is to assume that you *will* want to do a mailing eventually. Place a distinct button somewhere on a prominent page next to a sentence such as this:

```
Place yourself on our e-mail list to receive occasional,
hilarious newsletters (whenever we get around to writing
them). Our mothers tell us they're very well written.
```

Naturally, if you administer a public mailing list, promote *it* at your Web site, even if one of the primary functions of the list is to promote your Web site. Each marketing tool should help people find the other tool.

A company called Wishing offers e-mail "snoop" "plug-in CGI" that allows you to easily build a list made up of any site visitors who click on a button. Upon clicking the button, users are asked whether they wish to release their e-mail address. If they consent, then their browser automatically sends it without the user having to type anything. You can build multiple lists that divide visitors into categories by providing multiple choice buttons from which to choose (e.g., "Do you like CATS or DOGS better?" would build a list of cat-people and a list of dog-people). See Chapter 7 for information on Wishing's prices and other plug-in CGI products.

> **Defaulting Inclusion on Mailing Lists**
>
> If you provide any sort of online form to your users, it is fairly common to let them choose whether they would like to be included on your private mailing list. There are two ways to do it, depending on whether you would like to build a list emphasizing quantity or quality of names.
>
> 1. Default Places Them on List—Good for Building *Bigger* Lists
>   In this case, the user must take action (such as deselecting a preselected check box) to not be placed on the list. Most people either will or won't want to be on your list. But borderline cases will be more likely to allow themselves to be added to your list because this choice requires no action. As such, this will tend to create a larger list by including the people who don't have a strong feeling either way.
>
> 2. Default Does Not Place Them on List—Good for Building *Better* Lists
>   In this case, the user must take action (such as selecting a check box) to be placed on the list. This means that the borderline cases will be less likely to include themselves. As such, this practice will tend to create a list of more highly qualified members. This option might be better if you ever expect to spend money or time contacting individuals on the list, such as by sending them postal mail or calling them on the phone.

A Very Bad Idea: Sending Unsolicited Mail

With all of the great opportunities that e-mail provides for reaching potential customers, it is perhaps natural to consider the idea of sending e-mail announcing your site or selling products through e-mail sent to random strangers, whose e-mail addresses you've found elsewhere.

> DON'T DO IT.

At the time of this book's writing, there is a hot debate raging between two groups: The first group, 2 percent (I estimate) of the world that thinks unsolicited e-mail is the direct marketer's best dream-come-true since the invention of the business reply card; the other group, the 98 percent of the world that correctly believes that recipients of junk-e-mail (unlike postal junk mail) bear the costs associated with receiving unwanted mail. These costs come not only in the form of adding difficulty to the daily task of screening e-mail (looking for those that are important or wanted), but in the more tangible financial realities associated with the fact that Internet bandwidth and server capacity are not free. They are cheap, but not free. If every user on the planet began receiving a dozen unsolicited e-mails for every legitimate e-mail, then the entire system would be put under a tremendous, unnecessary burden. The only way to expand capacity to meet that burden would be to build more infrastructure—the costs of which would ultimately make their way down to the recipient, probably in the form of higher monthly fees paid to Internet service providers.

That would mean paying more money for something that you don't even want to read. Proponents of sending unsolicited e-mail, however, argue that some percentage of the population *does* want to receive this mail, particularly when the lists have been obtained from sources that are logically related to the sender's advertisement. The problem with this perspective is that, as long as sending e-mail costs the sender nothing, there is no incentive to discriminate among which addresses advertisers choose to use. After all, even when advertisers *do* have to pay the cost of delivery—as with postal mail—look how much junk people still receive. Now imagine how much junk we would all receive if postage were free!

While this battle rages on, sending unsolicited e-mail (which is coming to be known as "e-mail spamming") is considered to be every bit as rude and inappropriate as is spamming on Usenet or public mailing lists. Perpetrators are dealt with severely in many cases—such as Net-wide product boycotts—even though some of the perpetrators were hapless victims, inexperienced in Netiquette, who signed up for the services of unscrupulous Internet spammers calling themselves "marketing consultants."

The potential draw of the medium still remains, however. History shows that strong public resentment will not keep everybody from breaking rules that are hard to enforce. Somewhere in the Internet of the future, there may be a way for the most aggressive of direct marketers and Netizens to coexist happily. For example, some industry pundits have proposed e-mail labeling standards, "micro-payment" options and, "opt-out" methods. This means that you might automatically know which e-mail was commercial before you read it, you might be able to receive a 10 cent fee for every commercial e-mail you choose to read, and you might be able to classify yourself as somebody who would rather not receive any of these e-mails. With some or all of these conventions in place, marketers might be able to reach those people who don't mind receiving unsolicited e-mail while bearing the cost of taking up their time. Until that day, however, consider unsolicited e-mail off limits.

—three—

DESIGNING YOUR SITE TO MAKE MONEY

BUILDING A SITE
AROUND YOUR
BUSINESS MODEL

O nce you've decided on your business model and figured out which customers you're going to target, it's time to get down to the nitty-gritty of building a site that stands a chance of performing well.

"Design" Means More Than Pretty Graphics

Web designers do much more than pick out colors, resize photos of the CEO, and create cute navigational icons out of stick men. The word "design" refers to the holistic approach to solving the problem: How should your business or department best utilize the Web to achieve its marketing objectives? Site design encompasses decisions such as these:

- How long or short should your site be?

- In what style should your site's text be written?

- How should visitors navigate through the site?

- What features should be placed most prominently?

- What features should remain subtle?

- What characteristics should be added to appeal to your niche?

- What characteristics will make people want to return?

- What features should be added to make people tell their friends about it?

To do a good job of meshing your site's design with your intended strategy and business model requires a blend of talents that sometimes—rarely—exist in one person. Even many Web design firms have unevenly distributed skills in the areas that are required to do this job well.

If you hire a Web design firm or assemble a team, focus on finding a balance among the three requisite proficiencies:

1. Technical skills

2. Design/aesthetic perception

3. Marketing savvy and business sense

The person designing your site from the ground up must start by considering the site's intended purpose, the intended market, and how the business intends to engage that market both now and in the future. The designer should also have a fair grasp of current and anticipated competitive threats.

Chapter 4 is devoted to the factors that influence the selection of your strategy and business model. This chapter gives specific advice on building a site with these concerns in mind. If you are not reading this book from cover to cover and have not read Chapter 4, then I recommend that you skim its contents for salient points that apply to this discussion.

So You've Got Your Strategy... Now What?

Recall that marketers attempt to make their sites profitable in several different ways, such as streamlining operations in existing companies, seeking advertiser sponsorship, providing value-added services, and selling products and services. Naturally, these strategies are not mutually exclusive, and it is possible to employ all of them in one site, to varying degrees, if you choose to do so.

Implementing Advertising Strategy into Design

If you think you might be seeking advertiser sponsorship, then design your page format from the beginning with prominent links or banner ad spots in mind, rather than adding them as an afterthought. (See Chapter 10 for more on advertiser sponsorship.)

If you have long-term sponsors (more than 30 days), try to integrate their banners or logos attractively into your site. You might make their graphic element one of the linkable items an imagemap, rather than sticking it in the corner with a box around it. The idea is to keep its presence from being the only incongruous element on an otherwise great-looking page. If an advertiser has supplied a graphic that does not fit with your site's ambiance, work together to come up with something better. It's in the advertiser's interest as well as yours. (For a site design built to accommodate more than 50 long-term sponsors, see the case study, Year 2000, Chapter 10.)

If you participate in a banner exchange network, you never know what the banner your site displays will look like. Odds are, the colors will clash with your entire site. Many banner exchanges will stipulate placement at the top of the page. That's okay; this gets business out of the way before people start exploring your site.

Give these banners a place of their own so that they don't look like an afterthought. In this way, you can attempt to integrate them with your site, but still separate them from you.

Designing a Site Around a Value-Added Feature

For our purposes, "value-added" sites are those that utilize interactivity to "do something" for their visitors. The most well-known examples are the directories and search engines like Yahoo! and Infoseek. Other examples include stock look-up services, customized fitness routines, and mortgage calculators.

I have seen a few sites fumble in their attempts to offer this sort of customized page results because they made it too difficult for the user to reach the page offering the feature. Deciding which sections of an ordinary site to make the most prominent is usually a difficult decision for Web designers. But not in this case.

TIP: If your site offers an interactive, value-added service, then make the input for the service *impossible* to miss.

That might mean placing the input form directly on the front page. If it is relevant, you might even place it on *every* page of your site. Infoseek and other search engines, for instance, allow you to modify your search or begin a new search *directly on the results page from the last search*—you don't have to click the "back" button to use it again.

There are two strategies that nearly every site can (or should) utilize. You've already heard a lot about them. They are niche-exploitation and building a repeat customer base.

Exploiting Niches

We have already discussed the supreme importance of choosing a well-defined, targetable niche and staking a claim to your corner of the Web. But what does it actually mean to fill a niche? The metaphor comes from biology. Imagine a river with a swift current that has made all of the rocks on the sides and bottom of the river very smooth. Along comes a creature looking for a place to live. He can't hang onto slimy rocks, so he finds a crack in one of the rocks—an empty niche—and occupies it, living the rest of his days eating stuff that drifts by.

Think about how this applies to a business. If you find a good niche, food comes to you. It's better to find a niche that is unoccupied. To "fill" a niche suggests that you leave room for nobody else. Because there are few slimy rocks or cracks along the I-way, nichedom is totally virtual, totally nonphysical. The only thing that makes any site different from any other is the information provided at that site and people's perception of the site. The information you provide is the engine that drives your business. The perception you create is its body and wheels.

> Perception is created by *identity*.

Identity

Suppose somebody visits a page and then returns weeks later, after almost all of the content has changed. Yet the visitor also knows he or she has arrived at the same company's site. How does he or she know this is the same virtual space seen before?

> "Identity" is anything that identifies you as you.

Identity comes from a combination of things: background color, logo, the site's name, the style of artwork, the composition of page layout, and so on. Any Web consultant worth his or her fee would tell you that all of these should be crafted to appeal to the target audience. In fact, even the ones not worth their fee could probably clear this hurdle. The trick comes in *implementing* this profound—if obvious—wisdom. Here's the trick:

> **T I P :** When establishing your site's identity, don't focus on the audience, focus on the *niche—and the audience will follow!*

Distill the essence of whatever your niche is and *scream it at the top of your lungs* in every way you can think of. If you're creating a site about home-built submarines, don't bother with notions like, "Hmm—let's see, home-built submarine enthusiasts tend to be balding males between the age of 24 and 35, so let's show a bald guy." No, no, no! That's all backwards. If you scream "HOME-BUILT SUBMARINES" loudly enough, your audience *will find you.* And you will also appeal to enthusiasts who happen to be females with hair.

This is what Netscape has done for its product line. Other than the N-stepping-over-the-planet logo, all of its corporate communications center around the "navigator" theme.

> You know an identity is strong when you see a new piece and instantly recognize it as a member of its family.

If you've looked around much at Netscape's site, then you know what I mean. For server-throughput economy, its graphics need to be sparse, yet on almost every page, the site subtly manages to convey a flavor of adven-

FIGURE 14.1 Netscape's site has one of the strongest identities you will find on a site with quick-downloading pages. Great concept, brilliant execution. The color originals are worth checking out at http://www.netscape.com.

ture and exploration with a ubiquitous motif of nautical charts and sapphire-blue seas merging into starry skies. Pretty complex, when you think about it; stars connote both futuristic exploration, as well as historical navigation.

Figure 14.1 depicts a few of the graphics, reproduced in beautiful shades of splotchy gray for your viewing pleasure. I can almost hear Enya singing "Caribbean Blue" as I look at them.

The Home Page: What's the First Thing People See?

> **TIP:** Don't forget this—many people will not enter your site through the home page. (See Chapter 16.)

Consider these two home pages: Qualcomm (makers of Eudora E-mail software) and CommerceNet (a nonprofit consortium dedicated to accelerating electronic commerce) (see Figures 14.2 and 14.3).

I'm pitting these two sites against each other because both organizations are fairly well known, they are compositionally similar to one another (big globe plus navigational icons along the left), and both of these entities are directed at businesspeople who use the Internet. This means you are the target market. In all fairness, CommerceNet is a nonprofit organization. I would cut it some slack except that its raison d'être is "accelerating electronic commerce." As such, I am holding it to the standard of firms that engage in electronic commerce. (I discuss CommerceNet's navigational cues again in Chapter 16.)

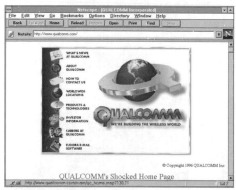

FIGURE 14.2 Organization: Qualcomm Site Identity Grade: B+

FIGURE 14.3 Organization: Commerce-Net Site Identity Grade: C

Analysis: Qualcomm

Site Identity Grade: B+

Personal aesthetic judgments will always vary, but the technical production of Qualcomm's graphics are among the best you'll see. Additionally, all elements are congruous with one another, created in the same clean style. You have a reasonably good idea what the company does based on its tag line, "We're building the wireless world." The globe/Q logo depicts this purpose; a Q (for "Qualcomm," of course) is literally surrounding and connecting everyone on the planet. The only reason Qualcomm doesn't get an A+ for site identity is that subsequent pages do not conform to the style or quality standards of the home page. At first glance, some interior pages even appear to belong to a different company, which is total failure from an identity perspective.

Analysis: CommerceNet

Site Identity Grade: C

Technical implementation of most of the graphics is reasonably good, but the inconsistency of style destroys any attempt at establishing a strong identity. The AT&T-like globe graphic and the Dr. Seuss-like navigational icons appear to have been created by different people in different rooms who never spoke to each other and may not even like each other. The name of the site's owner is not immediately clear to the random visitor. "CommerceNet" does appear several times, but there is no

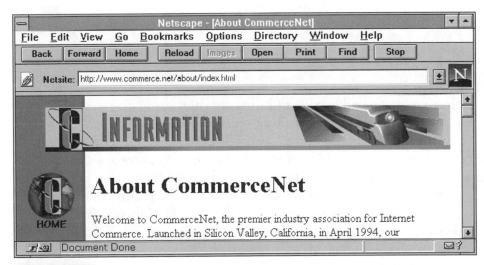

FIGURE 14.4 An eclectic choice of styles makes for a weak site identity.

masthead and the logo is virtually hidden in the small globe in the upper left-hand corner. Only on subsequent pages can the visitor get an idea of what the organization does. Subsequent pages are consistent only in that they are all *inconsistent*—styles seem to fluctuate randomly, as seen in Figure 14.4, which shows what users see after clicking on "About CommerceNet."

We see that clicking on "About CommerceNet" leads to a page entitled "Information," which depicts a 3D-rendered speeding train. Not only is the train a different artistic style from both the home page globe and the cartoon-style navigational icons, but what does a train have to do with either of the page's apparent names, "Information" or "About CommerceNet"? They might as well have used a photograph of a pizza slice.

Killer Copywriting

It goes without saying that poor writing has no place on a commercial Web site. "Good" writing, therefore, is what we'll call the minimum level of acceptability—it is that which clearly conveys pertinent information. "Great" copy is that which *strengthens identity* at the same time it conveys crucial information or persuades people to act.

Even many small companies have at least one person on staff who is a very good writer and who understands the business well enough to fill blank Web pages with words. If this person also has a mind for marketing, then he or she might be the ideal point-person for dealing with a Web design firm.

TIP: The members of a good Web design firm will deliver a site with strong visual identity. Persuasive copy, however, will depend on what you give them to work with.

Objectivity is one advantage of hiring a design firm—in essence, you benefit by what they *don't know* about your business. As such, they can try new angles that you would never have considered. But Web designers must concentrate most on the *delivery* of your message. That means they usually don't create that message. Ultimately, you must tell them what needs to be said, even if they have a professional copywriter on hand to make it sound good. Finding this skill at a small design firm can be difficult. If you hire one, check its portfolio sites to assess the quality of writing. If it isn't superb, then provide your own text, whether you write it yourself or hire a professional copywriter.

Niche Exploitation Case Study: Hot Hot Hot (http://www.hothothot.com)

Hot Hot Hot is a small company (three employees) that sells 450 varieties of hot sauce from all over the world. It has a physical store located in Pasadena, California. Web sales now account for 25 percent of its business (see Figure 14.5).

Niche Selection Grade: A+

This product category is a natural for the Web—the kind that lures investors after they've heard only two sentences. That's high concept. Consider the strategic advantages of selling exotic hot sauces:

- Unfilled niche—little or no direct competition

- Highly newsworthy due to its uniqueness

- Defensible niche—being "another hot sauce site" is not newsworthy; newcomers would have to establish relations with hundreds of obscure hot sauce manufacturers that one of the Hot Hot Hot owners developed while traveling the world in a jazz band

- Good margins on a relatively non-perishable food product

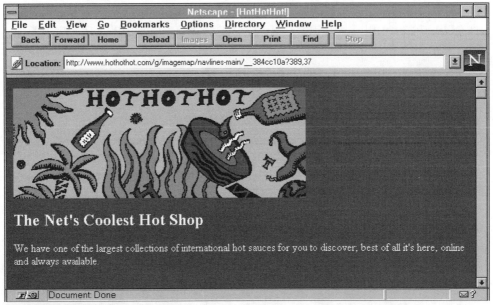

FIGURE 14.5 Hot Hot Hot's homepage (http://www.hothothot.com)

- One of the few experiential products (food, music, movies, etc.) that can be reasonably well described (by it's "heat level")

- Highly targetable—there are even print publications catering to "Chileheads"

- Yet generalizable—any culinary venue is potential exposure

- Excellent gift appeal—$5–25 items, small size, novel

- Product names that literally sell themselves (see below)

- Highly expandable site—could include recipes or country information, allowing marketing efforts to draw new people from different related niches

Site Identity Grade: A+

Graphics—The chosen graphical style of this site is perfect, feisty yet unintimidating (see Figure 14.6). The graphics somehow manage to make the idea of burning your mouth seem fun.

Site Structure—The structure of the site organizes a very large inventory into fun ways of exploring: by heat level, origin, ingredients, or name (see Figure 14.7).

Writing—This site sports some of the most clever sales copy you'll see on the Web. Again, the fear and anxiety we'd normally associate with eating fire is made to sound exciting or fun. Here are some samples of fun text from the Hot Hot Hot site:

> "Join our Frequent Fire(TM) Club"

Heat rating scale:

> "Fiery—For the truly dedicated culinary thrill seeker, these sauces are predominately Habanero pepper. Not for the shy, they're for the bungie-jumping, sky-diving thrill seekers of chile pepper pleasure."

FIGURE 14.6 Spicy graphics—very appropriate for a hot sauce site.

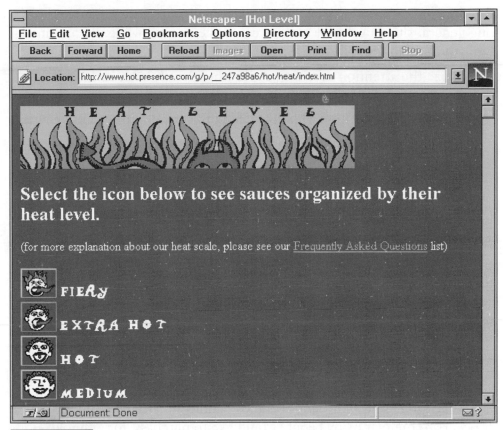

FIGURE 14.7 Visitors can look up sauces by their heat level.

Sample product names:

"Capital Punishment

This sauce was created for those who treat every
meal as if it were their last. Not even a call
from the Governor can save you. Imported from
Merida, in the Yucatan Peninsula..."

Multiple-Web Presences

One of the most clever ways that you can make your products appeal to
more people is to employ what I call *multiniching*. Rather than designing
your site to have general appeal, create several sites (related to your product or service) that each have an extremely targeted and narrow focus.

Building and promoting each of these sites will take more time than just one general site, but the advantages can make it worthwhile. By multiniching, you may so the following:

- Seize the attention of more people who identify with each site's sharper focus
- Outflank competitors who don't think to spread into separate niches
- Register each entry site separately with search engines
- Announce each site separately to newsgroups
- Avoid being off-topic with targeted newsgroups and mailing lists

Multiple Entry Points

In Chapter 7, I described a way of using "antechambers" or "portal pages" to measure which sources generate traffic for your site. In that description, several identical pages (with their own counters) all led visitors to your home page. To target different niches without creating entirely new sites, simply change the message of each of these points of entry. The changes could be as simple as modifying text or as sophisticated as creating unique identities or even "mini-sites" for each entry path (see Figure 14.8).

In this, my favorite example of this strategy, a hypothetical site called Terra Incognita sells indigenous people's handicrafts from around the world. It occurs to me that many people would like to purchase, for example, a Navajo rug or an aboriginal boomerang, but finding such people might be a challenge. The novelty of the product category makes it unlikely that anybody would do a search on "boomerang," for example, if he or she were doing Christmas shopping. However, if they were to chance on such an item, it might be the perfect bizarre gift they were looking for.

To attract these customers, and every other category of customers we can think of, we could create a mini-site (one to three pages, perhaps) based on each of the following topics:

- Handicrafts
- Adventure travel
- Home furnishings
- African art
- Environmentalism

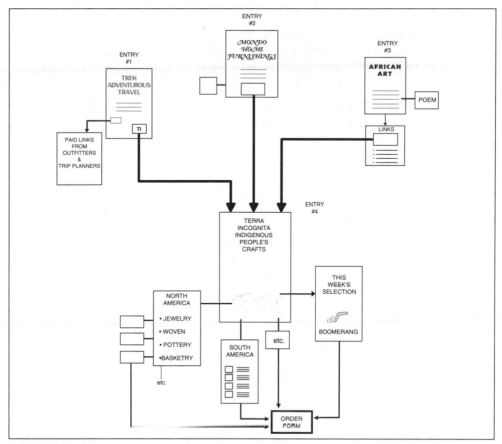

FIGURE 14.8 You can create several niche-specific entry points for one site.

On the environmentalism page, for example, you could tell stories about how indigenous cultures can help stem deforestation by selling hand-made crafts with local raw materials, much in the same way Ben & Jerry's Rainforest Crunch encourages Brazil-nut farmers to resist burning their lands in the Amazon river basin.

This ecological concept alone would generate amazing amounts of publicity for you in traditional media, but—if it were the only focus of your site—then you would niche yourself right out of other specialized markets such as adventure travel and home furnishings. The newsgroups addressing these categories would find an ecology-oriented announcement to be off topic and therefore inappropriate. However, you could be a regular contributor with an obvious link to many environmentally oriented newsgroups.

Likewise, if you were to create a separate entry point geared toward all of the people who like to (or wish they could) travel to places like Machu Picchu or Patagonia, then you could essentially bill a specialized entry site as "what to buy and what not to buy while you're there." This is a totally different angle, one that would allow you to post on topic to dozens of travel-related newsgroups—who just so happen to be read by people who would also be interested in buying your wares.

Parallel Sites

Parallel sites, as shown in Figure 14.9, a are sort of top-heavy variation on the multiple entry-points concept. That is, two fully grown sites exist as distinct entities, but they share some common elements, such as graphic elements or a centralized order-taking page. In the diagram, two sites have been created to appeal to two different niches. The two sites use the same design and utilize much of the same artwork and copywriting. They share

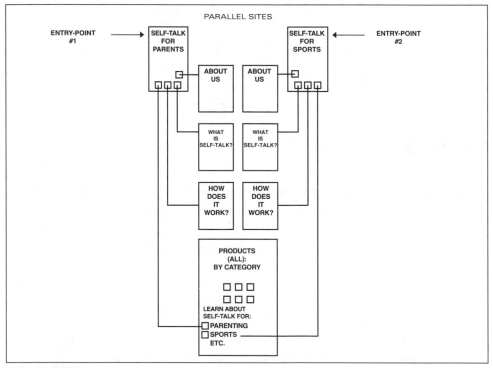

FIGURE 14.9 Appeal to different niches by erecting nearly identical sites that cater to different visitors.

a common products page. This allows customers to access more information (the other half of the site) that they might find interesting.

Why would anybody do this? Consider Self-Talk, a self-help product that we sell through http://monsoon.org/selftalk. Self-help products are a strange animal; some people like them, some people don't. Those who do tend to fall into three categories. The first is the mainstream group, such as moms and dads who want to raise their children to have good self-esteem, try hard at school, and so on. The second group is people who are perhaps down on their luck, searching for something to buoy their spirits or teach them how to regain control over their lives. The third category is what I affectionately call the "overachievers"; they are the unstoppable people ranging from people we know, to athletes, to Fortune 500 CEOs who are constantly looking for any little thing that will give them an extra edge.

Simultaneously reaching these three groups presents a challenge. The site offers products for everybody, but promoting a "jack-of-all-trades" site on the Web is the antithesis of niche marketing. Yet the mainstream group is hard to target because it's, well, mainstream. Some people in the second group—perhaps somebody who lives with an alcoholic—might be easier to target, but they aren't necessarily interested in the same things that would speak to the overachiever. Likewise, Fortune 500 CEOs probably won't respond well to a product that purports to help people "regain control of their lives."

This represents an extreme example of when parallel sites might be useful. Three different sites could be erected that are reasonably similar, but written with a different slant, such as providing different examples of people who have used the products. Other, more common examples exist for many product categories:

- Targeting experts versus novices
- Targeting wholesalers versus end consumers
- Targeting single people versus families

Interchangeable Parts: Designing Identity with Multiniching in Mind

If you foresee multiniching in your future, consider designing your logo and masthead so that you can carry a thread of identity across any parallel sites that allow access to one another. The degree of relatedness you'll want to establish between different sites or subsites will depend on your circumstances.

This concept applies well to malls: different stores should have their own subidentity, but you always want people to know they are still in the mall, if possible. You can accomplish this by carrying graphic elements across different sites, as seen in Figure 14.10. The "Self-Talk" logo appears on several home pages in different incarnations, depending on the niche being targeted. Additionally, the oval-shaped logo works as a stand-alone (with no masthead), which is useful as a unifying navigational element in many circumstances. For example, clicking on the logo in the upper-left corner of any page will always take users to the home page of that site.

Self-Sponsorship: Separating Commercial and Non-commercial

The Internet's history is steeped in what has been called a "gift culture." This ethos prevails even as the Web is consumed by the "Cult of Rampant Materialism." The difference is that people used to contribute to the Internet because they wanted to. Today's marketers contribute—for the

FIGURE 14.10 Mastheads with "interchangeable parts" will be cheaper to modify for niche-specific sites.

most part—because they must. We must offer something of value just to entice people to visit. This is a good thing; it seems to be working so far and balancing things on the whole.

As you think of things that you may provide, free of charge, for your viewers, recognize that some of the most popular sites on the Web give a lot while selling nothing. By separating your commercial activities and noncommercial "gift" activities, you gain several advantages:

- Potentially greater likelihood of having your site mentioned in the media

- Greater flexibility when posting to newsgroups

- Greater editorial flexibility

- Creating goodwill among the Internet community

This last point is more than touchy-feelie. Remember that, while Net culture—seen at its strongest in Usenet newsgroups—does not damn commercialism per se, so-called "blatant" commercialism leaves a bad taste in a lot of people's mouths. By separating the commercial and noncommercial aspects of your site in a church-and-state kind of way, you remove the blatantness (see Figure 14.11).

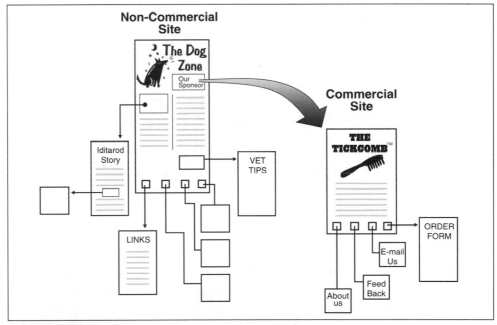

FIGURE 14.11 Splitting your site into commercial and noncommercial parts offers certain advantages.

If done properly, there is nothing deceptive about this site design. In fact, it would be foolish to even come close to misrepresenting yourself or obscuring the ownership relationship between the two sites. To make sure you're in the clear, do the following:

- Sell nothing (except ad space, if you like) on the noncommercial side.

- Provide one link to your commercial side, as prominently as good taste allows, with words such as "produced by," or "brought to you by." This is your commercial, so it's okay to add a tag line describing what you do, for example.

- On the noncommercial side, display the copyright owner's name— which will usually be the same owner as your commercial side. If you have a separate "legal" page for copyright information, you might even state the exact relationship between the two sites so that nobody can deny your forthrightness.

- There is probably no need for a separate domain. Part of sponsoring the noncommercial site means hosting its Web pages.

So long as you are honest and don't use the noncommercial site to attempt to sneak in endorsements of your products, then this gift to the Internet community will be appreciated by every Web user who feels that random banner ads are making the Web a slow-downloading eyesore. This strategy will make some of these Netizens more likely to tell their friends about you or promote you in public forums.

Building a Repeat-Customer Base

Generally speaking, you do want repeat customers. Even if your site sells just one item, of which people are not likely to buy more than one unit, remember one thing:

> Web customers usually don't buy on the first visit.

This may change as we become more accustomed to buying online. But for now, much evidence suggests that people frequently come back to visit *several* times before making a purchase. This happens even when the site does not change and when visitors have no reason to expect it to change. Presumably, customers just want to think it over first.

TIP: Utilize tactics that encourage repeat visits if your site sells items that cost more than $20. Large-ticket items are not impulse buys and require multiple visits before a purchase is made, except when the user has come looking for a specific item, such as a particular software package.

Even if a visitor to your site is not planning any immediate purchases, the mere fact that he or she is visiting you makes him or her a better-than-average future sales prospect. If you can use any tactics that will make this person more likely to bookmark your page or repeat on a regular basis, then you are increasing the odds that he or she will eventually buy.

However, in some extreme instances repeat visitors are less desirable. If your server is receiving sufficient traffic that it becomes the access bottleneck to users (meaning that even their slow modems are waiting on your slower server) then non-purchasing visitors may actually cause would-be customers to become frustrated by waiting, causing them to leave your site.

Increasing server capacity or your Internet hookup bandwidth is one way to fix this problem temporarily, but the problem can and does occur even among the world's fastest servers when traffic gets heavy. In particular, if you have server-intensive options on your site that have a broad appeal and could be drawing repeat customers who have no intention of ever buying anything, then you might want to rethink your strategy.

As an example, I personally visited a *USA Today* page, buried deep within its site, every day for several months to look up stock quotes (see Figure 14.12). Because I had bookmarked the stock quote page, I never saw any of the site's other pages. *USA Today* was either being philanthropic (thanks, guys) or making an oversight because this stock lookup page had no advertisement on it—which is how the site is supposed to make money. If other users were doing the same thing as I, then the publication missed out on a good opportunity to sell some ad impressions. Five views per week for 12 weeks times however many people bookmarked that page— there is no way of knowing how much ad revenue it lost (see Figure 14.13).

The stock-lookup CGI script, while somewhat server-intensive, is not the worst thing that a deadweight visitor like me could have been accessing. Just imagine if I had been visiting a page with a lot of graphics or some streamed audio. I would have become the online equivalent of the guy who sits at a bar and drinks only water while eating the free pretzels—in other words, a poor use of the bar stool in the eyes of the establishment's proprietor, who would rather have a paying customer eating his pretzels.

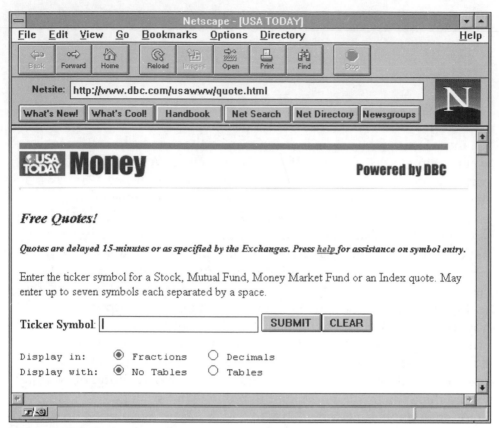

FIGURE 14.12 *USA Today* missed an opportunity to advertise on this page, which users may have bookmarked. "Powered by DBC" refers to the source of the stock quotes, but the words did not link anywhere and are useless unless one already knows what DBC is *and* how to reach it.

This insight should drive the design and strategy of your business model and site. Again, it goes without saying that repeat customers are good for almost everybody. But some Web businesses won't require them, whereas others will fundamentally depend on building repeat business. This suggests that sites geared toward impulse buyers or one-time purchases may wish to

FIGURE 14.13 This is an actual ad for Data Broadcasting Corporation that would have been perfect for USA Today's stock-lookup page.

make their site's most attractive features geared more toward generating word-of-mouth than generating repeat visits. The difference between these two is subtle, and usually involves *frequency of revision*.

> **T I P :** A "Joke of the Day" is better at drawing repeat visits. A list of great jokes is better at generating word-of-mouth.

Tips for Building Repeat Visits

Static site content cannot encourage repeat visits as much as constantly changing content. As such, building repeat visits is intimately tied to your decisions regarding how frequently to update your site. This decision has additional strategic implications, such as increasing costs of site maintenance.

Changing Content to Bring People Back

Most strategies related to building repeat business have one thing in common.

> **T I P :** Promise something people want. Tell them they must return later to get it. Give a specific time or day when it will be available.

Examples include the following:

- Contests (contestants must return to see if they've won)
- Weekly additions to substantive content (such as a newsletter)
- Weekly gimmicks (Top Ten lists, Joke-of-the-Day, etc.)
- Advice columns
- Public forums (chat, discussion group, guest books)

Ragu's Web site (http://www.eat.com) provides people with an easy way to receive updates regarding changes to the site. Users enter their e-mail addresses and push a button—very simple (see Figure 14.14). Ragu cleverly ties this technique in with the site's identity: "Don't forget your Mama!"

The following are some additional helpful hints:

- If you send out a newsletter; give it a name that is not only descriptive (so people will know what it is) but that also links it to the *identity* of your site.

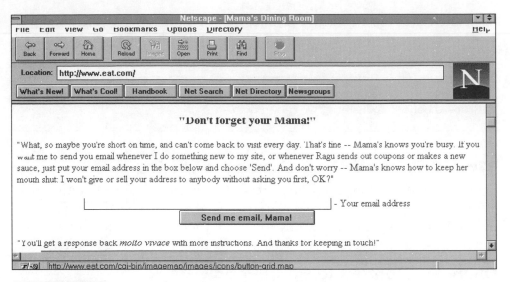

FIGURE 14.14 Ragu asks to keep in touch with visitors.

- If you use a Web service provider, ask it how much it would cost to include a "message board" on your site. This enables you to host public forums where your visitors can read or post their own messages. Prices will vary, but some providers offer message boards for a set-up fee of $100 plus $50 per month.

- For a one-time fee of $36 you can have six months of "WebGuest Plug-in CGI" provided by Wishing (http://www.wishing.com). This simple service creates a guest book on your site that your visitors can sign. While this is not as interactive as a public forum with separate threaded conversations, it is very inexpensive.

Interactivity Helps

According to Forrester Research, when a newspaper in Sydney, Australia, began putting interactive contests on its Web site, traffic jumped "2500 percent from 1,500 [visits] per day to nearly 40,000." One such contest allowed visitors to try to write the best caption for photographs depicting politicians in awkward poses.

Static Methods for Bringing People Back

Additionally, even if your site doesn't change, the sheer size and complexity of your site can keep people coming back to explore further, assuming your

FIGURE 14.15   MkzdK uses forms within tables within frames to navigate through a seemingly endless labyrinth of bizarre collections (http://www.envirolink.org/mkzdk/metadekon.html).

site is interesting. MkzdK's non-commercial, bizarre, and beautiful site almost seems to work by ensnaring visitors in a labyrinth-like world that is anything but simple to navigate (Figure 14.15). The sheer quantity and strangeness cause people who are interested in its esoteric subject matter to return again and again.

> **TIP:**   Implementing cookie technology is essential for ongoing "relationship marketing," in which you track preferences of individual site visitors or registered users. See Chapter 7 for more about cookies.

Asking Visitors to Bookmark Your Page

According to Intelliquest, as many as 44 percent of Web users "never" use bookmarks. If you're not familiar with the term, a bookmark is a feature on browsers such as Netscape Navigator that allows users to quickly tag any Web site they visit, recording the site's address onto a list stored by the browser software. By clicking on any item in this list of bookmarks, the user can later return instantly to that site without having to reenter the site's URL. If you are even considering operating a Web business, then I realize you probably know what bookmarks are.

> You should not assume that all users know what bookmarks are.

Tell people to bookmark your page, and tell them how to do it. Most Web sites do not tell visitors to bookmark them. Those that do usually assume that visitors know what bookmarking is. Such sites will sometimes suggest the best page for bookmarking, such as a home page or main menu that is guaranteed to exist in the future.

> You don't want people bookmarking your site's temporary pages.

Some sites go one step further and emphasize bookmarking heavily, including giving instructions on how to do it.

FIGURE 14.16 Deja News goes out of its way to encourage people to bookmark its site.

> If you teach a new user how to bookmark, you will probably be at the top of his or her list for a long time.

Deja News (http://www.dejanews.com) provides an excellent example of how to secure bookmarks with your visitors (see Figure 14.16). First, see how much prominence it gives the topic on its home page. There is always a trade-off when you choose navigational items. If you include too many, they all lose some impact. Deja News has been extremely judicious, allowing itself only four icons. One of these is called "Bookmark Deja News."

Once users click on this icon they arrive at a page that provides specific instructions for bookmarking the site (Figure 14.17).

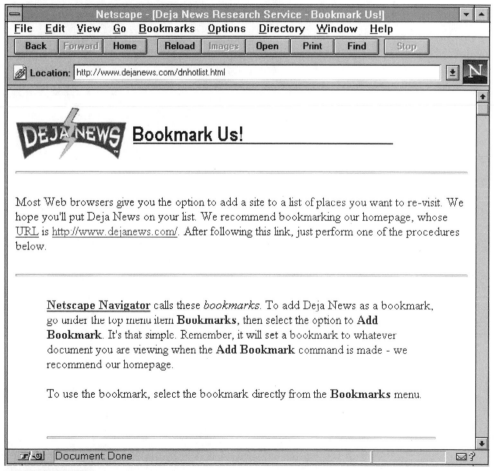

FIGURE 14.17 Deja News even explains how to bookmark pages for people who are not familiar with the technique.

A B S O L U T E
P R O F E S S I O N A L I S M

I f you read interviews conducted with owners of unprofitable Web sites, you will often hear about sales being poor due to users' fears regarding the security of credit card transactions. I find it remarkbly odd, however, that owners of *successful* sites indicate that users have little apprehension when it comes to giving out their credit card number online. Why this difference in beliefs?

The Importance of Looking Professional

As it turns out, surveys have shown that online shoppers are much more concerned about being ripped off by an incompetent or fraudulent Web-based company than they are about having their credit card number stolen by a hacker. The majority of Web customers aren't afraid of using their credit cards per se; they are only afraid of using them with some businesses. Without a person to talk to, a storefront to visit, or an address to send mail, shoppers can have a difficult time judging whether they're dealing with a reputable entity.

> **TIP:**   You need to look professional whether you are or not.

I say this only half-jokingly. On one hand, it goes without saying that anyone running or working for a business of any sort should endeavor to act with integrity at all times and strive to satisfy the customers. On the other hand, plenty of newcomers are venturing into unfamiliar realms of business, lacking the experience, skills, and resources required to do the job as well as it can be done. These individuals will, in time, become as professional as anybody else—if they survive long enough. That means attracting wary customers and serving them well, despite making beginners' mistakes, until eventually such mistakes rarely occur.

Tattoo this on the palm of your hand so you don't forget it:

> One of the primary objectives of your site is to remove customers' inherent fear of doing business online.

Given what we know about the source of customers' fear, this objective means you must do everything you can to come across as credible and competent.

> **TIP:** Worry more about your image than you worry about promoting transaction security.

The earliest commercial Web sites went to great lengths to explain how much safer it was to give your credit card number over an encrypted connection than it was to give it to your waiter at a restaurant. This sort of comparison was useful at the time. Now, however, if you are going to accept credit cards online, then it is probably enough to merely mention the word "secure" or "encrypted" somewhere on the page. People who are knowledgeable about network security won't gain anything from your discussing it further. People who don't know anything about security might actually have more anxiety if you dwell on the issue too much.

> **How Big a Hurdle Is Transaction Security Anxiety?**
> **Point:** Once a Web user has made his first online transaction, he is much more inclined to do it without hesitation the second time. Moreover, some users—even if they never had any fear of credit card fraud to begin with—report being more likely to buy something online once they've learned that a friend has done so.

These two factors will collectively help drive an exponential acceptance and adoption curve—the more people transact online, the more willing others will be to give it a try. Getting this snowball rolling—in effect, altering people's *habits*—is one of the significant hurdles to overcome with moving online commerce into the mainstream. Widespread adoption of network encryption and security standards is just one factor that tips the scale toward overcoming users' initial apprehension of using their credit card online. Recognize, however, that fear alone is not responsible for this resistance. Old habits die hard, and it is simply a slow process for a large group of people to change the way they do things.

Let's face it; a lot of commercial sites out there promote an image of professionalism that registers a notch or two below that of someone selling car stereos out of the trunk of a car. Have a little fun and try this experiment.

Your Mission: Buy two things online.

For your first item, select something specific and then go out and look for it on the Web. Don't choose a book or a CD—that's too easy. Look for something obscure (and probably cheap), like Nightcrawler earthworms for your compost pile—or whatever. For your second item, buy something online that you happen to find while browsing aimlessly—let it happen somewhat spontaneously.

For Web marketers who have never purchased anything online, this exercise is an absolute requirement. You will find out rather quickly how frustrating it can be to locate the right site and the right product. But even if you have purchased something on the Web already, conduct this exercise with the following specific purpose in mind.

As you look for your item, jot down notes about how you knew when you had arrived at the right kind of site. Specifically, how *comfortable* did you feel with respect to professionalism, competence, and sincerity at each of the sites you visited—and what specific cues conveyed these qualities? (See the case study at the end of this chapter for an example of a small company that conveys absolute professionalism despite working with very limited resources.) Your criteria might be different, but I find myself almost subconsciously asking questions such as these:

- Do they have their own domain?

- Do these people seem to know what they're talking about?

- Does their site seem to anticipate my questions and answer them? (This is usually a sign of experience—they actually *have* been asked these questions before.)

- Do they take pride in or exude confidence about their work?
- Do they rely too heavily on hype to make their point?
- Does the site look clean, sharp, and well planned?
- Is it well written?

Maybe you observed subtle cues—things you hadn't even realized—that give away something about the quality of the company behind the Web site:

- Providing a physical mailing address will suggest to people that you are a real entity. A street address lends more credibility than a P.O. box.

- If your business happens to occupy space in an attractive building, consider including a photograph to convey prestige (Figure 15.1). If you rent such space, the landlord may have existing photography that you may use for free.

- Including full names of company officers, complete with photographs and biographical information, can be useful for establishing credibility. Make sure the photos are professionally produced—preferably all

FIGURE 15.1 Showing a photograph of your building subliminally suggests you really exist to wary Web users.

by the same photographer and on location, as opposed to using standard portrait photography.

- Have one person write all biographical pages in a consistent format. Avoid anything that makes these look or feel like personal home pages. This doesn't mean they have to be stuffy or conservative; they just need to be professional and relevant. Nobody cares if the president water skis unless you happen to sell water skis.

- Adding a phone number increases credibility. Providing an 800 number is even better.

Making Small Companies Sound Big on the Phone

If you are operating a small business (even out of your home), don't be afraid to include your business phone number on the Web site. Using your PC, you can install sophisticated voicemail using software such as Microsoft Phone. Callers will have no idea how large you are when they hear, "Hello, you've reached Hoskyns and Associates' corporate office. If you know the extension of your party, please enter it now, followed by the pound sign. For domestic sales, press one. For international sales, press two…"

Your business may also benefit by outsourcing telephone order taking, with a 24-hour, 800 line, for example. Callers will not know that they have not reached your own company's calling center. See Chapter 5 for details on outsourcing.

A higher overall level of commitment suggests that your Web business is legitimate and serious about doing good work for the long term. Expensive sites, registered trademarks (®), 800 phone lines, and huge product selections or inventories all suggest a bigger investment on your part—which will make customers feel more comfortable dealing with you.

Once you have compiled a list of questions that you might ask in order to determine your comfort level in buying something from a site, visit *your* site and apply your list of questions to yourself. Try to think like an objective, first-time visitor. Would you feel comfortable doing business with you? If you have not yet built your site, keep these issues in mind as you design it.

Image

As you conduct your shopping experiment on the Web, you might even notice that certain companies looked more professional than others just by seeing their brief descriptions on the search results page of Infoseek, for example. Do a search on something with thousands of responses such as "travel agency." Scan the results of this search and notice what cues make you want to select one site over another.

Design

For better or worse, the biggest determinant of how professional you look will probably be how much money you spend creating your site. Interactive features and, in particular, snazzy graphics are simply beyond the scope (and budgets) of most amateurs.

Although your site will not necessarily have to be huge or highly interactive, there is probably no getting around the need for grade-A graphics.

> **TIP:** Bite the bullet and pay for good graphics.

Depending on your business model, you may not need to frequently revise your site's basic graphic elements (logo, masthead, and navigational icons). If so, shelling out big bucks to buy a little professionalism might be a very appropriate one-time charge. See Chapter 5 for tips on hiring this expertise, whether it be a Web design firm, a freelancer, or an employee. Just be sure to look at actual work created by the *same person* who will be doing your work. Design firms sometimes display portfolio pieces created by employees who left the firm years earlier.

When hiring or contracting with individuals, be skeptical. A lot of people selling this sort of work aren't very good. The really good people are pretty expensive. If you're ever going to make a serious commitment to your dream of Web profits, this might be the time.

Language

Chapter 14 discusses ways to reinforce your site's identity using effective writing of body copy. The words you use can also be used to make people feel comfortable about doing business with you.

If you were to ask a habitual liar, "Do you tell lies?" that person would probably say "no." But for some strange psychological reason, habitual liars never seem to *volunteer* the phrase, "I don't tell lies." They could say it if they thought to do it—they are liars, after all. My pet theory is that it simply doesn't occur to them to say this because they don't place much value on telling the truth. For this reason, I think we tend to believe people who look us in the eye and say, "I don't tell lies."

If my theory is correct, then there might be corrolaries in marketing communications. For example, if a business owner didn't really care about providing superior customer service, would he or she be likely to proclaim, "We strive to offer the best customer service in the industry"? I don't think he or she would. In fact, every time I've heard a proprietor who comes across as zealous about service, for example, the service has usually been pretty good. Therefore, if you do strive to provide great service, products, workmanship—by all means—tell the world.

- Say that quality is important to you. State it outright. Use compelling language, or give an example to prove your point.

- Also state that customer service is important to you. If you feel this sort of phrase is overused, then go a step further and explain *why* it's so important to you. Most businesses don't go this far, and if you are sincere, it will be apparent.

Attention to Detail

I've stated earlier that successful Web businesses are successful only partly because they began with a sound business model, and mostly because they successfully implemented or followed through on a thousand tiny details.

To pull an example from the world of commercial graphics, I've seen a number of small companies use slightly different versions of their own logo for all the wrong reasons. I'm not talking about how MasterCard has different approved versions of its logo for one-color and two-color applications. No, I'm talking about instances where nobody in the office of some small firm knew where the original artwork was kept so that person attempted to re-create the logo by eye-balling it and substituting the closest fonts available. Sick. Or sometimes a company will have its logo printed large onto corrugated boxes for shipping—and ask the box printer just to reproduce the logo from a fax because nobody has time to send real artwork.

Big, sharp, snazzy, have-their-act-together companies simply don't do things like this. They are meticulous about the minutia of how their company is represented, and the impression that they make on *anybody*, not just customers.

Once a style is created for your site, don't let independent contributors deviate from the style. You want every page to instantly look like part of the same site. Ideally (if your site is small enough), one person is responsible for site consistency.

Quality Assurance of the Site

I've stated throughout this book that the Web is flexible enough to allow you to try things and make mistakes. This fact does not leave the door open to careless or lazy site creation and upkeep. Quality assurance (QA), as it relates to your Web site, refers to the procedures by which you assure that everything about the site works as it should and conforms to your standards of quality. This means your site:

- Should possess no typographical errors

- Should provide no links to sites that no longer exist

- Should accurately reflect company information, such as current prices

And so on.

You've probably seen sites that promised to have something added by a certain date—and you're reading this announcement months after that date, but the new element wasn't added yet. I'm not saying you must keep your word on things like this—anything could happen that might prevent you from adding something by a certain time. But it is only sheer ignorance of attention to details that would allow this site to continue to display a message promising something by a date that has already come and gone.

- Each month, browse your own site. You will be surprised how quickly little comments can become outdated simply by recent events in the news.

- Formalize your QA procedures. Make a list of requirements. Make one person accountable. If the site is too large to be scanned and policed by one person, then assign parts to different people and either make all of them accountable or have them report to one individual who is accountable for the entire site's QA.

- If you have an anal-retentive person on staff, make that person the one in charge. If you don't, hire one. You want someone who will actually feel physically uncomfortable if a subhead is the wrong point size.

- If you do have an anal-retentive person in charge of your site's QA, make sure he or she is aware of the differences between formal writing and marketing copy. Comfortable with appropriate sentence fragments. And so on.

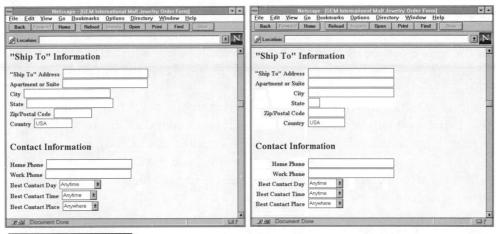

FIGURE 15.2 & 15.3 Sloppy forms are a dead giveaway of an unprofessional site.

Details Count: Nice-Looking Forms

The typical Web user may not consciously pay attention to such things, but clean, neat design makes a huge difference on how all visitors will perceive your business. Compare Figures 15.2 and 15.3, for example.

Many less professional sites contain forms like the one on the left— nonaligned data fields of random length. The corrected form on the right was created by using tables to align the fields. If you are going to create your own pages, you must master tables. If you hire somebody to do the work, make certain that he or she pays attention to details like this.

The purpose of installing such compulsive obsession with site quality, by the way, is not to ferret out every minor error before the public sees each page. The purpose is to catch and correct 95 percent of the mistakes before the pages go public. Inevitably, something will get by unnoticed. In fact, if you have a frequently updated site in which no error ever gets through, then it's possible that you are spending too much time screening for quality breaches. You could be introducing a bottle-neck suboptimally. That is, if QA delays your site's changes long enough, then the advantage of being perfect will not justify the disadvantage of being late.

You might as well exploit the fact that the Web is fluid enough to allow a certain amount of mistakes without doing much damage. This facet should be exploited by moving faster rather than being overly cautious, proofreading something a dozen times, getting multiple people's approval, and so on, in the interest of certifying ultra professionalism to an unhealthy extreme. Strike a balance. The potential damage to your image of imperfections is mitigated by a couple of factors.

Quick Fixes

Unlike printed brochures, with a Web site errors that are discovered late in the game can be corrected cheaply and instantly with little disruption in operation. The trick here is to jump on problems the moment you notice them.

If a customer provides feedback about your site regarding a typo or factual error, you will be in the top league if you make corrections within 24 hours. To reap the full benefit, e-mail the customer, thanking him or her for the feedback, and inform that person that you have already corrected it. This visitor will assume that your business is just as diligent in other facets of its operation.

Visitor Turnover

If a Web site is able to draw heavy traffic one week, then there is a good chance it can draw heavy traffic, made up of new people, next week also. Even sites with a lot of repeat visitors may have completely different people visiting each day if the repeaters visit only weekly, for example. If a handful of visitors witness some gruesome error, they are the only ones who will know—if you fix it right away.

> **TIP:**   Offer something for free to the site visitor who spots an error.

This provides an incentive for people to find and report mistakes, as well as providing an incentive for employees to check their work. But it also provides a sort of meta-effect; by demonstrating that correcting these details is *so* important that you offer to *pay* people to report them, you convey that you are a perfectionist. I would rather buy something from a perfectionist. So would everyone else.

To put it bluntly, Web sites can screw up and still recover quickly. Usually there will be few costly or long-term adverse effects. An obvious exception to this would be any blunder that angers a user to the point that he or she launches a hate campaign against the company.

> ### Go International
> The BUCKMASTER® Survival Knife page at http://www.finest1.com/buck makes an interesting claim:
>
> "We can handle E-Mail and Postal Mail in: English, Spanish, French, German, Italian, Vietnamese, Japanese, Chinese Mandarin, Chinese Taiwanese, Russian, Ukrainian, Arabic, Persian, Amharic, & Malay. Our phone answering

Quality Assurance of Non-Web Aspects of Your Business

Established businesses have a decided advantage over new businesses in this department. For many small, new, Web-only businesses, all of the attention of the small group of founders is dedicated to building a site and promoting it. The many details required to pull this part of the project off successfully can be so overwhelming that nobody remembers to make sure that the boring, low-tech operations of the business are running smoothly.

I was involved with a Web start-up that directed orders to another company, which fulfilled the orders with products that they themselves produced. They had been in business for years and were very experienced, but we had a minor breakdown in communication that could have easily gone unnoticed until a problem occurred. The order fulfillment department of this company was not accustomed to our format of orders, which we sent via e-mail; they had previously taken orders only by phone, using a different form. This led them to not see the "special instructions" field of our forms. As luck would have it, a friend of mine ordered some products through the site and gave special instructions to have the products shipped to an address different from her own (she was purchasing these items as a gift). Because the special instructions went unnoticed, she received the package at her home address. Fortunately, nothing bad resulted from this. We were lucky to discover the problem with a "friendly" customer. Not all visitors would have been so understanding.

Competent individuals charged with specific tasks generally perform them correctly. We e-mailed orders to them and they fulfilled them—just as we all had agreed. But nobody had caught the error in our communication process. No individual person did anything wrong. This error occurred because of a weak linkage in our *system*.

TIP: Look for weaknesses in your business systems in the linkages between entities. This is where problems can go undetected the longest.

If your company has more than just a few employees, periodically shop yourself. Have a friend place an order to your company using his name and e-mail address. Have him include some complicated, special instructions on the online ordering form. Wait and see how well your company handles the order. If you discover problems, realize that poor systems could be as much to blame as careless employees.

Guarantees

As with traditional businesses, guarantees are a great way of boosting customer confidence. Because the Web introduces additional forms of uncertainty, it is more important than ever to offer guarantees if possible.

Uncertainty About the Company

Are you legitimate? Are you going to be at the same URL a month from now? Will the customer have recourse if something is wrong with the order? Will you even return their e-mails if they send a complaint? These are valid concerns in general and particularly on the Web. It is much easier to ignore an irate customer's e-mail than it is to ignore an irate customer who is standing at your checkout counter screaming and scaring away other customers.

Merely mentioning "guarantee" on your site is not strong enough to combat this uncertainty, in my opinion. The word is almost a cliché. Many firms "guarantee" their work but don't offer an explanation of exactly what that means. Does that mean they'll give you a refund? Or will they fix it? If so, how soon?

Communicate your guarantee with intensity.

- Say it three times, in three different ways, close to the order form.

- Make it visually impossible to miss.

- Explain the exact terms (on a separate page if the terms are complex).

The Secret to Good Customer Relations: Feedback

If you manage the creation of even a modest Web site—such as five pages—you will lose all objectivity by the time you finish the task. Site navigation that seems obvious to you might confuse a first-time visitor. Additionally, you will mentally possess all of the site's information as a whole, whereas visitors may not understand certain things if they haven't read other things first. It will be harder for you to spot errors such as misspelled words because your brain is prone to skip past sentences that it has read a dozen times.

Solicit feedback first from people you know. You will be amazed by how they instantly spot gigantic problems that were invisible to you. Next, solicit feedback from people in your target market by sending *personalized* e-mails to a handful of people whose names you find on related Web sites and on newsgroups. I emphasize "personalized" because this is neither a mass mailing nor an attempt to promote yourself. Be sure to explain this when you contact them.

Soliciting Feedback from the Net

Step 1: Visit a related site, analyze it thoroughly, and offer useful commentary to its owner. Then ask if he or she wouldn't mind looking over your site. You're asking a pretty big favor, but you have offered value in exchange, and he or she should be interested if your site is related. This technique works well, sometimes generating an 80 percent response rate.

Step 2: Visit a related site and ask its owner *a specific question* about your site. This is asking only a small favor, and he or she is likely to volunteer more if he or she does visit your site. Mention something specific about his or her site so that they know you're not conducting a mass mailing.

Step 3: Send a personalized e-mail to someone who posted a message on a relevant newsgroup. Comment on the specific post so that he or she knows this is a personalized message. Add something brief and useful if you're able (again, always attempt to provide value). Ask him or her to visit your site. Specify that it is brand new, not yet promoted, and that you seek feedback.

Step 4: When sending a personalized request to an individual, avoid saying "I invite you to visit..." because that sounds too much like an ad. I ask people to visit with something like,

```
I wonder if you wouldn't mind taking a look at my site
to see if you notice any glaring errors or ways I could
improve it.
```

Step 5: Appeal to people's fondness for recognition. Don't kiss up; just be genuine. The reality is that you have singled this person out because he or she is more appropriate than somebody else. Let him or her know this.

```
I assume from posts like this one that you know a lot
about such-and-such. I was wondering if you wouldn't mind
looking at my new site on the subject. It hasn't offi-
cially gone public yet, and I'm looking for feedback from
knowledgeable people at this point...
```

If you're up-front and honest with people in your quest for feedback, many of them are more than happy to help. I've had these intro letters turn into dialogues lasting a week or more.

You'll know other people want to continue the discussion when any of these occur:

- They ask you a question

- They invite you to write again

- (Probably) when they write lengthy e-mails

Soliciting Feedback from Site Visitors

Naturally, you will also want to hear what ordinary visitors to your site have to say about it. There are several common methods to do so.

1. Simplest: Provide a mailto link that says something like, "We'd love to hear what you think about this site." The problem with this method is that it's a little too passive. It doesn't ask a specific question. It does provide an easy route for people who spot a typo, for example. Other than that, about the only people who will respond to this method are people new to browsing. Be aware that their comments might not be representative of the browsing public.

2. Provide a link to a page with an open-ended feedback form (Figure 15.4). This approach is useful because you can include a couple of fields in your form to find out certain things, such as asking where the person found out about you.

3. Use a straw-poll. Provide a very streamlined, targeted form using radio buttons to find out one thing only. Place this on a relevant page, side by side with other content (see Figure 15.5). Many people will respond to this, but you will not get much qualitative information.

Other types of questions you might ask include these:

- Who do you plan to vote for in the election? (Demographics research in the guise of a general interest survey—sneaky.)

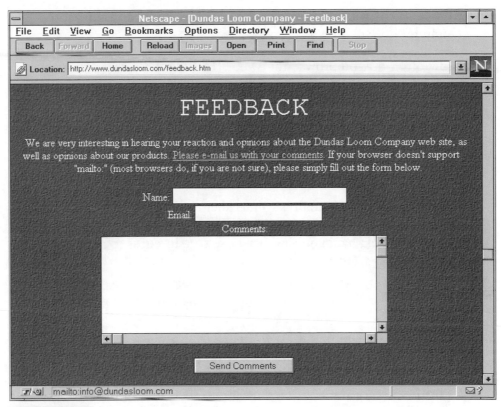

FIGURE 15.4 Dundas Loom dedicates one of its main pages to asking for open-ended feedback.

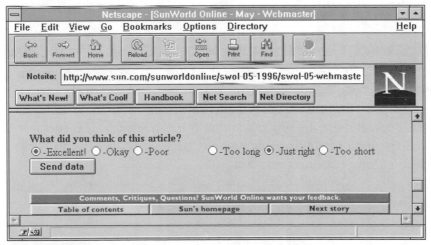

FIGURE 15.5 Simple, specific queries for feedback will generate more responses than open-ended forms.

- Which of the following would you like to see added to this site? (Include three choices.)

- How often do you browse the Web? (Include three choices, such as "Less than once a week," "One to five times per week," and "More than five times per week.")

4. Include a couple of questions on your registration form, if you require registration (see Chapter 7). Be careful not to ask too many questions on any form—this almost always decreases the response rate.

5. Send e-mail questionnaires to members of your house e-mail list. Chapter 13 discusses house-list mailings at greater length. If you're after feedback, avoid questions whose true intent is to advertise—it's pretty transparent to ask things like this:

```
12. Were you aware that we offer the lowest prices on
    such-and-such on the entire World Wide Web?
    yes_____    no_____
```

6. Most importantly, you want feedback from the people who *aren't* buying (hence, they probably aren't on your house-list). You want to find out what, if anything, was wrong with your site or products. This is some of the best information to seek and, unfortunately, some of the most difficult to obtain. The best solution I've seen is to offer a freebie to anyone who fills out a questionnaire or to enter all respondents in a contest.

Unsolicited Feedback from Site Visitors

Sometimes people will contact you out of the blue and tell you something useful, even though you didn't ask for it. Always respond promptly with gratitude to people who provide such feedback. Invite them to write back anytime. Ask them if there are any questions you can answer. It is possible, however, that the bulk of your unsolicited feedback will come from people who are upset for one reason or another.

> **TIP:** Turn hate mail into gold.

Think of hate mail as a pile of gold coins. It is the best feedback you will ever get because it usually contains *exact prescriptions* for the following:

- Improving your product
- Making your promotion more appealing
- Improving your site
- Improving your company

It is possible that the only qualitative feedback you ever get will be from people who have something to complain about. That's okay—you want to know about these complaints because of the Cockroach Theory: For every one you see, there are a hundred you don't see.

Don't waste this opportunity to connect with these people who bothered to contact you directly. This may be the only contact you have with surfers who have found your site. Write back to them. Learn from them. Many people are too busy to respond to your e-mailed requests for feedback. Ironically, those who took time out of their day to send you a complaint are generally the most willing to take another moment to give you another piece of their mind.

I was involved with a site that published some audiotape products designed to help those with HIV deal with fear and depression. The publisher offered the product to individuals below wholesale prices and made free albums available to qualifying organizations. Despite this fact, the mere presence of a for-profit, AIDS-related product on the Web upset a number of the site's visitors who felt it was exploitative. I got the fun job of fielding these flames and responding to them as best I could.

I took an open-minded approach and resisted any urge to behave defensively. It wasn't always easy because I felt that some of the flames were completely off-base. Instead of defending the actions of this company, however, I engaged the most venomous of the flamers with honest and probing questions: "How can we make these available and still cover our costs?" and "What should have been different about the site," for example. An amazing thing happened. First, these people's rage upgraded to just mildly annoyed. Second, excellent suggestions began pouring in. They wrote screen after screen of e-mail, telling us how we ought to be doing things. The funny thing is, I agreed with almost all of the suggestions. Quite a lesson in humility.

> **TIP:** Read hate mail with an open mind. Respond kindly without sounding defensive. Ask for more input. You will receive it, and you may possibly convert an enemy into an ally in the process.

After the Sale

Ideally, when a customer purchases from you, it is the beginning of a relationship rather than the end. Positive word-of-mouth does wonders for many Web businesses. At the very least, make certain that the customer received everything that he or she hoped to receive.

> **TIP:** Send an e-mailed verification within 24 hours of receiving an online order. If the order contained any special instructions, refer to them specifically.

Have your order form contain a field that the customer can deselect if he or she does not want to be included on your house mailing list (see Chapter 13). Consider maintaining separate mailing lists distinguishing those who have actually purchased something from you. After enough time has passed for your customer to have received his or her order, send an e-mail note that either looks personalized or is personalized.

First, ask if everything was correct with the order, and then ask the person a couple of specific questions involving an issue for which you would like some feedback. This one-time, order-related follow-up is appropriate, even if the customer asked not to be placed on your mailing list. If your letter doesn't look like a form letter, even Web veterans will usually respond favorably, impressed by your follow-through. Use the opportunity for what it is—a chance to connect with your customers and find out how you may better serve them. If you don't usually contact customers directly, let them know why they are the rare exception. Most customers will be flattered to be singled out as useful sources of information. Some will even invite you to write back any time or even call them on the phone. Consider keeping these "friendly customers" on file for future reference.

> **TIP:** Try new product ideas or promotional ideas on your "friendly customers" before releasing your idea to the general public. Some early feedback might help you avoid mistakes.

Don't just find out how your *visitors* found you; find out how your *customers* found you. People who actually pay you money may be randomly distributed throughout your site visitors, or they may be coming predominantly from one or two sources, such as a well-placed advertisement. It is therefore important to, at least, find out where the paying customers are coming from.

TIP: On online order forms, ask how they found you.

Don't make the field required—capturing the information is not worth losing a sale. With telephone orders, always ask how customers found you. If you aren't taking orders yourself, train the order-takers to do so and include the question as a field on their order form. Have the order-takers press for more information as appropriate. If the customer says he saw your ad, ask if he remembers in which magazine. If another customer says she saw your site mentioned in a newsgroup, ask if she remembers which newsgoup.

If you consistently gather just this information, you will be ahead of 90 percent of the marketers on the Web—just browse and see for yourself how few online order forms even ask you where you found them.

If you take the analysis one more step, you will be even further ahead of the pack. First, tally these results and create a bar chart to see which promotional avenues provide your site with the greatest number of visitors. Then create other charts for subsets of your dataset, such as buyers, small-purchase buyers, large-purchase buyers, people who request more information, people who responded to contests, and so on.

If you have enough data points, you may discover, for example, that your paid advertising is generating a lot of hits but few buyers. And perhaps your newsgroup postings are generating only modest traffic but from people who end up buying big-ticket items.

Case Study: The Dundas Loom Company
http://www.dundasloom.com

A number of the recommendations in this chapter had already been implemented when I discovered Dundas Loom Company (see Figure 15.6). With one part-time and two full-time employees, Dundas Loom certainly qualifies as a small company.

I chose Dundas Loom not because it has the best Web site on the Internet—in fact, its site is very modest and could even use a little work, such as lightening

---

the tiled background and color-correcting the photographs. I chose it because it has done so much with so little. With a site that cost only about $400 to create, it has managed to pass my acid test:

> Would I feel comfortable buying online from this firm? Absolutely.

FIGURE 15.6 The Dundas Loom Company (http://www.dundasloom.com) promotes true professionalism despite limited site production resources.

This case study points out exactly why I would feel so confident purchasing something from it, even for hundreds of dollars. I encourage you to visit the site. If you were in the market for a loom, would you feel comfortable ordering from this company?

Dundas Loom was created in 1988 by Stephen and Judy Dundas of Missoula, Montana. Their passions for woodworking and weaving turned into a thriving wholesale business with about a hundred dealers nationwide. They also sell directly through craft catalogues and run ads in publications called *Handwoven* and *Spinoff*.

If you visit Dundas Loom's site, you will not be met with stunning graphics or interactive wizardry. You will, however, learn about this little family business that loves making looms. Their small size works for them. Their Montana location works for them. These quotes provide an example of the simple philosophy that their site consitently conveys:

Welcome

Dundas Loom Company is a family owned business located in Missoula, Montana. We make Weaving and Spinning products that are simple, artistic and durable. We take pride in crafting tools for other artisans.

We are zealots about service.

The Company We Keep

Stephen Dundas is an extraordinary designer and woodworker. He loves jazz, gardening and plays the flute and cello.

Judy Dundas is the self declared queen of Dundas Loom Company. She is a weaver, nurse and fledgling marketer.

Notice the use of "other artisans." Very subtle. Confident but not hypish.

Another passage follows from a product page (see Figure 15.7). Remember that list of questions you might pose to a Web business? Do these people seem to know what they're talking about? Does their language suggest attention to detail and quality?

"This artistic wheel is made from cherry with purple heart highlights. The Dundas Wheel has a double drive with Scotch tension. Ratios available are from 6 - 18. The double treadle wheel has a built in lazy Kate with generous 6 ounce bobbins. The wheel is balanced to start with either foot or the spinner can treadle with one foot. Hand-rubbed oil finish."

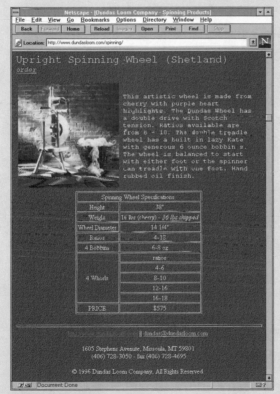

FIGURE 15.7 Good photography, good writing, and thorough specifications eliminate all doubt from the minds of shoppers looking at this Dundas Loom spinning wheel.

Dundas Loom custom manufactures an amazing 82 SKUs (stock-keeping units) and presents them all in an extremely easy-to-read table on its online ordering form. Its prices were dated just two weeks before I saw the site, suggesting it maintains the site with regular updates. The following is an example of the shipping information.

> "Shipping: UPS where possible. If item(s) exceed UPS size limitations shipping will be COD by motor freight.
>
> Canadian Citizens: Prices are U.S. currency.
>
> Returns: Accepted if returned within 6 months of purchase. Customer is responsible for crating/shipping on returns.
>
> Feel free to leave any comments. Thank you!"

Strangely, even though these are restrictions, I sensed myself feeling more comfortable because the employees obviously knew what they were doing. Notice how just a few words can convey that they have been doing this for a while. With no expensive graphics, they make navigation simple with a no-frills box situated consistently in the upper-left corner of each page (see Figure 15.8).

```
Weaving Products
Spinning Products
Weaving Accessories
Order Form
Feedback
Other Interesting Stuff
```

FIGURE 15.8 Expensive graphics are always nice, but text-based navigation is all this site needs for now.

Perhaps what impressed me most of all was the degree of detail of its technical specifications. By using tables well, the site manages to keep a lot of information from becoming overwhelming.

Spinning Wheel Specifications	
Height	38"
Weight	16 lbs (cherry) - *36 lbs shipped*
Wheel Diameter	14 1/4"
Ratios	6-18
3 Bobbins	6-8 oz
3 Whorls	ratios
	6-8
	10-12
	16-18
PRICE	$475

FIGURE 15.9 Ample and easy-to-understand technical information eliminates uncertainty from buyers' minds.

FIGURE 15.10 Ample and easy-to-understand technical information eliminates uncertainty from buyers' minds.

The Dundas Loom site was created by Internet Services Montana, who also provides Web service for the site. Stephen Dundas says they hope to learn HTML soon so that they can make regular site changes themselves.

DESIGNING YOUR SITE'S
LOGIC AND NAVIGATION

G ood promotion of your site brings customers to your front door. Building an attractive and professional-looking site around a good concept makes them eager to stay and look around. But how do you help guide their movements once they're in your site? Should you? Or should you simply let them explore? The answer depends on your business model.

Influencing Your Visitor's Use of the Site

If your site generates money primarily by selling banner advertising, then your overriding goal is to get visitors to view as many pages (hence, banners) as possible. This means using a higher number of shorter pages, each of which ends with a reason to make the user eager to continue to the next. Encouraging a high number of page views also means providing many different areas to explore, with little regard for the path taken by the user or the sequence of pages he or she views.

If your site sells products directly, then you have an entirely different set of goals. Your primary goals are to convey the information that people need to make a purchase, and you want to guide them to place an order. Secondarily, you want to give them a reason to tell their friends about the site and return themselves. But too many Web site developers fail to recognize one fundamental fact.

For sites selling products that must first be explained, the perfect balance between "too much" and "not enough" information is best achieved by doing two things simultaneously. First, make available more information than the average user requires to make a purchase. Second, emphasize a default path that bypasses much of this information and leads users directly to your order form. In this way, quests for additional information are perceived by the browser as optional excursions away from the primary path, as opposed to necessary prerequisites for making a decision (see Figure 16.1).

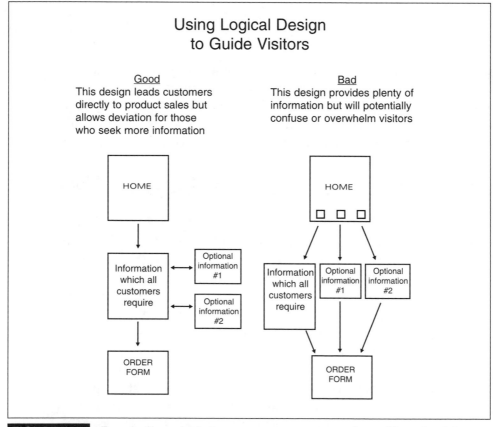

FIGURE 16.1 By selecting which pages users may access from different points, you can help guide them through your site.

"Guiding" the customer is achieved through both the logical and navigational design of your site:

- **Logical Design**—What pages exist? How do they interlink? Variables of logical design *impose* which paths are available and not available.

- **Navigational Design**—Graphical cues and the prominence of linked elements on the page *suggest* a path or *provide information* about the different options.

The Acid Test of Good Logical and Navigational Design

Two types of users usually visit commercial Web sites, each arriving with one of the following thoughts in mind:

1. "I know what I want. Where can I find it?"

or

2. "I don't know what I want. What should I do next?"

Good design will provide clear answers to both of these categories of visitors. Some sites fail at both. Most sites do a good job of answering one of these questions. Only the best sites adequately address both. Unfortunately, some of the coolest-looking sites were built with the following attitude:

"Our site offers one thousand pages with cryptic names. Have at it."

Such sites fail at both of these tests but are potentially appropriate for advertiser-sponsored sites whose prime objective is to get users to click on as many pages as possible.

Logic

For those sites that are not primarily advertiser-sponsored, your choice of logical design will depend on what you sell, how you sell it, and how you expect to change these variables over time.

The Company-centric Design

This design promotes the entire company rather than one product or one of several product lines. This is a good option for large companies because their individual divisions or product lines may come and go, but the company remains. As such, this design also works well for small companies that offer a variety of products, particularly when not all the products are tightly related. In this case, the unifying element is the company itself.

Company-centric Web sites are also typically used by firms that sell services rather than products—in essence, the company *is* the product. This model focuses on delivering the following information:

- Who you are

- What you do or sell

- Why you're better at it than anybody else (or why your products are better)

- How to contact you

- (For some businesses) where to find your products

The most noteworthy aspect of company-centric sites is that they tend to lack a suggested path. Instead, they present a variety of options and let the user decide what to do next. Sometimes this is unavoidable. If you have a dozen different product lines, then you can't try to lead the visitors; they will have to lead

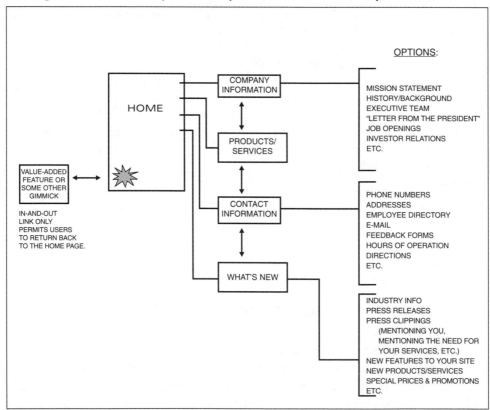

FIGURE 16.2 Company-centric Web sites revolve around the organization rather than products or special features of the site itself.

themselves. Other times, this lack of a "suggested path" is a shortcoming. In particular, companies that sell services (which can be thought of as product-oriented sites because the company is the product) often neglect to guide the visitor to a logical conclusion—a call to action. They provide a lot of information about themselves and then leave the customer thinking, "Okay, now what?"

If your site promotes a service-oriented business, make the next step clear. Don't just provide your phone number. You must tell them to call you and provide a context in which they understand *why* they must call you. The more specific, the better. For example, "To talk about ways that our booth designers can make you stand out from the crowd at your next trade show, call our Design Center at 800-555-1234."

You can assemble company-centric sites in an infinite number of ways, selecting exactly those options that suit your needs. Figure 16.2 diagrams the logic of a generic example.

The "Newspaper" Design

Even though this design appeals to information publishers, it is not limited to online newspapers and magazines (Figure 16.3). The newspaper format

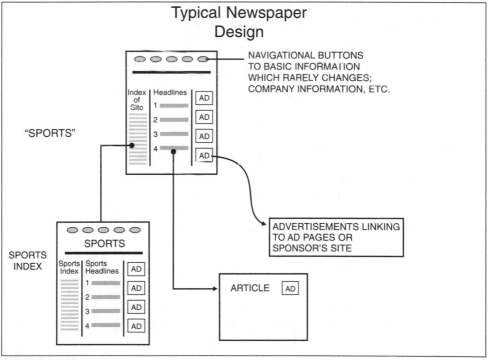

FIGURE 16.3 Large sites with much frequently changing information often use a "newspaper" site design.

is useful for any site that has large quantities of frequently updated content, including large-scale catalog sites (see "Case Study: Internet Shopping Network," later in this chapter).

The design usually consists of two or three columns on very deep pages (those requiring vertical scrolling to see entirely). On each page with columns, the format should remain the same, such as something like this:

- Column 1: Indexed links to pages

- Column 2: Current stories

- Column 3: Advertisements

Direct Product Sales Sites

Perhaps the most exciting of all commercial sites are those that actually let shoppers buy things from you and charge their credit cards even while you sleep. If you spend some time surfing the Web, you will probably find a few different formats used to sell things.

You will want to structure your direct sales site differently depending on such factors as these:

- The type of information the customer requires to make a purchase

- The amount of information the customer requires

- Whether the product category is familiar or unfamiliar

- How many product categories you offer

- How many products you offer in each category

- Whether the purchase is likely to be one-time or ongoing

Depending on your particular mix of the above variables, you can choose from several site design models described below.

Request for Print Catalogs

Even though these sites don't actually sell online, they present a good way for existing companies to ease into online sales. By providing an easy way for customers to request already existing company catalogs or brochures, the company can dramatically extend its reach (see Figure 16.4). These companies can gradually convert the site into an online catalog with order-processing capabilities.

Catalogs generate much higher sales from individuals who request them than from those who have received them unsolicited—no matter how good

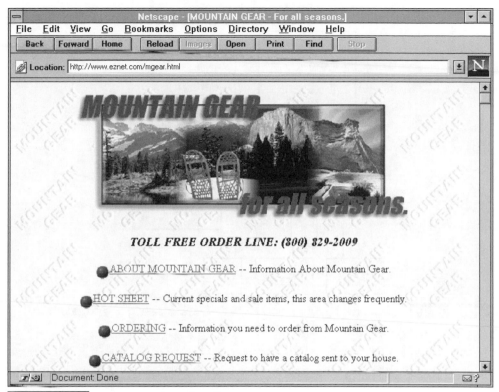

FIGURE 16.4 Mountain Gear (http://www.eznet.com/mgear.html) uses its Web site primarily for letting users request print catalogs to be sent by ordinary mail.

your mailing list is. One company that accepts no orders online but mails catalogs reported mailing 2,000 catalogs to users in the first three months of being online. Nearly half of these requests came from overseas.

Billboard Sites

Billboard sites (see Figure 16.5) are small sites with perhaps one to two pages of product-related content, plus an order form (there may be additional, out-of-the-way pages such as legal disclaimers, production credits, and so on). These sites are short and sweet. Not too much information, not many products to choose from. If you are a small company that sells one version of just one item, the billboard may be perfect for you.

If you sell a handful of different items that don't relate to each other through a common theme, it may be better to create multiple billboard sites rather than one catalog site. This allows each object (and its respective site) to appeal more directly to people who found that page, looking for

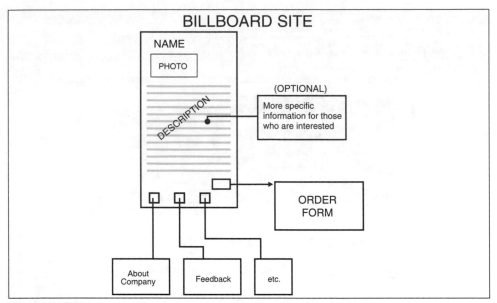

FIGURE 16.5   Billboard sites are a good way to focus on selling one product that doesn't require much explanation.

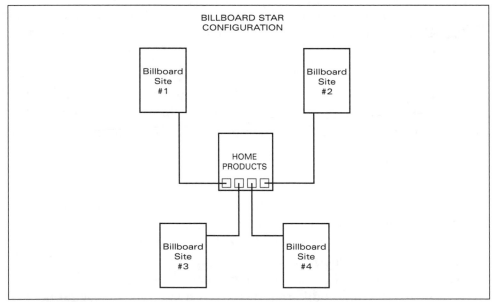

FIGURE 16.6   If you sell several unrelated products, you can have multiple, single-product billboard sites that are all connected to your company's home page.

that item in particular. Additionally, this will allow you to promote each site independently, with its own singular focus. You might interconnect these billboard pages in a star configuration, with your company home page at the hub (see Figure 16.6).

Infomercial Site

Occasionally, a product comes along that requires lengthy explanation for customers to understand why the product works or what benefits they can expect from it (see Figure 16.7). In the mid-eighties, this realization (and lots of empty cable channels) led to an explosion of so-called "infomercials," which spent anywhere from five minutes to one hour pitching products like courses on investing in real estate or tooth-whitening agents.

The Web is an excellent medium for some of these products. Intangible products (such as training courses) or those requiring detailed explanation work better than those requiring demonstrations because the Web is not yet well suited for video communications. The risk with presenting large amounts of intellectual information is that it is easy to overwhelm or bore the site visitor. The effort you take to design and test your presentation

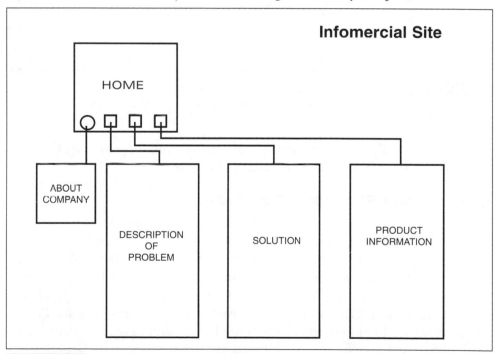

FIGURE 16.7 Infomercial site designs are good for selling products that require lengthy explanations.

FIGURE 16.8 This page from Netscape's General Store offers an item that nobody could live without—Netscape golf balls. The page neglects to mention how many balls you get for $31. I hope that's not the price for one ball.

format will greatly impact how many of your visitors actually read the information that they require to make a purchase.

Catalog and Shopping-Cart Sales

As the name suggests, these sites offer a wider array of products that customers select as they browse, making only one order at the end of their session. "Shopping-cart" technology is server software that enables the server to keep track of the customer's selected items prior to his or her reaching the ordering page (see Figures 16.8, 16.9, and 16.10). This higher level of complexity is most useful in large sites, with many products for sale. The added functionality also costs more to implement and may be initially cost-prohibitive for lower-budget Web businesses.

Catalog sites can be logically configured in many ways. For example, the hot sauce Web site described in Chapter 14 allows visitors to look up

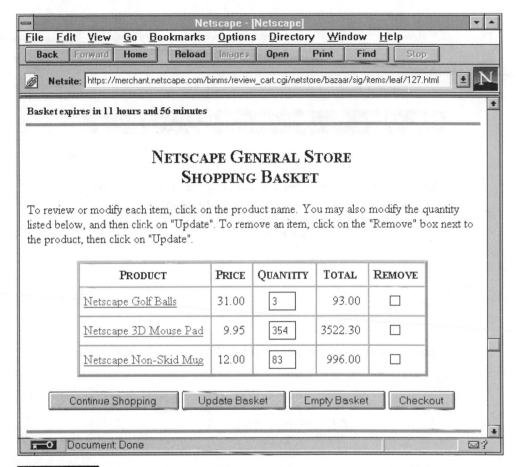

FIGURE 16.9 Netscape's General Store provides a good example of "shopping-cart" technology that runs on their own commerce server software. The server keeps track of which items the user has selected and tallies up a total so that the user has to make only one financial transaction to buy multiple items.

450 stock-keeping units (SKUs) by heat level, origin, ingredients, or name. A much larger site, the Internet Shopping Network, carries more than 25,000 SKUs of computer-related products. For this large number of products it employs a newspaper design. For details on this large-scale catalog's design logic, see "Case Study: Internet Shopping Network," below.

Online Malls

Online malls are often similar to the star configuration of unrelated sites described in the "Billboard Sites" section above. Instead of having a com-

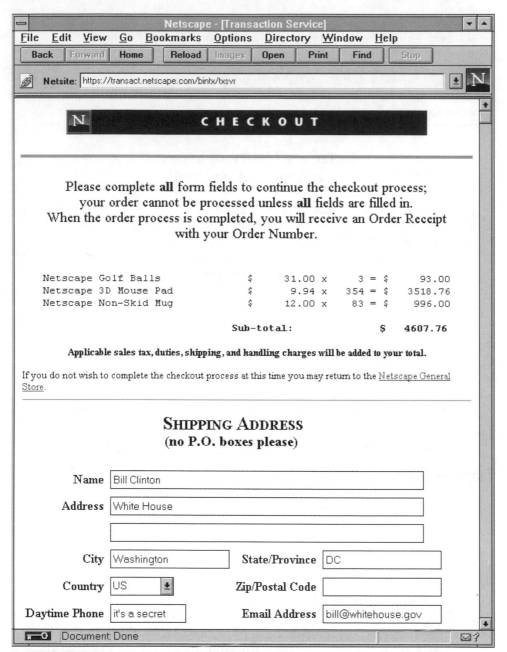

FIGURE 16.10 The shopping-cart at Netscape's General Store has kept track of my selections and now lets me "check out" (a euphemism for "pay"). In addition to providing credit card information, the purchase form allows me to ship the items to anybody whom I think might need 354 Netscape 3D mouse pads.

pany home page at the hub of the star, a mall owner (or "landlord") has his or her mall page in the center, with connections to each store (or "tenant") sites (see Figure 16.11).

Business arrangements of online malls vary. Sometimes the landlord rents virtual space to companies that need only one page and don't want to create a stand-alone site. The tenant may pay a monthly fee to be represented in the mall, or the landlord may alternately take a percentage of sales.

Most landlords create the tenant pages—if the tenants knew how to do it themselves, they would often create their own independent site instead. All tenants of a given mall benefit from the traffic generated by the other stores and the landlord's promotional efforts. Some landlords take any tenant who wants to sign on; others seek out only specific tenants, particularly if the mall has a theme. Sometimes, a company with an existing Web site will pay to have its site included in a mall. However, the distinction begins to blur here between what is a mall versus what is any site that will provide a link to your site for a fee—otherwise known as "advertising."

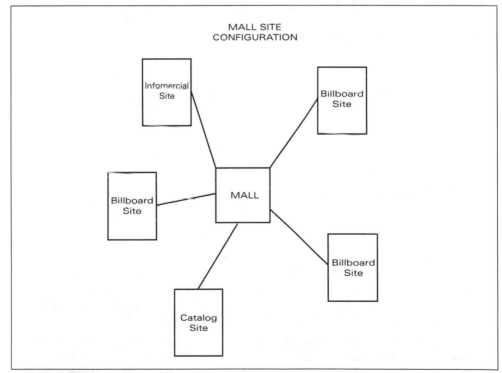

MALL SITE
CONFIGURATION

FIGURE 16.11 Malls are logically similar to a star configuration of billboard sites, except that each node is a store rather than a stand-alone product.

Case Study: Internet Shopping Network

http://www.internet.net

Internet Shopping Network (ISN) is a wholly owned subsidiary of Home Shopping Network, Inc., the $1 billion company that sells products directly on television. ISN sells more than 25,000 computer products from over 600 manufacturers through its site on the World Wide Web.

Each week, 3,000 new shoppers join ISN. To allow these people to efficiently navigate their way through so many products while being exposed to ads for particular products, ISN has adopted the newspaper logical design described earlier in this chapter (Figure 16.12).

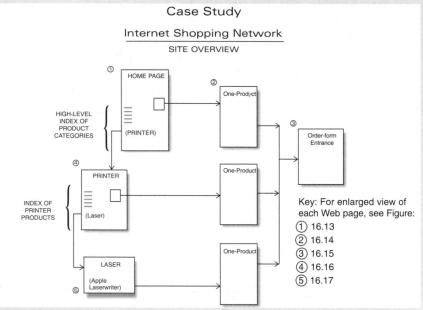

FIGURE 16.12 This is an overview of Internet Shopping Network's site.

① The Home Page (Figure 16.13)

This is ISN's site entry point. From here, visitors can access administrative pages for such tasks as becoming a member or checking the status of an order. They can also search for an item, select from 12 product categories along the left side of the page, or find out more about "Today's Hot Deals," the spotlighted products along the right side of the page.

Different online catalogs have different policies, but many charge manufacturers a fee to give their products such prominent placement. This is a specialized form of advertiser sponsorship—selling ads for products contained

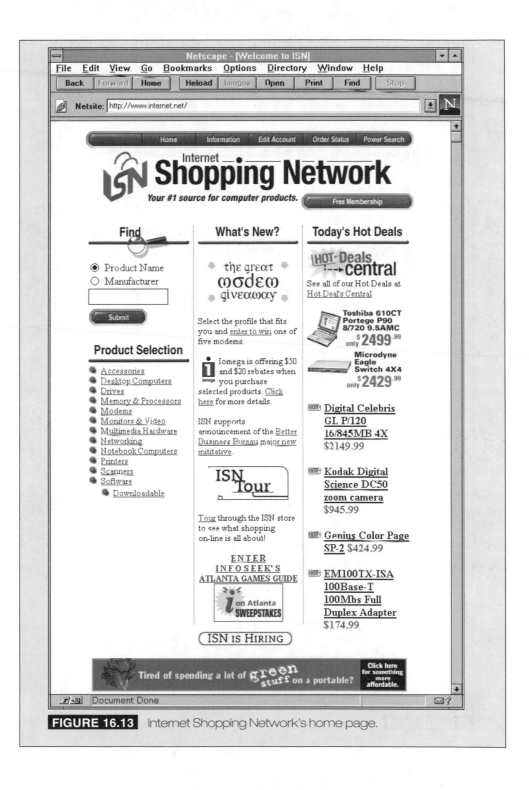

FIGURE 16.13 Internet Shopping Network's home page.

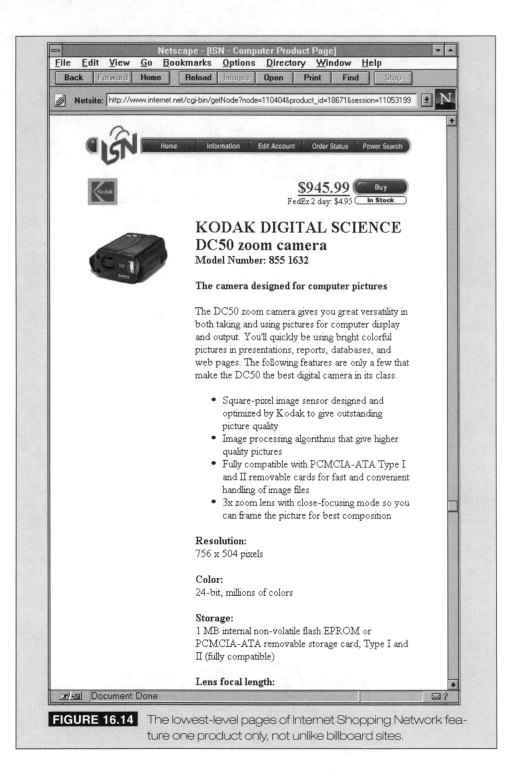

FIGURE 16.14 The lowest-level pages of Internet Shopping Network feature one product only, not unlike billboard sites.

elsewhere within your site. These ads link directly to their products pages, as in the case of this Kodak digital camera.

② A One-product Page (Figure 16.14)

This page is similar to the "billboard" site design described earlier in this chapter. It features one product and gives specific information about it, including its price and technical specifications. From here, the customer can proceed to ③, the online ordering section, if he or she decides to purchase the product.

③ Order-form Entrance (Figure 16.15)

FIGURE 16.15 This page is the entrance to the online ordering section of Internet Shopping Network.

If users do not wish to purchase the camera, they may press "Home" or their browser's "back" button to return to the home page. If they were looking for an Apple Laserwriter printer, they might select "Printers" from the product selection index in the left column.

④ Printer Products Category Page (Figure 16.16)

FIGURE 16.16 This midlevel page in Internet Shopping Network's hierarchical site displays an index of products within one category.

This separates printer products by their type. Notice how this page uses a format similar to the home page. Categories are indexed along the left, and "Today's Hot Deals" related to printers are displayed along the right. Like those on the home page, these prominent ads also link to their respective product's pages. Because the user is looking for an Apple Laserwriter, he or she would select "Laser," which links to a page of various manufacturers' laser printers.

⑤ Laser Printers Page (Figure 16.17)

As you see, there are two Apple Laserwriters from which to choose. Either of these links to its own product page. From any product page, users may enter the online order section of the site.

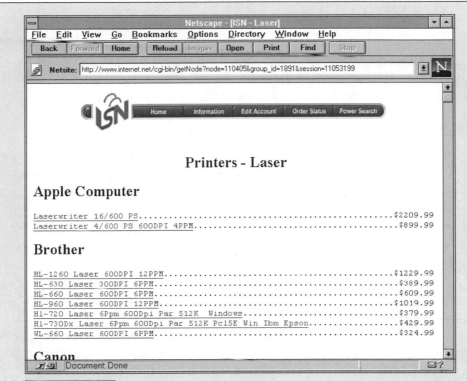

FIGURE 16.17 This page in Internet Shopping Network's hierarchy displays laser printers according to their manufacturer.

If you'll recall the Acid Test of Good Logical and Navigational Site Design, a good site will do two things:

1. Let people who know what they're looking for find it easily.
2. Make suggestions to people who don't know what they're looking for.

This site accomplishes the first of these requirements by systematically organizing more than 25,000 products in a hierarchical series of indexes that start at a general level (product type) and become more specific with each selection, all the way down to individual products.

At the same time, the site does a great job of making suggestions to the user by displaying "What's New" features and "Today's Hot Deals" at each step of the way. Even if the user knows only that he or she wants a printer but doesn't know which kind, the hot deals related to printers will make a suggestion that is relevant to his or her quest.

Site Logic Design Grade: A+

Navigation

Remember that the dual objectives driving the design of your site's navigational features are to make things easy to find and to suggest options for visitors who are not looking for something in particular. There are several standard ways to accomplish these objectives.

The Primacy of the Home Page

> **TIP:** Make it extremely easy and obvious for visitors to get to your home page from *anywhere* in your site.

Occasionally, you may have a reason to strictly control the user's path by using what I call an "in-and-out" page, meaning the only way out is to push a "back" button such as the one in Figure 16.18.

Other than with rare exceptions such as these, I recommend placing a direct link to the home page on every page of your site. This is easily accomplished by placing your logo in the upper left-hand corner of each page, with the linked word, *home*, beneath it. Many sites take this degree of consistency a step further by placing their standard navigational bar at the top (or top and bottom) of every page, such as on Internet Shopping Network's pages, shown in Figure 16.19.

The reasons for doing this are very compelling. First, it would be a challenge to make every page easy to find from every other page—impossible with a large site. However, making every page easy to find from the home page *is* feasible. Therefore, all you have to do is make the home page easy to find from every page, and you have accomplished one of your two overriding objectives: making things easy to find for visitors who know what they're looking for. This is reasonably well understood by site designers—after all, that is why it's called a "home" page. Another less-known reason for making your home page easily accessible from every other page is this.

FIGURE 16.18   "Back" buttons are useful for "in-and-out" pages that are a dead end.

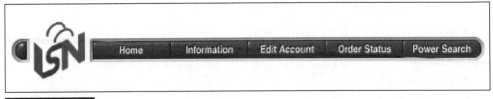

FIGURE 16.19 Internet Shopping Network uses a consistent navigational bar at the top of its site pages.

> **TIP:** Many—perhaps most—of your site visitors will not enter through the home page.

The majority of Web surfers find sites by using search engines or by linking from different sites. Search engines like Infoseek systematically comb the entire World Wide Web by following and indexing every link they find on every page. If your site is about garden equipment and, buried on an obscure page deep within your site, you tell a story about baking chocolate-chip muffins, then the search engines will find that page and potentially list it to people who do a search on chocolate-chip muffins. When this muffin-seeker arrives in the nether regions of your site, he or she will have about as good a point-of-reference as you would have trying to understand the plot of a movie walking into a theater an hour after the feature started. Providing a one-step route to the front door of your site is essential for orienting any visitor who wishes to find something particular.

Be aware that many visitors who bookmark your site will not bookmark the home page. This might mean you have frequent visitors who are unaware of new site features. Consider placing a "What's New" icon along with a home page link at the top of each page.

Next, the home page must make suggestions for people who don't know what they're looking for. Even though it may seem counter-intuitive, depending on your site, many if not most of your visitors will arrive not looking for anything in particular. Perhaps they've heard from a friend that your site is "worth looking at"—and that's all they know. Perhaps they've read one sentence about your site on a search engine's results. Perhaps they linked from one site expecting one thing, only to find another.

Assuming a good percentage of your visitors are just "browsing"—literally—then it is your duty as a good host to take them by the hand and guide them. For example, your home page might sport any of the following links, displayed prominently near the top:

- Overview of this site

- Is this your first time to our site?

- Beginners start here

- Who we are

- This site's mission

- Welcome to our little corner of the Web!

Hand-holding is also accomplished by a number of other means.

Emphasis of Features

The size, position, and context of each link you create will determine how likely people are to select it. Many sites feature a prominent graphic with the words, "Our Products" on the same page with a line of mouse-type at the bottom of the page providing copyright information. Naturally, you would expect more people to investigate products than the copyright information. However, the name of these links is not the only factor determining click-through. The *prominence* you provide for these—or any links competing for attention—will play a big role in determining which page people visit next.

- In any horizontal row of navigational buttons, assume browsing visitors will start at the left and work their way to the right.

- In any vertical column of navigational buttons, assume browsing visitors will start at the top and work their way down.

Witness this profound example. Observe the two nearly identical pages shown in Figure 16.20 and 16.21.

The older version on the left was intended to downplay the site's commercialism by putting the only link to "Products" in the navigational bar at the bottom of the page. On this site, approximately 25 percent of site visitors clicked-through to the products page. Then we conducted an experiment, placing the large "Products" button in the vertical row, as seen on the image to the right. The percentage of site visitors who clicked-through to the products page *doubled to roughly half!* The people were the same. Only now, we were suggesting that they go look at the products page—and they did.

Note: Do you know what percentage of your site visitors buy? They can't buy if they never see your products or your order form. If you can get more people to your ordering page, your orders will usually increase.

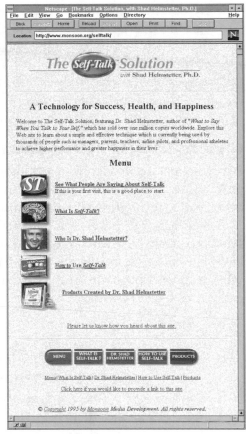

FIGURE 16.20 & 16.21 These two pages are identical except for the inclusion of a prominent "Products" button in the figure on the right. This addition doubled the number of people who looked at the product page.

Test to see which features are most prominent on any page by opening that page and observing where your eye travels. Your eye will go to the most prominent feature first. Have other people look at the page but don't tell them why. After they have looked at it for about 10 seconds, stop and ask them the *order* of things they viewed. Prominent features draw people's attention not only early, but repeatedly while looking at a page. The following are additional tips to keep in mind:

- Avoid using flashing text to increase its emphasis. Users universally agree that this is more of an annoyance than a help. As always, there may be exceptions. Be judicious.

- Animated icons will draw attention. Beware, however, that users may focus on the animation itself and not the subject to which it pertains.

- By definition, you cannot emphasize every feature on a page. Use varying degrees of emphasis to express varying degrees of importance. Too much of any technique will ruin its effect, like trying to use neon to get someone's attention in Las Vegas. Multiple, large graphics will only delay download times. Multiple animated icons on one page will lose their impact and display poorly on slower computers.

Creating Useful Menus

Navigational design requires a trade-off. On one hand, you would like users to be able to access anything with as few clicks as possible. On the other hand, presenting too many options overwhelms users.

Exception: From my own personal experience, the "Rule of Seven" seems to apply best when the menu options are unrelated, such as "Home" and "E-mail" used on a site's menu bar. However, more options do not seem to pose a problem when the options are related, as with these product categories listed on Internet Shopping Network's index (Figure 16.22).

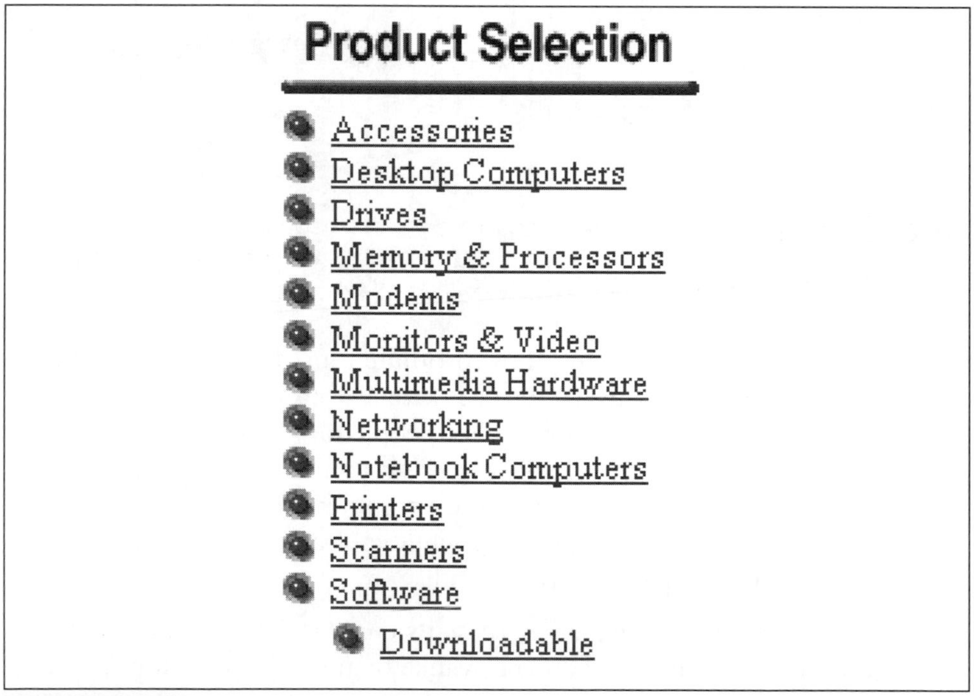

Product Selection

- Accessories
- Desktop Computers
- Drives
- Memory & Processors
- Modems
- Monitors & Video
- Multimedia Hardware
- Networking
- Notebook Computers
- Printers
- Scanners
- Software
  - Downloadable

FIGURE 16.22 More than seven options will not overwhelm the user if the options are all members of one narrowly defined category.

Mama's Favorite Places	Soap Opera	Mama's Lookalike Contest
Italian Art & Architecture	Pizza Party	Italian Desserts Guide
Presents From Mama	What's Next?	Mama Wants to Know
Mama's Links	Talk to Mama	Little Italy Tour

Mama's Favorite Places | Soap Opera | Mama's Lookalike Contest
Italian Art & Architecture | Pizza Party | Italian Desserts Guide
Presents From Mama | What's Next? | Mama Wants to Know
Mama's Links | Talk to Mama | Little Italy Tour

FIGURE 16.23   Ragu's (http://www.eat.com) menu has too many options, some of which are cryptically named.

> **TIP:**   Human factors experts advise against using more than seven selections in a menu.

The brain seems to know that it can ignore all options that do not apply, making the maximum number of choices much greater before the user becomes overwhelmed.

Observe the bewildering array of options at Ragu's site (Figure 16.23).

Some of the names are intuitive; others are cryptic or confusingly similar ("Mama Wants to Know" and "Talk to Mama"), meaning visitors must select that option in order to know what it is about. This fact alone suggests that these labels fail at both parts of the Acid Test of Good Navigation—they are useless to people who know what they're looking for, and useless to people seeking suggestions.

Using Cool Names for Parts of Your Site

Using cryptic names for the right reason is okay.

First, use non-intuitive names to make people curious—but only do this one or two times, suggesting a path for wandering users to follow. Example:

Check out The Haven.

Oooh, makes you wonder what The Haven is, right? But, if *every* option on your home page is cryptically named, then you have given users no direction and they may become frustrated, particularly on graphics-intensive sites in which every new page viewed means waiting in agony while the graphics download.

Second, use cryptic names to add style. Then add a brief description so that people know what it means. For example, instead of labeling a link with the

---

> words, "Links to Cool Dinosaur Sites" (which has about as much flair as tundra), use something more imaginative such as:
>
> The Lava Pit
> *Our Collection of the Hottest Dinosaur Sites on the Web*
>
> Naturally, "The Lava Pit" has an identity of its own that could be executed on the dinosaur links page with a lot of creativity.

Any first-time visitor to the Ragu site may, before going any further, look at his watch and think, "Do I really have time to get into this?" A better approach would have been to lump some of these into categories while naming others so that we instantly know what they mean. Rather than trying to represent dozens of features in a menu bar, many sites successfully employ a "site map" to show users every option available.

> **TIP:** The "Rule of Seven" options in a menu is an upper limit, remember. If you can narrow the options down further, such as to just four options, then each item on the menu will receive more attention than each item on a seven-option menu.

Multiple Menus

Many site developers need to present more than seven features. One of the best ways to handle this is to display multiple menus, with each menu representing members of a clearly defined category. For example, the following home page design (which was never used) for an executive and specialized talent search firm uses two menus simultaneously (Figure 16.24).

- An "Our Company"-type menu bar along the top with the selections, "Main Menu," "Letter from the President," "Success Stories," and "Contact Us"

- An "Industry" matrix menu for the fields in which the firm can locate managerial and technical talent: "Telecommunications," "Semiconductors," "Executive," "Medical," and so on

The final version of this design would have implemented an introductory paragraph briefly describing what the company does. While the tag line ("Search Consultants, Executive and Specialized Talent") is pretty clear, visitors do not know whether the site is intended to appeal to company recruiters or job candidates.

FIGURE 16.24 Splitting navigational options into multiple menus works when the logical division between the categories is self-evident, as with these two menus for company-related pages versus industry-related pages.

The company icons logically flow from left to right, though their names are perhaps not as clear as they could be. If a visitor were to visit them sequentially, he or she would learn first what the company does ("President's Page"), next hear about the company's track record and read

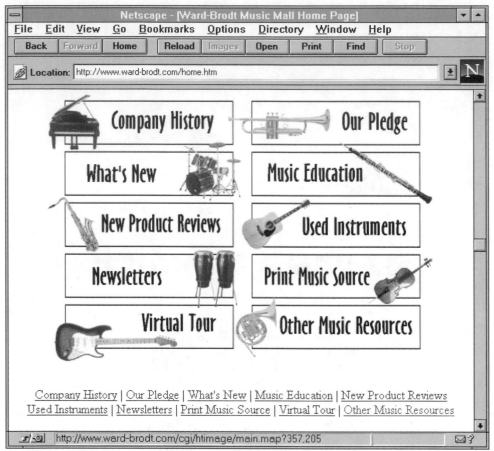

FIGURE 16.25 Each text link corresponds exactly to the words in the graphical links. If two versions of the same link use inconsistent words, then users might think they lead to two different locations.

testimonials from satisfied customers ("Success Stories"), and then learn how to contact the company and whether he or she *should* contact the company ("Contact Us"). As it happens, this company wanted to hear only from employers, not experts seeking jobs. This important point is not made by any of the elements depicted here.

More important, however, is that the industry icons are graphically very distinct from the company icons. Because they are all members of a well-defined category (industries), the "Rule of Seven" does not apply, and many industry icons (with their accompanying text labels) could be shown without overwhelming anybody.

Graphical navigational icons should always be accompanied with a text version so that users who have set their browsers to ignore graphics will still be able to navigate through your site.

> **TIP:** Make the text version read exactly like any text in the graphics version. Make the punctuation and capitalization consistent also (Figure 16.25). For instance, if your button says "our home!" then your text-link to that same page should not say "HOME" or you will risk confusing your visitors.

Using Frames to Aid Navigation

Newer browsers support multiple frames to appear at once on the user's screen, with each frame corresponding to a separate HTML page. This feature is useful for breaking pages into sections that will and won't be changing during the user's visit. For instance, your logo and navigational icons might be the same regardless of which page the user visits. You could place these elements into their own frames so that only one element, such as body text, changes when the user travels through your site (Figure 16.26).

In this example, IMGIS (http://www.imgis.com) uses frames to separate an animated spinning logo (upper-left frame), the site's masthead (upper-right), high-level navigational buttons (lower-left), and a more detailed "site map" of the site's interior (lower-right).

"Site maps" are text-based lists that name all or most of a site's pages, usually in a hierarchical framework such as an outline format. Site maps are very useful for helping users navigate through larger sites, such as those with more than 20 pages.

This particular site map used by IMGIS is somewhat confusing because we are not sure if it corresponds directly with the navigational buttons in the left frame. For example, is "Advertisers" the same section as "Advertising"? Once again, consistent word usage is extremely important when developing your site's navigation. If you used slightly different names when created the road signs for a city, you would expect drivers to get confused. The same goes for the online world.

Additional Navigation Design Tips

If your site is very large or if you access information from a database, consider making your site "searchable." For example, Internet Shopping Network allows visitors to search by keyword to find a particular item out of the 25,000 products that it carries. The technology behind making your

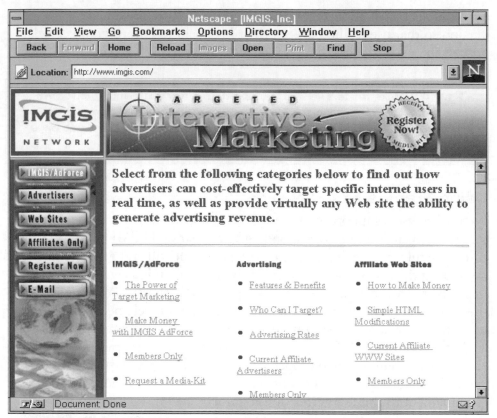

FIGURE 16.26 IMGIS (http://www.imgis.com) uses frames to separate navigational elements.

site searchable is more complicated than the average do-it-yourself HTML coder will want to handle. If you are using a Web service provider, you should work with it to add this functionality.

Use of the phrase, "Click Here" is largely considered to be unhip by Web veterans. However, as usual, the economics of scarce space and limited creative thinking have led very many respectable Web sites to use the phrase when the situation warrants (see Figure 16.27).

FIGURE 16.27 Two of these ads tell you to click. One doesn't. Hip or not, which would you be more likely to click?

Simply put, there are cases when terming an object "clickable" is simply the most efficient and understandable way to instruct users. Go with what you find works for you.

Very inexperienced Web users are afraid to select a button labeled "To Order." They fear they will automatically be billed somehow. This fear seems highest among members of large online services because these companies have not always made it easy for their subscribers to know which services were free and which started a meter ticking.

TIP: To overcome users' fear of being automatically billed, label your button "Information about Ordering," which leads directly to the page containing the order form.

This is usually an accurate label because most online ordering form pages provide a lot of information that people need before they decide to purchase, such as warranties or shipping costs. You must do anything you can to encourage people to see this page.

CHAPTER 17

FOREVER UNDER
CONSTRUCTION

Once a site is up and running, the fun part begins. There is no end to improvements that could potentially lead to more sales. The trick is to focus on those improvements most likely to make the biggest difference.

Upgrading Your Site

You have probably seen sites that are dated a year ago, promising something new "next week." Sometimes these sites are the orphaned projects of the summer intern, the only person who knew HTML, who left the company to return to school. Or perhaps the Webmaster has left the company or has redirected his or her focus to another project within the firm. Perhaps the manager in charge of the Web project is chomping at the bit—with dozens of new ideas planned—just waiting for budget approval from the powers that be. Or maybe this manager has all but forgotten that he or she has a quiet little Web site running in the background, perhaps earning money, perhaps not.

On the other end of the spectrum, I see some Web owners who change their site too frequently, without regard for whether anybody has even see the last two versions of the site. To these people, the update schedule is driven by a "what can I do to it now?" mentality that has nothing to do with any plan or defined objectives.

> **TIP:** If you want to tinker aimlessly with a site, then create a personal home page or create a site for a local charity. Changes to commercial sites should be done for a reason, in accordance with a plan or certain objectives.

Naturally, if you are paying for outside Web production services at $100 per hour, then you will want to think long and hard about what features you add, when, and why. If you possess all Web creation skills internally, then you might build an argument that experimentation is cheap—that you might as well throw things up and see what sticks.

True, your risks are lower. But a haphazard approach to modifying your site has the dual risks of implementing some aspect that is not on track with your overall company strategy, and more importantly, ignores the opportunity cost of development. That is, if you are busy creating one thing, that means that you cannot be doing another thing at the same time. If some feature would boost site sales by 25 percent but you don't get around to it because you are fiddling with a feature that boosts sales by only 5 percent, then you have failed to optimize.

Unfortunately, many sites' original designs and subsequent improvements are driven by what the designer thinks "would be cool" or as a real-life tutorial for learning a new technical skill, such as a developer who is looking for a way to earn money while learning Java. That's called looking for a problem to fit the solution; you want to avoid such backward approaches to any investment of time or capital.

> **TIP:** Before rushing ahead with any major improvement, pause and think.

Generating and Weeding Out Ideas

> **TIP:** Never consider one idea in isolation. Match it against other ideas for alternate site improvements. Solicit ideas from visitors, co-workers, friends, and people on the internet whose opinion you respect. To develop more ideas, subject all concepts to traditional group brainstorming.

When brainstorming ideas for site improvements, start with the questions focusing on your niche:

- What would make our site land at the top of the list of sites devoted to such-and-such? What element would make us *the* place on the Web related to this? (Review Chapter 2's discussion of "Staking a Claim.")

Once you have narrowed the ideas down to the short list, focus your study on ways to bolster your site's and company's identity:

- What new feature would make our identity strong and clear? Or, how could this new feature be used to strengthen our identity? For example, you might offer reviews for something on your site, such as movies or new products. Instead of giving one to four stars, use something clever—such as one to four *bear claws* for reviews of fishing spots on a "Travel Alaska" site.

And before you move forward with any concept, apply it to the following series of questions, just to make yourself think things through systematically. Also consider applying these questions to all of your other ideas, for comparison.

- Will this change improve the company's image?
- Is this change consistent with our site's identity?
- Will this change create heavier traffic?
- Will it generate word of mouth?
- Does it have press-release appeal? (Is it high-concept, or does it solve a problem?)
- Will it generate repeat business?
- Will it make home page visitors explore more deeply into the site?
- Will it increase sales?
- Will it provide ancillary marketing opportunities (generating e-mail addresses for a direct e-mail campaign at a later date, for example)?
- Will this change divert customers' attention from the primary goal of the site?
- Will it introduce performance problems for users with slower connections?
- Will it alienate users with older or non-Netscape browsers?

A proposed improvement need not perform well in accordance with all of these questions—that would be difficult or impossible. But it should appeal very strongly to at least one of them. These questions should be weighted depending on your current situation. For example, if your site already has high press-release appeal and is getting mentioned in the press constantly, then focus instead on ways of getting home page visitors to explore more deeply into your site, for example. Or, you may have no problem getting a good sales rate from your site visitors, but traffic may be low. In this case you would need to focus on site improvements that would be geared more toward generating word of mouth.

Quantify your intuition. Attach numbers to your ideas. If you are not soliciting user feedback or practicing advanced traffic monitoring (see Chapter 7), then your decisions regarding site changes are rooted in intuition—shooting in the dark. Study the traffic numbers to avoid making changes that hurt your site's overall performance.

> **TIP:** Use cookie technology to determine if visitors are new or repeat visitors (see Chapter 10).

Refer to your server's agent logs to see what type of browser people are using to access your site. As of this writing, you probably need only worry about *which version* of Netscape people are using. If you offer features that are viewable only by later versions, you will alienate users of older versions. Always provide alternate options for these people, unless they equal less than 15 percent of your total traffic.

If sophisticated analysis is not available to you (due to log unavailability, for example) it is probably better to make intuitive changes than to leave your site stagnant indefinitely. But to avoid making your site worse somehow, first try *adding* features rather than changing or replacing features.

Forecasting the benefits of site improvements may be anybody's guess, but forecasting their costs are not. Never embark on an involved improvement without estimating how much time and money it will take to implement.

"Last Updated"

> **TIP:** Don't display a "Last Updated" date if you don't update your site at least once every three months.

There is little worse you could do than to proudly declare that your site was last updated eight months ago. If someone sees that your site hasn't been updated in four months, then it begins to looks as if your Web site is only an intermittent project—or maybe abandoned altogether. If your site has been updated in less than three months, it will appear as though the site is updated regularly, but perhaps only as a part-time project by one of your employees. If your site is consistently updated every two to four weeks, it will appear as though you have a dedicated Web-oriented business. If your site is substantively updated more frequently than every two weeks, it will appear as though you have a full-time employee dedicated to Web maintenance. In fact, it *will probably require* a dedicated employee to make such frequent updates.

Frequently updated sites (let us say, those updated more often than once per month) are usually designed to cater to repeat visitors. Other than changing pertinent, up-to-the-minute information, such as important industry news, market prices, or job openings, it would be a wasteful use of resources to replace content before many people have had a chance to see it for the first time. As such, some effort should be spent discerning *how often* people visit your site. Plan your update frequency accordingly. If many people are regular repeaters and many are first-timers, then accommodate both of these segments by keeping some of your site consistent over time (such as company information) while frequently updating portions of your site to appeal to the repeaters. Offering archives of past content allows new visitors to get up to speed with the regulars, possibly making them more likely to become regular visitors themselves.

Different business models derive more benefits from attracting repeat visitors than do others (for example, sites that are advertiser-sponsored usually want all the hits they can take). Those sites that thrive most on repeat visits must be willing to update their content more frequently than those that do not. But even sites that would not ordinarily expect people to visit a second time should update their content at least once every three months (and display the "last updated" date) simply to appear timely to first-time visitors.

Experimentation

Before sinking a lot of money or effort into an idea, test the water. Install a minor version of the idea, for example, and see how your users respond. Let them know it is a test, and they might be more willing to provide feedback that will help you decide whether to fully implement the idea or refine the idea as you are creating it.

If you have several features in mind, take a straw poll of your visitors' preferences. You could do this by having them select one option out of four on a form. Or you could make the test more transparent instead by putting up four navigational buttons leading to "under construction" pages for one day only, for example. By counting relative hits on each of these four pages, you would have an idea which concepts appealed most to your visitors.

Shuffle Your Existing Content

If you have limited development resources, you can always try refining what you already have. This includes modifying your text on existing pages. It also might mean rearranging the order of icons and links leading to pages, changing the icons, or emphasizing new sections that were previously played down. To avoid confusing repeat visitors, test new configurations for only a week and see what happens to your internal page counters. If the modifications seem to help, leave them. If not, switch back to the previous configuration.

> **TIP:** If you are creating your own pages, save previous versions so that switching back and forth between new and old will not be complicated.

New Features: Low Tech

There is no end to the list of things a site might feature. Your existing or intended site may already possess some of the following options, but no site has all of them (and, I suspect, none would want to). If nothing else, these may provide the starting point for your own brainstorming sessions:

- Text-only version (for the graphics-impaired and bandwidth-impaired; see Figure 17.1)
- Foreign language version
- What's New page
- Employee pages
- Hot links
- Funny horror stories from your tech support department
- Little-known facts about such-and-such
- The history of such-and-such
- Gallery of art related to such-and-such
- Famous quotes related to such-and-such
- Scavenger hunt (requiring thorough exploration of your site)

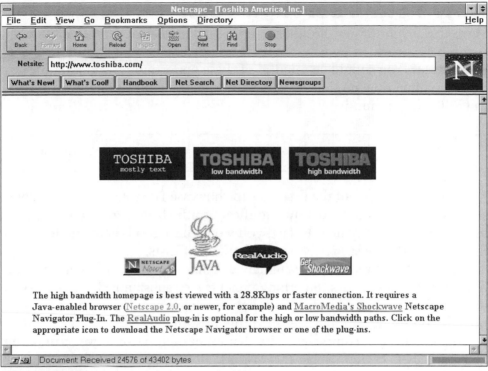

FIGURE 17.1 Toshiba's site offers users three versions of the site ranging from text-only to graphics-intensive, as well as features geared toward multiple plug-ins.

- Free thing to sites that provide a link
- Essay contest
- Contest: add the funniest caption to this photo
- Contest: name our new product, site, Web page, mascot, etc.
- Contests designed to *build traffic* should make the contestants' odds of winning improve by getting friends to enter.
- Contests designed to *sell* should force contestants to explore your site, assimilate information, or prove that they understand something (such as a contest for the best one-paragraph description of your site).
- Foreign language versions—Check your access logs to learn from which countries users are visiting. Before creating an entire parallel site in another language, do a test page and see how many people access it.

New Features: High Tech

With the advent of new browser plug-ins and cross-platform development capabilities provided by Java, the world is opening to an unknown array of possibilities. You should be mindful of these opportunities and look for ways in which they might add significant value to your site. However, keep the following in mind:

> **TIP:** Don't invest in high technology or gimmickry without good reason.

If you can be one of the first sites to showcase late-breaking technology, then you might be able to draw significant traffic from people coming to see something totally new. In fact, you would be a good candidate for inclusion in the most prestigious "What's Cool" lists.

Another good reason for using fancy technology—the best reason, actually—is when it conveys something beneficial or substantively related to your site's purpose and business model; in other words, when your gimmick is "on topic," it might be worth the investment.

Implementing technical wizardry that is not on topic, however, can have a detrimental effect. Remember that visitors' attention spans are finite. If you show them something that draws too much attention but doesn't relate very well to your site's nature or identity, then you risk distracting visitors. True, the feature may enhance your site's word-of-mouth appeal, but it is worthwhile to study traffic data within your site, both with and without the feature, to determine if it has an effect on your visitors' usage habits. If it draws traffic and does not distract people or dilute your identity, then that's great.

However, all of these problems can be avoided by planning to use only features that are specifically designed to promote your identity and niche exploitation. Using technology for technology's sake is a poor use of resources and usually looks incongruent to visitors. Think about this the next time you visit a site that features a box with scrolling text saying "Have a nice day." Doesn't that just make you want to reach for your credit card? Or tell all your friends? No, it makes you wonder why it's there.

As stated in Chapter 1, eventually, high degrees of interactivity will be common or even expected on Web sites. By then, there will be so many varieties and applications of technology that sites will be able to choose the features that really make sense for their business. Concepts will drive the selection of technology, rather than available technology driving which concepts are employed, as they frequently do today.

Expanding Your *Business* Rather than Just Your Site

Until the day when using more advanced technology is common, expected, or inexpensive, there are probably better ways for small Web businesses to attempt to increase their revenue. The exception here, again, occurs when technology is perfectly suited to the business model—such as implementing streamed audio to allow visitors to sample audio products. This might partly be a gimmick, but it primarily adds value.

Most businesses should probably look at alternate ways of using their resources to increase revenue. For example, in Chapter 14, several techniques were discussed for multiniching, or creating multiple Web sites that appeal to different target audiences (even though both sites may sell the same thing). Of course, all sites and businesses are different, but, once a site has reached a certain level of value to its customers, expanding that value may not increase traffic proportionally due to the Law of Diminishing Returns. I believe this is why some of the largest online newspaper publishers—despite offering tremendous amounts of content—are having difficulty turning a profit.

Look at it another way. You can be a generalist or a niche player. If you are a generalist, then you have the difficulties supporting your expensive daily operations and possibly end up like a huge online newspaper, swimming in millions of dollars' worth of red ink. Or you can occupy a niche and live comfortably. But niches, by definition, are small. Doubling the appeal of your site might only create a 20 percent increase in traffic because the market simply isn't big enough to support you at a larger size.

Imagine, for example, that you manufacture balsa wood dinosaur-skeleton models. You have a great-looking, 30-page site featuring interesting facts and a dozen different models. Also assume you are profitable. Does it follow that doubling your size, offering twice as many interesting facts and twice as many skeleton models, will double your profits? Probably not because you are really only giving the same group of skeleton-model-builders more options from which to choose. Your sales might increase some—perhaps from the one guy who must own every model you make. But your sales won't double.

A better idea than doubling the size of the site would be to build a new site that sells whale-skeleton models. Maybe you offered these all along, but your site was geared toward dinosaurs because reptiles represent 80 percent of your product line. The most natural expansion route—the best use of your investment dollar—would probably be to create a full-blown whale site, only loosely connected to the dinosaur site. Give it its own identity. Market it as its own business.

Balsa wood dinosaur-skeleton and whale-skeleton models provide a clean illustration of this concept. Your business might not be so obviously adapted to other subniches. Perhaps not, but multimillion dollar manufacturers have had to do this in the past. Successful companies focus on what they do best and then grow by finding other applications for that core competency.

If you cannot expand into other niches, consider expanding the umbrella of products and services that your niche customers will find attractive—even if it means working with other companies. For example, your Web site may promote an existing business, such as a roofing business. Rather than adding roofing-related facts, it might make sense to devote your time to creating a cooperative page with a bank promoting home-improvement loans. You may find a way to earn revenue by referring leads to the bank. You may also acquire site visitors who found you while originally looking for a loan.

The Evolution of Everything

Throughout this book, I've drawn on examples from biology to explain concepts related to evolution of markets and technology, as well as competition between individual rivals. One of the best ways to predict the future of any economy, market, or technology is to study and understand the forces that drive and guide all innovation and change. If you are intrigued by this sort of cross-disciplinary synthesis of concepts, then I highly recommend *Bionomics: Economy as Ecosystem* by Michael Rothschild, which can be found at http://www.bionomics.org (Figure 17.2).

Keeping Your Eyes on the Horizon

A little success can be a bad thing when it causes someone to stop working on getting things right. A reasonably well-constructed Web site that plugs along, barely paying for itself each month, is a prime candidate for the "site that doesn't change for nine months." But who knows? Maybe that same site would have been generating a lot of money with just a little extra work.

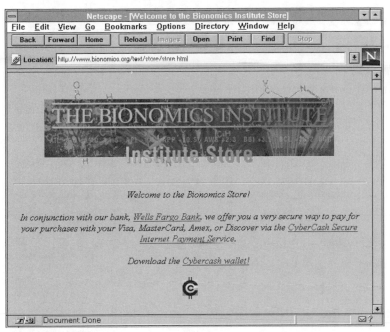

FIGURE 17.2   Visit The Bionomics Institute to learn more about the big-picture shifts in technology and commerce (http//www.bionomics.org).

And even those who keep tinkering with their sites often fail to take a step back and address the fundamentals. For example, many people create a site and spend a solid chunk of time soliciting links from other related sites. This is good. But then they fail to repeat the process three months later, even though many of the sites that provided links may have disappeared, or there may be a dozen new sites that would be happy to provide links.

Finally, there are destined to be businesses that got in early and did things right that nevertheless collapse because they fail to take a big step back periodically and look at what's happening in their industry, and with Web marketing in general. Again, this is not to say that all sites should constantly upgrade to every new type of technology, but they should at least be aware of the implications that accompany each new technology. The forward-looking manager is always asking, "How could this affect me?" and that manager will be the least likely to be surprised.

Always keep browsing—sometimes aimlessly, sometimes with purpose. See what others are doing. See what your competitors are doing.

Make it a weekly ritual, and have fun.

Don't Stop Here, Visit the "Increasing Hits" Web Site

http://www.monsoon.org/book

The pages of this book contain information you need to make your commercial Web site succesfull. But don't stop there. The Web is changing every day and new opportunities and threats are constantly arriving in the Web marketing arena.

Visit this book's online companion, "Increasing Hits." There you will find additional ways to maximize your site's revenue, including brand new tips and tricks pertaining to the rapid changes occurring on the Web. The site also provides links to many online resources, such as the following:

- Current Web statistics and market research
- Site promotion services and software
- Traffic log analysis shareware
- HTML editing software
- Trademark search reasources
- Order fulfillment and outsourcing services
- Specialized Web attorneys and free legal advice

I also invite you to drop by the site to contact me directly. Stay wired, stay informed. Hope to see you soon.

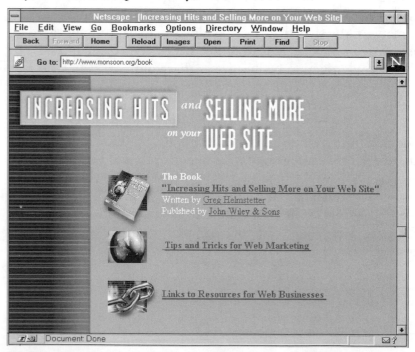

INDEX